THERE COMES A TIME

A Challenge to the Two Party System

Gerald John Fresia

 PRAEGER

New York
Westport, Connecticut
London

Library of Congress Cataloging-in-Publication Data

Fresia, Gerald John.
    There comes a time.

    Bibliography: p.
    Includes indexes.
    1. Political parties—United States. 2. Third
parties (United States politics) 3. Opposition
(Political science)—United States. 4. Political
participation—United States. I. Title.
JK2261.F84 1986   324'..0973   86-12190
ISBN 0-275-92095-X (alk. paper)

Library of Congress Catalog Card Number: 86-12190
ISBN: 0-275-92095-X

First published in 1986

Praeger Publishers, 521 Fifth Avenue, New York, NY 10175
A division of Greenwood Press, Inc.

Printed in the United States of America

∞

The paper used in this book complies with the Permanent
Paper Standard issued by the National Information Standards
Organization (Z39.48-1984)

10 9 8 7 6 5 4 3 2 1

IN MEMORY OF

Anzannia Surrechio Chiacchiaretta

and

Josephine Dellea Fresia

PREFACE AND ACKNOWLEDGEMENTS

This study is intended to serve three groups of people. One group consists of the growing number of disaffected citizens for whom electoral politics in the United States holds little appeal. It is hoped that the analysis here will assist them in clarifying and expressing that disaffection in ways which help to empower the disenfranchised. The second group consists of teachers and students of the two party system who have had little choice but to wade through sanitized texts whose purpose is to encourage us to believe rather than to think. The attempt here to pull together and explain the political history of people with little or no property as well as to link party and economic activity, I trust, will be of value to those troubled by the existing literature. The third group consists of progressive political activists who are building a movement. It is to them that my most direct appeal is made—that we place high on our agenda the need to call attention to and confront the failure of the two party system as a democratic form.

This study began as a dissertation directed by Kenneth M. Dolbeare and critically reviewed by Herbert Gintis and Linda Metcalf. South End Press encouraged me to broaden and bring up to the present what was then a class analysis of party realignments during the 19th century. Christine DiStefano read and commented upon the entire first draft of the present study. Robert Higgins and Peter Bohmer provided suggestions for the introductory chapters. Dan Clawson and Mary Ann Clawson each permitted me to examine related works of their own which have not as yet been published. Angel Nieto allowed me to use his poetry. Several others contributed in numerous additional ways. They are: Sherry Blankenship, Ida and Carl Joslyn, P. Anandan, and Pak Yung Suk. Jean Caiani deserves special thanks for her constant support and encouragement.

March 1986
Worthington, Massachusetts

CONTENTS

PART I

The Personality and Character of the Two Party System

Here we are again
apparently invisible
in the history that is made implacably:
a whiff of air,
a drop of water,
barely a whisper.

Here we are again
apparently invisible.
We look around
and recognize ourselves.
We've seen each other often
on similar occasions,
applauding distant revolutions,
protesting invasions and massacres.

Here we are again
apparently invisible
and we look at
and recognize ourselves,
give each other strength
with our own presence,
do not lose hope, for,
apparently invisible,
we know that:
a hurricane is made of whiffs of air,
a flood comes one drop at a time,
whispers can create a clamor.

Angel Nieto

1

THINKING TWICE ABOUT THE
TWO PARTY SYSTEM

The parties...have played a major role as *makers* of government, more especially they have been the makers of democratic government. It should be stated flatly...that the political parties created democracy and that modern democracy is unthinkable save in terms of the parties.[1]

—E.E. Schattschneider

Most political activity in America is the province of millionaires, or of those favored by foundations and think tanks controlled by millionaires. It is time to recognize that political action is a special form of investment—one which is usually far beyond the means of most citizens.[2]

—Thomas Ferguson

If we were either unaware or uninterested in the barriers that have prevented meaningful political participation by "marginal" constituencies, we might be inclined to side with Schattschneider. It might make sense, then, to view the political struggles among elites within the party system—who for the most part have been white, wealthy, and male—as a democratic process. If we were to seriously value the aspirations of subordinate peoples, however, it is probable that we would explore, with a felt sense of concern, any number of disturbing features of the two party system.

For example, we might question why barriers to political participation (such as property qualifications, literacy tests, poll taxes, voter registration, residency requirements, the disfranchisement of convicted felons and so on) have been a systematic part of our electoral history. We may wonder why Schattschneider and others, given the insistent celebration of majority rule within the social order, ignore the fact that no president of the United States has ever been elected by a *majority* of the nation's *adult citizens*.[3]

3

Somewhat disconcerted by the long history of suffrage restrictions, we might then be inclined to investigate the impact of the structure of electoral competition (single member district, plurality elections, the electoral college, the weakening of the convention system, the establishment of the primary system) on our opportunity as common citizens to organize serious political opposition to those with significant political power. We might be compelled to inquire whether or not the structure of the two party system, as opposed to multi-party sytems or systems of proportional representation found in most other western democracies, filters out serious critical thought. Does the two party system undermine the possibility of ideologically distinct parties? Does it virtually eliminate the possibility of major parties other than Democrats and Republicans? In light of our fear of the type of single party domination that marks totalitarian societies, we would have to ask why our two party system seems to sanction regional and, at times, national domination by single parties. If we were to do all this, it is also probable that we would move on to explore *movement* politics or the rich but lesser known history of political activity which has flourished *outside* the party system. And once having acquired an appreciation of the political imagination, courage, and creativity of those citizens denied access to the two party system, we would, quite likely, tend to lean toward Ferguson's interpretation. Indeed, our tendency, after having acquainted ourselves with this line of reasoning, might be to state quite flatly that Schattschneider is not only wrong but that by taking the position that he does, he inadvertently helps to obscure subtle but significant forms of political repression.

As political activists we might be inclined to follow Albert Camus's suggestion and view history not through the eyes of elites but through the eyes of those who find themselves at the bottom of the political heap. Besides, any political order which itself claims to be of, for, and by the people ought to be viewed through the eyes of its most politically disadvantaged citizens. After all, we might be moved to suggest that it makes no sense to celebrate a government of "the people" if what is meant by "the people" is the more successful half. True enough, a test of this sort might conjure a simple sympathy for the victims of bigotry. And it might swell the ranks of those who are enamored with a sense of distributive justice and whose vision of a better society is but a variation of the "Great Society." But a central theme of this essay is that we, as political activists, must get beyond the self-indulgence of conjuring simple sympathy. As impassioned thinkers, the test we would do well to apply is one of critical reflection. Our assessment of the two party system ought to rest on its ability *to provide space for serious intellectual confrontation and spontaneity and for processes which illuminate rather than mystify the inner connections of our social relationships and collective arrangements.*

* * *

In this chapter our questioning shall be exploratory and rudimentary. Our first task is to get a sense of the success which subordinate
people have had in working within the two party system. In other
words, has the two party system worked for those who have not had
significant economic power and political influence? We shall answer
this question by contrasting the aspirations of those who organized
broad political movements that penetrated the two party system with
the final rewards which the two party system provided. What, in the
end, did the party system help these people achieve?

But we also need to get a more intimate sense of party politics. We
need to get a sense of its personality. What are the rules governing the
party process? What does it take to win an election or effect public
policy? Which principles must be compromised? To what degree is
self-examination as a nation allowed or encouraged? Why do men seem
to have more influence than women? Whites than people of color?
Owners of property than the propertyless? Do we all have equal access?

We shall also try to understand the motivations of those who have
chosen to work outside the party system, who see politics more as the
"building of a movement" rather than the mobilization of support
around a single issue. What are the rewards of movement politics? Its
limitations? Its possibilities? The premise here is that to know or
become familiar with only one kind of politics, in this case the politics
of the two party system, is really to know none at all. Therefore, in this
chapter we shall also begin an exploration of what movement politics
are all about.

Politics Inside the Two Party System

Political parties ostensibly exist in order that citizens may join
with others through them and win governmental representation by
means of electoral competition. The two party system, therefore, allows
dissident coalitions, ultimately, to capture control of the government.
One of the most respected scholars on this subject, V.O. Key, Jr., has
characterized this opportunity as "a functional equivalent of revolution."[4]

One wonders, are the narrow uses of the terms "dissident" and
"revolution" by Key intended to save the democratic appearance of the
party system? Even the most cursory survey of transformative periods in
party history raises doubts as to validity of this claim. For example, the
"Reagan Revolution" was mandated only by 27 percent of the potential
electoral. Although embarrassingly skimpy among western democracies, within the United States this sort of mandate is not atypical.
Lyndon Johnson polled approximately 38 percent of the potential

electorate in 1964. Richard Nixon, in his massive landslide of 1972, won only 34 percent of the potential electorate. If we look at elections marking "critical realignments" we find that Andrew Jackson registered 25 percent support of the adult population in 1828, Lincoln 32.6 percent in 1860, McKinley 40.6 percent in 1896, and Roosevelt 32.6 in 1932. But even if we were to ignore participation measures, we would likely be alarmed by the analysis of Walter Dean Burnham which concludes that the "'golden age' of the American party system and of democratic participation as well, took place in the last half of the nineteenth century....the twentieth-century history of American electoral politics has been essentially...a history of excluded political alternatives."[5]

To those who applaud the victories in this century with respect to suffrage reform, particularly of blacks and women, Burnham's statement must seem somewhat puzzling. Implicitly Burnham is telling us that the broader 20th century participation within the party system did *not* enhance democratic chances within the party system. Does this suggest that there are reasons why those who benefit from the two party system might want to construct democratic facades? We are led to suspect that the more recent participation of blacks, women, and others of similar political status, perhaps male immigrant wage earners, may have somehow been used to mask or otherwise put a democratic face upon the process by which political alternatives (and one could argue alternative politics) were "excluded." Let us begin our survey of party politics, therefore, by looking at the role it has played in the lives of women, blacks, and white male wage earners.

* * *

The subordination of women prior to the 19th century had not been crystalized as a political issue. In part, this was due to the unreflective acceptance of Puritan thought. The subordination of women was thought to be as natural as the subordination of children to parents or lay adults to ministers and the courts. Differences in status were part of the mutual dependence, the binding together by one's need for one another and dedication to serving God.[6] As evangelical reformers helped to organize abolitionist and temperance movements, however, political space was unintentionally provided for women who understood slavery and excessive drinking not only in religious terms but also in secular terms. These abuses, to many women, were, plain and simple, a form of male irresponsibility. In other words, evangelical reform movements inadvertently encouraged women to probe the legitimacy of male domination. But lodged within the broader religious context, the very first challenges to male authority were at best indirect and perhaps even unclear. As is the case with political activity organized by women against militarism today, the broader challenge to male authority is implicit. Such criticisms might be said to be more symptomatic than self-conscious.

Connections between issues become clearer, however, when politics consists of the process of rigorous and repeated expression and reflection. Once 30,000 women from Britain, Sweden, Holland, West Germany and Ireland encircled the air base at Greenham Common to protest the deployment of U.S. nuclear missiles and women began to clarify the reasons for being there, the connections between militarism and a gender based social order were made explicit.[7] Similarly, as women converged, talked about and wrote about their experience as women at the turn of the 19th century, the linkages between particular institutions, male authority, and female subordination at the onset of the industrial age no longer remained shadowy and vague, no longer seemed appropriate or natural. The critical insights of Abigail Adams, Judith Murray, Mary Wollstonecraft, and Frances Wright also helped transform the disaffection of women into a political force. The gradual creation of a female identity laid the foundation of a divergent world view, one upon which women could confidently press demands for redress.

The bond between coming to know oneself and the need to create political space for that new identity is always very tight. It may have been the writings of these women or others like them that gave a group of female workers the confidence to publically take defiant actions against male domination on a Friday in late December 1828. Four hundred young women "turned out" to protest working conditions at a textile factory, the Cocheco Company in Dover. After parading about the town to the sound of martial music, they burned several casks of gun powder.[8] As women were "turning out," others were lecturing publicly. Wright, for example, was speaking out on the issue of woman's rights while Maria W. Stewart, a free black in New England, was advocating abolition as well as educational opportunities for women. As Howard Zinn points out, "...by the time a clear feminist movement emerged in the 1840s, women had become practiced organizers, agitators, speakers."[9]

For women, the process of individual expression and prolonged collective self-examination, a process central to critical thought and collective struggle, had begun outside the two party system. At the first women's rights convention in 1848, women listed specific grievances in a Declaration of Sentiments and Resolutions. Among these were disenfranchisement, the inability to have a voice in the formation of laws to which they had to submit, the false supposition of the supremacy of men (especially in the context of the family and the home), legal, professional, and educational discrimination, and exploitation at work. Notice that disenfranchisement was considered as but one facet of the female experience which women resented. In 1876, a Declaration of Rights for Women was issued by the National Woman Suffrage Association which again stressed that "many forms of flagrant discrimination were still prevalent."[10] In 1967, women activists within the Civil Rights and peace movements took a bold new stance that fundamentally altered politics outside the party system. Stating that "We are oppressed as women, and our oppression is as real, as legitimate, as necessary to fight against as that of blacks, Chicanos, or the Vietnamese," women activists demanded that men deal with their male chauvinism "in their personal, social, and political relationships."[11] The process internal to relationships and institutions now seemed as important as the purposes to which such things were committed.

The breath of the feminist indictment is generally ignored. The most recent phase of feminist political expression, consequently, is often severed from its anti-patriarchal moorings and cast in cryptic, quantitative terms which in themselves accommodate both the misogyny and positivist science that permeates our way of politics. I am referring to the term "gender gap." The term effectively reduces a burgeoning cultural alternative to a trivial measure of electoral preference. To the degree that citizens view the political activity of women through this conceptual lens, feminist aspirations are forced to serve phallocentric policy options. And the harsh illumination of feminist thought is reflected outward toward the fringe of illegitimacy.

To be sure, the suffrage and temperance movements brought women into contact with major and minor parties repeatedly. Writes Aileen Kraditor, "From 1868 on, suffragist speakers made the rounds of the political conventions presenting petitions and testifying at hearings of resolutions or platform comittees."[12] But has not such contact been made necessary by the fact that the party system has been a kind of "office of admissions" for the disenfranchised? Women, minorities, and immigrants, in order to gain recognition as *citizens* or equality before the law first have had to win the franchise. The privilege (right) of voting has been the proverbial ticket in.

What is particularly interesting here is that because they have been pushed to the outside of the two party system, women have been free to pursue a much broader investigation of their experiences. They have been less constrained by the need to understand the dominant culture in the same terms that the culture understands itself; and they have been less constrained to build electoral coalitions or frame their grievances in terms of party-system-single-issues (as had suffragists). Indeed there is a thread running throughout the history of feminist activism from the abolitionist movement, when women first established a foothold on the public stage, to the consciousness raising groups of the 1960s, the politicization of personal relationships in the 1970s, to the linkage of militarism and a gender based order in the 1980s. And that thread has been the introduction of *competing perspectives*.

It is in light of potentially transformative politics of women that the gender gap analyses (roughly 10 percent fewer women than men had approved of Reagan's performance as president prior to the 1984 election) are most worrisome. Are we being sidetracked without knowing it? Is our own assumption that politics is only electoral politics limiting the impact or vision of feminism in some way? For example, it is quite possible that the presidency of Ronald Reagan has helped feminists make the point that many of our worst social ills are rooted in a socially destructive configuration of several concepts: masculinity, control, authority, conquest, force, expansion, etc. It may very well be the case that feminist values, consciously or otherwise, simmer beneath the surface of electoral politics threatening to erupt as a polar force around which political opposition to environmental degradation, militarism, and cuts in social expenditures could effectively rally. But the cutting edge of feminism, which has the potential of becoming an antipode of sorts, not only in the West but within Eastern European countries and the Soviet Union, *may have been blunted by the nomination of Geraldine Ferraro as vice-president.* Although the Ferraro nomination has been vigorously and widely applauded, a less innocent inspection suggests that the nomination legitimizes system-accommodating aspects of feminism—woman as chief administrator—while it delegitimizes those aspects which collide with the management of global militarism. The larger question becomes this: are there biases internal to the processes of the two party system which we unwittingly perpetuate by our support and acceptance of them? To further illuminiate this question let us go back to the suffragists and their fundamental appeal.

As suffragists made their rounds from convention to convention, suffrage planks were repeatedly rejected. Why? It may be that moral appeals, even ones so basic as the demand to be counted as a citizen, carry little weight in the pragmatic, hard ball world of party politics.[13] On the other hand, pragmatists are always ready to make a bargain. Worthy ends, rejected out of hand, can be slipped back into the political mainstream if they are useful as bargaining chips. But to what larger end? "Politicos" have an easy answer: forget the sentimentality about right and wrong and think seriously about that which advances the "success" of the party. Indeed, the proponents of this perspective suggest that the steady advancement of the temperance movement (which culminated with the 18th Amendment or national liquor prohibition) and the passage of the 19th Amendment, which granted women the vote, came during the "Red Scare" when party elites desperately hoped that prohibition and the influx of "pure" female voters would contribute to the success of both major parties generally by counteracting the increased identification among immigrant workers with leftist ideologies. And in this context, we can better appreciate the nomination of Geraldine Ferraro. A woman's presence on the ticket was intended to advance the cause of Democrats. But notice that the converse may not be true. That is, it is unlikely that a woman was placed on the ticket because Democratic party elites were awash with feminism. No policy blueprints, for example, were advanced in order to rivet public attention on even the most basic of feminist complaints, such as violence (within the home or in the context of militarism) or the "feminization of poverty."[14]

The distinction between the visibility and the genuine influence of subordinant groups within the party system is terribly important. Parties permit the enlistment of the support of a disadvantaged constituency in order to popularize its agenda without really having to understand or work for the interests of such constituencies. In this case, women will vote in record numbers for the 1984 Democratic platform which some observors have described as "immoderate and regressive as any to be found in the Democratic Party archives since John W. Davis's unremembered candidacy of 1924." The voice of women *as Democrats opposed to Reaganomics* has finally been solicited by Democratic elites. But it may also be said that the voice of women, *not as servicers of men but as women,* has yet to be heard clearly within the party system.[15]

One is tempted to conclude that within the two party system, justice—as the term is used within the context of family life, close friendships, or communities—has little meaning because it rarely has value in the bargaining process. But the elimination of the concept of justice from party activity as a meaningful concept does not explain the divorce of the interest of party elites from the real interests of disadvantaged groups. Perhaps a broader inspection will help us to clarify the questions we need to ask. Let us, therefore, look at the general experience of blacks within the two party system.

Consider the situation following the Civil War when the struggle for change was acute. Leading Republicans proposed that black males be allowed to vote in those Southern states that rejoined the Union. This proposal, the Fourteenth Amendment, was put forward to ensure Republican domination in the South. We notice once again that the aspiration of black males, worthy as ends in themselves, were *used* to advance the success of the party for political control in the South. Democrats responded by championing the cause of woman's suffrage. Why? Because they hoped that the linkage of woman's suffrage to black male suffrage would ultimately jeopardize the Republican amendment. Notice again the instrumental use of political expression. This time women were *used.* Accepting the Democrats' assistance, the suffragists abandoned their initial petition to enfranchise both blacks and women. Notice the result. One group is played off against the other. When politics is reduced to bargaining, disadvantaged groups have always their unity with which to bargain.[17] Tentatively, we might explain the divorce of the interests of party elites from the real interests of disadvantaged constituencies this way: the aspirations of disadvantaged constituencies are important to political parties primarily to the extent that they contribute to a party's success. For example, in light of the widespread protests against apartheid, Congressperson Vin Webber, a conservative Republican from Minnesota, stated in early 1985, "If we 'Republicans' are to become the majority party we have to change the perception of conservatives on civil rights...we need to shuck the baggage of an ugly strain of American conservatism in the past, the baggage of racism." Note the essential concern is not with the plight of the black South Africans or black Americans. It is obtaining majority status. *Implicit is the notion that the conservative Republican political-economic agenda needs to be popularized, not democratized.* The aspirations or interests of political have-nots, therefore, are regularly transformed from meaningful ends in themselves to political instruments which may or may not help the powerful. The divorce is one, not surprisingly, that reflects the reality of an order organized around the pursuit of individual self-interest.

Could it be that our particular form of democracy, while it accepts individual initiatives, works to check the coalition of rebellious factions? The experience of blacks helps us to address this question. Let us begin with the experience of abolitionists. Black abolitionists had been actively organizing conventions (the Negro Convention Movement) since 1817. It was not until the late 1830s, however, when two leaders of the predominantly white American Anti-Slavery Society, William L. Garrison and James G. Birney, together with Myron Holly of upstate New York, began to organize abolitionists in time for the 1840 election that the abolitionist movement entered the party arena.[18] The Second Great Awakening (1795 to 1835) had provided the political tone of the period. Individual salvation turned on one's ability to make morally responsible contributions to the community. Generally, this meant the exercise of self-denial and an earnest commitment to industry and the discipline of the burgeoning factory system. It also meant the support of specific evangelical reforms which also legitimized factory discipline such as temperance and abolition. The anxiety to develop morally by developing industrially was exacerbated by the 1837 depression. But the depression alerted party elites to the possibilities of mobilizing abolitionists. By explaining the depression as having been created by a "spendthrift, slaveholding South upon a frugal, industrious and unsuspecting free labor North," white abolitionists made the accumulation process appear as a liberation movement. The situation was tailor made for party politics. The energy of the abolitionist *movement* would be used to power the emergence of competitive capitalism.[19]

The party that transformed this movement energy into a pillar of private interests was the Liberty Party, the only party ever to have direct roots in an abolitionist organization. Julian P. Bretz points out how the transformation was made:

> The Liberty party might continue to insist that its paramount object was human freedom, but the fact remained that its activities were chiefly directed against the slave power as a political and economic force, and not against the existence of slavery in the states. The separation of the national government from slavery was, politically an attainable end, while emancipation was not.[20] By 1844 the Liberty Party had retreated from a call for federal interference with slave labor in the states and simply supported "the absolute and unqualified divorce of the General Government from slavery."[21]

Let us summarize the impact of the two party system upon the abolitionist movement: 1) the   collective interests of abolitionist politics was attached to the development of private interests or the property relations of competitive capitalism; 2) this was accomplished by leaving unclear, perhaps purposefully so, the distinction between criticisms of slavery and criticisms of policy positions of slave owners; 3) the resulting policy initiatives were limited to what was politically attainable. But why is the process so mystified? Why didn't abolitionists understand or object to the fact that abolition was not an obtainable end or that it was being pushed aside in favor of someone else's interests? What structures the range of policy options? And whose interests become the public interest? We shall come back to these questions throughout but let us continue, for now, our preliminary critical evaluation.

One senses that there is a kind of calculating rationality at work here, the kind of rationality that places a woman on a ticket primarily because it is likely to increase electoral support. There is the kind of thinking that is required when it is assumed that the point of political activity is one of essentially effecting public policy as opposed to effecting social change, personal growth, and critical insight. Therefore, *as a party leader* who unreflectively accepts the party system as it is, my interest in other citizens (and their aspirations) would rest primarily upon my conception of them as potential contributors to the building of winning coalitions organized around *my* interests. The conception of citizens as people capable of imagining and creating alternative institutions with fewer and less severe defects would be unavailable to me. But if it were available to me, it is probable that I might find the notion to be threatening. For if the structure of party politics functions, in part, to validate the pursuit of private interests, collective aspirations, especially ones steeped in a desire for social change, would challenge who I am and the way I am living my life. And if the pursuit of private interests were a central pillar in an order perceived as democratic, unity among those attempting to change the order would be considered a very serious threat indeed, particularly if that unity were among those perceived to be lacking self-discipline, logical acumen, or industriousness. It appears, then, that the two party system gives expression to a thin conception of "popular government," one that gives life to the conception of popular government prescribed by James Madison in *Federalist No. 10.* : a popular government is one in which people "without property" (or who have become property) who are "united and actuated by some common impulse of passion" are prevented from weakening "the rights of property."[22]

The influence of this Madisonian conception of popular government is central to the coalition building process within two party politics. It at once protects the freedom bestowed by property rights at the same time that it makes it difficult for those without property or who have become property to "discover their own strength and to act in unison with each other."

For example, white abolitionists thought that by excluding blacks from the party process they could build a broader base of support within the white community and more quickly move toward the policy of abolition. It is the time worn strategy, now so salient among Democrats, to capture the middle ground. But this strategy is a sanitizing process. In this example, the coalition was able to achieve broader support only by shifting the policy focus from abolition to the separation of the national government from slavery. As Bretz pointed out, this was done because the separation of the national government was politically an attainable end. Or in Madisonian language, it was consistent with property rights as they were then defined. Does traditional coalition building tend to filter out critical thought? In this case, it was required that 1) black abolitionists be excluded, and 2) that white abolitionists appeal to the broader white (supremacist) community. It appears that as the two party system supports the conditions of property rights and the particular kind of freedom internal to those conditions, it blocks the political opposition of those whose subordination is a direct outcome of property rights.

One could argue that the mobilization of the broad sectors of the white community behind the separation of the national government from slavery was a step forward in any case. To be sure, no single group was able to get all that it wanted. Yet each group got something that it wanted. Isn't this the stuff of political compromise? Weren't the interests of blacks advanced? Let us look at the process from a different angle. The effect of the party process was the abandonment of the principle around which black abolitionists had organized and the acceptance of the principles around which the party system was organized (gaining control of government and passing legislation). This shift in principle reenforced the vastly unequal portions of political power shared by the participants. Much like the contemporary situation where the aspirations of feminists are misused, the aspirations of blacks, once an end in themselves, became valuable only to the extent that they contributed to the private interests of those seeking to topple slave-owners as a political economic force. Leading black political figures were denied their subjectivity as white supremacists were allowed to shape the legislative agenda. The movement, which had abolition as it goal, required social and institutional change and divergent norms with which to personally identify. The coalition which had the separation of the national government from slavery as its goal required that institutional inter-connections and social norms, which rested upon slavery, not be changed.[23]

A more recent example of way in which the coalition building process tends to block the political expression of subordinant groups was the unwillingness of left of center groups to link up with or endorse the 1984 presidential campaign of Jesse Jackson. The refusal of the National Organization for Women (NOW) to join the "Rainbow Coalition"[24] was made primarily on the basis of building a coalition that could win, and in so doing advance the cause of women. Stated one NOW member, "If we were going to make the first presidential endorsement in our 17-year history, we wanted to get the biggest bang for our buck."[25] That this broader coalition consisted of men and women who did not profess feminism or support for a woman as a vice-presidential candidate (as had Jackson) seems to have mattered little. And with the nomination of Ferraro, NOW's strategy may have been effective in the short run. But notice: the interests of feminists with respect to cuts in social programs and militarism, which probably would have been better protected by an explicit alliance with people of color, may have been sacrificed in the interest of making, if not keeping, the woman's movement white and middle class. As in the case with abolition, making a wealthy white woman a vice-president is more politically attainable end than is strengthening the social wage or supporting liberation movements in the Third World, especially when the freedom of investors increasingly turns upon the political control of the Third World.

The gains disadvantaged people make, then, appear to be due less to the democratic nature of the party system (these groups hardly have equal say or access) than to the chance that their misfortune might be used by one set of elites as a brickbat against their political opponents. Republican elites established public school systems in the South and supported the enfranchisement of blacks during Reconstruction in their struggle with Democrats over the consolidation of political and economic power in the South. So blacks got something. Republicans later were quick not to enforce the enfranchisement of black men (the Fifthteenth Amendment). Why? Because the Democrats agreed to allow, in 1877, the electoral commission to declare Republican R. Blaine Hayes the winner in the electoral college even though the Democratic candidate, Samuel J. Tilden, had received more popular votes.[26] Following that historic "compromise," the fate of blacks was sealed. The forty years of work by blacks within the party system was rewarded not only with disfranchisement but with what became the most severe and extended period of racist violence excepting slavery itself.

During periods when party participation has been particularly ineffective, blacks have tried to make the bargaining process work for them by switching party allegiance. The 1970s was just such a time. The number of blacks below the poverty line grew from 8 million to 9 million (34 percent of all "poor"). Between 1972 and 1982, black unemployment grew 140 percent while unemployment among black teenagers in 1982 was 48 percent. In 1978, white high school dropouts had a lower unemployment rate than did black youths with a college education. In 1971, black families averaged 60 percent of the income of white families, but by 1981 that percentage had dropped to 56 percent.[27] Frustrated with the inability of the Democratic party to "deliver" for blacks, a few blacks have rejoined the Republican party as Freedom Republicans. A woman spokesperson for the group explained,

"Democrats don't need to bait the hook if they already got the fish. Besides, Jesse Jackson got only 5 percent of the white (Democratic) vote. They love to have us in their party, but they're not going to vote for any of us."

In 1980, Ralph Abernathy, a major figure in the Southern Christian Leadership Conference, abandoned the "Democrats only" strategy and threw his support to Ronald Reagan. This attempt to wrestle with the limitations of only two major parties was no less blasphemous than the late 19th century plan of Blanche K. Bruce's, who was a black Mississippi planter. With the Supreme Court approving segregation and with the disfranchisement of blacks underway in the South, Bruce urged blacks to abandon Frederick Douglass' political strategy of "Republicans-only." By 1900 a Negro National Democratic League was organized. When the Democrats finally reached the White House in 1917, the fortune of blacks seemed to decline further. The election of Woodrow Wilson, according to Harvard Sitkof, led to the most Southern dominated, anti-Negro administration since the 1850s.[28] Not one black delegate was seated at a national Democratic convention until 1936. And the attention blacks received in 1936 appears to have been due less to the progressive thinking of Democrats than to the "Great Migration." As blacks left the South and became northern urban industrialists, their political stock began to rise, ever so slowly. Manning Marable argues that it was not until 1948 "that the Democratic party even took a lukewarm, public stand in favor of civil rights for Blacks." Marable concludes that "Black accommodation to the Democratic Party" has been "bitter fruit."[29]

Perhaps Henry MacNeal Turner's statement in 1868 before the Georgia legislature after that body voted to expel all its Negro members best captures the relationship of blacks to the party system: "we are told that if black men want to speak, they must speak through white trumpets...." It is his defiance, however, that is most intriguing to the student of party politics: "I hold that I am a member of this body....I shall neither fawn nor cringe before any party, nor stoop to beg them for my rights." It may be this sense of dignity, this unwillingness to stoop or beg that transforms very limited gains within the party system into the great accomplishments of history. Ironically, it may be what Francis Fox Piven and Richard Cloward have termed "defiant mass protest" that is most responsible for the democratic appearance of our political institutions. But before we glimpse the activity which takes place outside the party system, let us examine that other great movement, the labor movement. What has been the political party experience of white male wage earners?

The gap between what wage earners sought in the party system and what they got is, as in the case of women and blacks, quite striking. The party history of white male wage earners is different, however. We find that while wage earners have experienced discrimination in terms of their access to the party system (see Chapter 4), particularly among immigrants, their discrimination compared to women and blacks in this regard has been less severe. In a word, the explanation of why the voice of the males has been more easily heard within the party than that of females is *patriarchy*. The concept of patriarchy used in this study, however, extends into the complex linkages between religious and scientific beliefs. We shall come back to a discussion of patriarchy more systematically in Chapter 4.

The limitations of the party system, both with regard to its structure (only two parties) and its processes (politics as bargaining) are hardly arbitrary as we have seen. The history of the party experience of wage earners suggests that the party system is, as we have suspected, very much an institutional support of what we shall call property relations, or the set of social relations organized around the freedom of individuals to own and control productive and reproductive property. Before we get ahead of ourselves, let us briefly review the party history of the white male wage earner.

In response to the introduction of the factory system, small farmers and wage earners protested the discipline of wage labor imposed by factory owners, and the disruption of community life which the factory system generated. Discriminated against by factory and slave owners who together ran both major parties (the Whigs and the Democrats), wage earners joined in creating a degree of political space (during the 1820s and 1830s) by helping to organize a number of minor parties such as the Workingmen's Party, the Antimasons, and the Locofoco's.[30] For the most part, these parties were led by reformers who were troubled by the extraordinary privileges enjoyed by "monopolies" or financiers and the burgeoning captains of industry. Whig and Democratic elites, troubled by the domination of slave owners within each of their parties formed splinter parties. For example, dissident Democrats in New York formed the Barnburners while in Massachusetts dissident Whig leaders formed the Conscience Whigs.

As the chorus of condemnation of "wage slavery" grew, and it should be pointed out that women were among the most militant wage earners, white male wage earners became the central grassroots constituency in a constellation of parties that eventually evolved into the Republican party, as the Whigs collapsed in the 1850s.[31] Yet, the Republican party was the political dimension of an expanding wage system. This meant that honest and genuine reform of the workplace, the issue which had initially brought workers into the party system, would be indefinitely postponed. In a word, the participation of the toiling masses prior to the Civil War had backfired. Vis-a-vis slavery, Republicans held up the wage system as a model of freedom. What so many workers had termed wage slavery was *free labor* to Republican elites challenging the economic policies of slave-plantation owners.

If the two party system functions to insure that disadvantaged constituencies advance only when their advancement contributes to the development of property relations, the world view and private interest of political elites bears special consideration. The Republican triumph following the Civil War, by giving full expression to competitive capitalism, completed the American Revolution. Who were Republican elites? There were two basic groups. One group represented the program of the Free Soilers or the preservation of the territories for entrepreneurs, developers, and free labor. The other group of elites were northern industrial and mercantile capitalists who were anxious to initiate protective tariffs, appropriate money for railroads, create a national bank and a uniform currency, and exploit the rich resources of the public domain.[32] The gains that would come to disadvantaged classes, therefore, would have to compliment the private ownership of property, expansion of the private economy, and the conquest and development of nature.

For example, one major factor underlying the personal identification of wage earners with Republicans was the hope that "the virgin soil, rich and wild as at the dawn of creation, might be preserved, a free asylum for the oppressed and a safe retreat for the slaves of wages...."[33] Republicans responded to this desire for "free soil" with the Homestead Act of 1861. It granted 160 acres of unoccupied and publicly owned western land to anyone who was able to purchase it and then cultivate it for five years. Was this a political victory for workers? At $1.25 an acre few wage earners were able to come up with the necessary $200 or pay for the required transportation. Most of the 50 million acres was purchased by speculators. If Republicans were unable to provide workers with free homesteads, we would be less inclined to suspect that the advancement of property relations define the political rewards made available to disadvantaged classes. But during the Civil War the President and Congress *gave* over 100 million acres to the railroads free of charge.[34]

Or consider the People's Party. It was the party that grew out of what may have been the most massive and extended period of protest in the nation's history. Involving small farmers and wage earners in all sectors of the economy (but largely avoiding blacks and ignoring women), spawning a plethora of creative policies, such as the "sub-treasury plan" designed to democratize the monetary system, and boasting of several thousand co-operatives and millions of partici-pants, the party arose (1894) when the Democrats had collapsed in Kansas, Nebraska, Minnesota, the Dakotas, Colorado, Montana, and Oregon and when there was support for programs of small farmers "of anywhere from 25 to 45 percent of the electorate in twenty-odd states."[35] Yet by 1896, the People's Party had been taken over by an elite group of mine owners ("silverites") and ambitious politicians. The creative policy initiatives advanced by farmers were reduced to a "free silver" plank, or unlimited silver coinage, within the Democratic platform. Moreover, organized labor and socialist elements of the party were eventually purged. Wrote the *National Watchman*, the official People's Party organ, "Let us be conservative, in order to secure the support of the businessmen, the professional men, and the well to do. These are elements we must use if ever success comes to our party. For every loud voiced socialist who declares war on us we will get a hundred of the conservative element in our society."[36]

It is worth noting the contrast between interpretations of protests of the late 19th century which suggest that the party process captures the essence of democracy and the interpretation presented here. V.O. Key, Jr., for example, has written that, "The Populists...had an influence that extended beyond Democratic acceptance of their doc-trines. Their energetic agitation in support of their cause gave currency to ideas that eventually gained wide support and became law." It sounds good, but it is an academic rendition of people's history which by adopting the Madisonian perspective is able to interpret rule by financial and commercial elite as "popular government." Ignored are larger *structural* changes in the social system. A *monopoly sector* was constructed upon the systematic erosion of the little economic power that had been preserved by the skilled worker. This transformation of skilled work into mindless work and of the skilled worker into what critics of the process have called the "rump of human nature" was accomplished largely through *scientific management*. Whereas Key believes that the ideas of Populists were being turned into law, the reality is that the rise of a monopoly sector and arbitrary control in the workplace during the Populist moment mocked workers who had long expressed hostility within the party system toward the economic "tyranny" of monopolies. Indeed, it was precisely this expressed hostility that had motivated many wage earners to work within the party system nearly seventy years earlier.[37]

Discussions of the changes in work processes such as the introduction of scientific managment, which was essential to monopoly capital and the triumph of Republicans at the turn of the century, are clearly avoided in the literature on political parties. The reason may be that the domination of one person by another, either by class, race, gender, or through the forces of production, is often assumed as natural, just as women seemed to have viewed their own subordination during the 18th century as divine providence. Therefore, it is not really perceived, either by many party elites or many scholars who study the party system. When Key states that the Federal Reserve Act coped with problems "by means different from that urged by the Populists" he reveals the degree to which he and others who have adopted similar interpretations of party politics are unaware of its *undemocratic* dynamics. The Federal Reserve Act: 1) was written J. Laurence Laughlin and associates *on behalf of the banking community*; 2) it placed in private hands the decisions effecting the extention of credit to farmers, not in public hands as Populists had urged; and 3) it insulated the bankers within the Federal Reserve from the political criticism of public inspection. The end result according to Lawrence Goodwyn was "a loss of autonomy by millions of Americans on the land." Certainly, the proposition that the party system thwarted what democratic thrust there was to the Populist movement ought to be seriously considered.

Mike Davis suggests that the political experience of workers during the transformative period of the Great Depression furnishes us with the "most ironic" experience of all. Writes Davis:

> The same workers who defied the machine guns of the National Guard at Flint or chased the deputies off the streets during the semi-insurrectionary Minneapolis General strike were also the cornerstone of electoral support for Roosevelt. The millions of young workers aroused by the struggle for industrial unionism were simultaneously mobilized as the shock troops of a pseudo-aristocratic politician whose avowed ambition was 'the salvation of American capitalism.' To the extent that so-called 'labour' or 'farmer-labour' parties emerged in industrial areas of the midwest or northeast they remained scarcely more than advance detachments and satellites of the New Deal.[38]

Davis goes on to add that "fledgling 'labour parties' collapsed as workers were successfully reabsorbed into a capitalist two-party system that brilliantly manipulated and accentuated cultural schisms in the working class."

Davis is surely on to something, but to suggest that disadvantaged classes have been or could be "brilliantly manipulated" may be a bit too tidy. Something is missing. Only dupes are ever "brilliantly manipulated." The reabsortion of fledgling labor parties by the two party system may have been due in part to the belief shared among workers that the two party system was capable of working for them. It was largely through the two party system during the 1930s, after all, that workers obtained the minimum wage and the right to bargain collectively. Weren't these solid achievements? Is it probable, after so many years, that disadvantaged constituencies demand essentially that which the two party system can deliver? If so, the question becomes, is it possible to speak of manipulation when the disadvantaged get much of what they want?

First, let us recall that organized labor actively opposed government intervention into labor-managment relations prior to the 1930s.[39] The national minimum wage and hours law within the cotton-textile industry in 1937 was pushed through by a coalition of conservative northern mill owners and liberal politicians who were anxious to stabilize the industry by equalizing (labor) costs. The losers in this case were southern mill owners whose market position had been propped up by their ability to get away with paying very low wages. The United Mine Workers and the Teamsters worked with owners in their respective industries to effect similar legislation.[40] Only as an instrument which strengthened the market position of large owners and contributed to the stability of an industry did the issue of poorly compensated labor become an important issue to elites. Gabriel Kolko argues further that the minimum wage was "both irrelevant to human needs and surely did nothing to sustain the postwar prosperity celebrated as the triumph of the 'welfare state.'"[41] But what it seems to have done was to shore up the appearence of a democratic party system, and, more important, it was precisely this appearance that helped satisfy the democratic appetite of those in undignified situations such as wage earners.

The Wagner Act or the right of workers to bargain collectively is similar in this regard. By validating trade unions as legitimate institutions, the Wagner Act stands as one of the major rewards of party participation. After nearly forty years of collective bargaining, however, its limitations are becoming well known. The "great bargain," notes David Milton was an arrangement "whereby a number of material demands of the new industrial unions were legitimated in exchange for the renunciation by labor of its independent political power." In other words, adds Milton, it was a classic trade-off, power was exchanged for money.[42] Again, this charge like the one of manipulation, fails to grasp the need of so many to accept the appearances of democracy as reality. One cannot be charged with exchanging something when the exchange is not clear, when one is not conscious of what is going on. And this is the crux of the manipulation internal to the two party system. Disadvantaged classes (and it is becoming clear that one is disadvantaged when one is not an owner of productive property), and elites surely to a large degree, neither understand nor control the party process. The manipulation in question is part structural (our option of one or sometimes two major parties is as limited as can be); but it is also partially self-constructed. There is security, as partial objects in a process, to pretend that we are full subjects. Where does it lead?

It leads to an acceptance, even at times a celebration, of the loss of our ability to collectively control our lives. The acceptance of larger pieces of the pie by workers (economism) during the 1930s after having lost control of the workplace is no different in one respect than the acceptance of the reduction of Populist demands to the remonitization of silver as the outcome of a democratic process. Hindsight affords us this critical perspective. We can argue, with some detachment, that while the crop lien system allowed merchants to control nearly every aspect of a small farmer's life, the best the People's party could come up with was changing the monetary standard from gold to silver. But what about the "modern victims"?

> ...the American people, who are forced to purchase homes, automobiles, and other goods under undemocratic and highly usurious credit procedures, have been socialized into such an ethos of mass deference that they no longer contest the matter, as their eighteenth- and nineteenth-century predecessors did. This is so despite the fact that millions of working Americans, who could enjoy the dignity of owning their own homes under ground rules of a democratic system of money and credit, are forced under the prevailing system to spend their lifetimes as transient renters. The relevant long-term development is that the American people understandably no longer even comprehend the financial formulas that ensnare them, since such matters are no longer on the agenda of national political discussion.[43]

We would be remiss if we were to let stand the characterization "socialized into such an ethos" stand. True, we seem to be lodged deeply within the bowels of a dreadful ethos, but there is a degree of pitiable comfort there. There is comfort in avoiding questions of power, in assuming that much of what happens to us is *not* due to decisions made in corporate board rooms, in accepting the agenda of the party system as a complete one, and in believing that the purpose of political work is essentially one of passing legislation or electing someone to speak for us. In short, there is comfort in ignoring clues of domination. Indeed, it is the widely shared belief, or should we say need to believe, that all is well that may be the most important constitutive

element in our "democratic order." The notion that politics entails a
social and public process of self-examination and personal growth is
one that is foreign to us. Consequently, the need to engage in serious
critical thought, join together in order to learn from one another, or in
general to work collectively, recedes. The need to trust authorities,
experts, and party leaders and distrust the "uninformed" and the
"uneducated" advances. Class identities are fragmented. Interest
groups multiply. I am no longer a black, a woman, or a worker. I am
someone working to pass a minimum wage law or an equal rights bill. I
am a private citizen seeking to protect *my* interests and *my* rights.
Participating in party politics is to accept party politics as politics. It is
to personally identify with it, to value and protect it, to defend it from
criticisms.

But notice the severity of the problem. As long as we believe that a
party system which excludes on the basis of access and on the basis of
ideology is also one that is essentially democratic, we risk complicity in
political repression. For example, if men and women in the economically powerful echelons of growth industries have greater access in a
party system that appears democratic, how do they explain the failure
of other broad constituencies such as the 3 million clerical and blue-
collar medical workers, the largest single segment of low-wage labor in
the United States, to use the system effectively? Will the need to see their
own rise to power as valid lead the wealthy to see the politically less
powerful as apathetic? Ignorant? Lazy?

The upshot of all this is that organizing within the two party
system carries with it the illusion of democracy and a misunderstanding
of the political space the two parties provide. Obscured are the linkages
between the authority of the state and the private interests of large
property owners as well as the gender, racial and class biases of a social
order organized around economic conquest and control, patriarchy and
racism. Silent are the constraints of single-member districts, plurality
elections, the electoral college, the primary system and other rules of
the game which give rise to a highly individuated or atomized political
process.

Between 1965 and 1980, the share of the U.S. market income going
to the poorest 40 percent fell from 11 percent to 8.5 percent. Black male
participation in the labor force between 1945 and 1983 fell from 80
percent to 60 percent while 60 percent of employed black males (and 50
percent of Hispanics) are concentrated in the spectrum of the lowest
paid jobs. Mike Davis points out that a generation after the first March
on Washington, black unemployment remains double that of whites,
while black poverty is three times more common. While the number of
working women doubled between the Eisenhower and Reagan Administrations, their earnings dropped to 59 percent of the average for
men. As the decade of the 1980s began, one third of all full-time women
workers were earning less than $7,000 a year yet the white male median

income was $17,000. And despite organized labor's supposed power within the Democratic Party, it has, according to Richard Edwards, difficulty obtaining the party's approval even for the highest labor priorities such as public jobs bills, labor law reform, repeal of the Taft-Hartley Section 14-B, a higher minimum wage, or national health insurance. With the return of a Democratic administration in 1977, the AFL-CIO, depending on the Democratic party to halt organized labor's decline,[44] sought legislation to speed up representation elections, increase penalties for unfair labor practices, and generally strengthen the National Labor Relations Board's ability to mitigate the rise in union-busting tactics. The AFL-CIO was defeated, however. Thomas Ferguson and Joel Rogers suggest that the defeat ("a catastrophe for organized labor") "underscored labor's inability to extract concessions or support from the putatively friendly ranks of the Democratic party.[45]

Women, people of color, and wage earners have made gains within the two party system to be sure. Most of these gains, as we have noted, were won because they happened to have helped shore up the political-economic hegemony of certain groups of large property owners. The access to the ranks of elites that has been achieved by a tiny handful of women, blacks, and labor leaders is significant, but such gains are not the hallmark of a democratic party structure but of a party structure where political expression is reduced to an instrument and where individual success is tainted by complicity in domination.

As economic and political power has become more concentrated, the visibility of a few women, a few labor leaders, and even a fewer number of dark faces at the top has given many citizens an excuse to repress their own sense of powerlessness, their hunch that all is not right. Still other citizens have become conscious of the systematic disparity between appearance and reality. As political activists they work primarily outside the party system. And by building their own political processes and structures, however inadequate they may or may not be, the institutional barriers to empowerment are at once transcended.

Movement Politics

> ...the river of black struggle is people, but it is also the hope, the movement, the transformative power that humans create and that create them, us, and makes them, us, new persons....And at its best the river of our struggle has mov- ed...forever seeking what black people in South Carolina said they sought in 1865: "the right to develop our whole *being*."[46]
> —Vincent Harding

> If there is no space for us, then we create space.[47]
> —Jean Caiani, political activist

Harding's use of a river as a metaphor to capture the mood and timeless quality of movement politics is particularly apt; "for the black

river in the United States has always taken on more than blackness,"
writes Harding. "The dynamics and justice of its movement have
continually gathered others to itself, have persistently filled other men
and women with the force of its vision, its indomitable hope."
Movement politics is trans-historical. Engaged in by those who share a
sense of powerlessness or discrimination, it is a struggle to create space
for the development of the whole person, or the full human personality.
Institutional arrangements which obstruct such development vary
across time, but the river, the struggle, the movement continues.

Movement politics is also historically specific. Creating the space
for the development of the full human personality in any given age
particularlizes the struggle, carries the struggle into confrontation with
those institutions which at any given time limit and constrain the full
play of creative expression. Movement politics, in our own age, is the
rejection, often implicitly, of the two party system. It is the rejection of
politics as competition among temporary coalitions of distinct autonomous groups, each pursuing "opposed aims...[which attempt] either
to vote down the opposition or push it into a settlement on the most
favorable possible terms for themselves." Implicitly, it is a rejection of
the win-loose mentality that permeates party politics.[48]

As Jean Caiani suggests, movement politics arises out of the need
to create the space for political expression that is denied to certain
groups or classes in general. But in particular it is the creation of space
for an emerging human personality and space for a different kind of
politics as well. Growing out of a collective sense of discrimination,
movement politics becomes a source of hope for the oppressed. It raises
the possibility of creating new and dignified life situations where
cooperation and mutual concern displace competition and individual
self-interest. The first trade unions arose out of the collective struggle to
restore the dignity of autonomous craft production. Constrained
politically, the movement eventually became organized around higher
wages and shorter hours as well as the need for assistance during
periods of sickness. The early Farmers Alliance grew out of the
collective desire of small farmers to avoid the crop lien system and to go
beyond the cash stores of the Grange. It led to cooperative marketing
and purchasing arrangements that shook "inherited forms of deference" and moved farmers to revolt throughout the South, Texas, and
the Western Plains. During the 1950s and 1960s, southern blacks,
working together, transformed their church into a rampart from which
a moral indictment of the American conscience would spawn a
relentless crusade for civil rights which in turn set the stage for a
renewed push for black nationalism. Out of the sharing of personal
experiences in the 1960s, women with new and broader self-understandings would go on to create the space for health clinics, rape-crisis
centers, shelters for battered women, and a voice for the lesbian

community. Unlike party politics, movement politics augments instead of fractures the collective spirit or what many have termed simple civic virtue.

Sharp divisions, of course, exist within movement politics, but as illustrated by the woman's movement (the principles of socialist feminists differ from those of radical feminists which differ from those of NOW, etc.), the divisions do not obscure the notion of solidarity that is shared among women. Nor do such divisions obstruct the exploration of the idea that the social order is gender based. Indeed, much as Harding suggests, each faction is more like a tributary to a river, a common purpose, than it is like the factionalism of self-interest within the party system. Unlike party politics where the dovetailing of self-interests (we can help each other help ourselves) forms the basis of collective action, the collective spirit within movement politics flows more out of the understanding that politics' greatest rewards are contained within the very process of working together. For the activist, politics has more to do with the empowerment of common citizens than with the accountability of elites. Political activity has more to do with prolonged discussion, criticism, and self-criticism among concerned citizens than with listening to candidates and media experts. Voting, in this context, is but one aspect of political expression, not the first and last.

That politics can be an enriching experience separate from assessments of "victory" or "defeat" is evident in the statements of fulfillment expressed by 1960s activists.

> The flood broke loose gradually and then more swiftly. We talked about our families, our mothers, our fathers, our siblings; we talked about our men; we talked about school; we talked about "the movement" (which meant new left men). For hours we talked and unburdened our souls and left feeling high and planning to meet again the following week.)
>
> The women's movement really gave me my voice. Before I was never very good, but with the women's movement I was really thunderingly effective...)
>
> Once you start talking to people and bring them together you can start moving to do something for your neighborhood....- We called a meeting with the people and discussed our problems. We found that most all of us had the same problems. We decided to go on a rent strike.[49]

Making space, creating new forms of political expression, new ways of seeing and of working together, appears to fill out the meaning of political activity in a way that is strikingly different from the way in which the term "politics" is ordinarily used in connection with the party system. Issues are not separated but connected together. There is internal gratification (personal growth, discovery) in addition to external rewards (cleaner air, safer work environment, etc.). The process is social as opposed to individualistic, supportive as opposed to combative.

Moreover, the range of external objectives often extend beyond the range of legislative boundaries (establishing feminist publishing houses or Afro-American studies, for example) and, therefore, often broadens the scope of government. That is, movement politics is part of the struggle that broadens what government can do as well as the concept of what is possible. Legislation intended to support halfway houses for battered women, worker controlled factories, or to prevent discrimination within the private sector were government responses directly related to movement politics. Movement politics also impacts in ways that are fundamental but in ways that are not considered political. Cafes, clinics, and shelters are created. Activists in southern Florida raised money to search for a Kanjobal interpreter in order that Guatemalan refugees be clearly understood in their testimony before a federal judge. The challenge which women posed to those of us who might have used the concept "girl" unreflectively, for example, has altered everyday life. Indeed, it is quite doubtful that the Democratic nomination of Geraldine Ferraro for vice-president could have preceded this sort of conceptual change. Although the two party system is the gate through which official policy makers pass, the process of making policy is lodged within the more politically creative milieu of everyday life. Significant social change which marks history begins not with voting, writing letters to Congress people, or with signing petitions. Rather it begins with the meeting that is called by those at the bottom of the political heap.

The implicit rejection of party politics that is internal to the process of building a movement, therefore, is not a simple rejection of ideas in the heads of Democrats and Republicans or of the goals to which they subscribe. Rather it is a rejection of the meaning—the norms, values, and standards—that is part of the political practice of Democrats and Republicans, of "liberals and conservatives." Moreover, because the norms and values that are rejected cannot be attributed simply to individual party elites or to a particular set of party actions (they are the glue of the practice presently termed "politics"), movement politics is an implicit re-evaluation of the standards, meanings, norms, and social bonds which define our way of life.

Using Key's terminology, we could say that movement politics, not the two party system, is the "functional equivalent of revolution." Suffice it to say that it is the primary basis of genuine political opposition. The point is that as one engages in movement politics, one crosses a threshold of sorts. The actions one participates in, if not the professed beliefs of the participants themselves, express a discontent that appears unjustified, if not irrational, from the point of view of citizens who believe politics to be party politics and democracy to be electoral competition.

To those who are disenchanted with the rewards and the processes of the two party system, movement politics stirs the imagination. It once again becomes possible to feel good about political participation. And because of the ability to broaden the range of debate and to make politics an enriching and empowering experience, activists tend to weaken the legitimacy of party elites. Indeed, it is upon the shared sense of legitimacy that activists base their appeal, just as party elites base their appeal upon the right to own property. Movement politics, therefore, more than the two party system, often becomes the last line of defense for those whose economic dependence makes them politically vulnerable. Consequently, participation within movement politics invites cooptation and repression. It is within this very precarious space, the space between co-optation and repression, that activists have worked, whether it has been reducing the number of working hours in a day from 10 to 8, amending the Constitution, securing affirmative action programs, or generally creating the space for egalitarian practices. Francis Fox Piven and Richard Cloward have argued that "Whatever influence lower-class groups occasionally exert in American politics does not result from organization, but from mass protest and the disruptive consequences of protest." But must it be this way? Is it not possible to synthesize the best that movement politics and party politics have to offer?[50]

Sara Evans' work regarding the linkages of the peace, civil rights, and the women's movements of the 1950s and 1960s brings us to our concluding point. Many of the activists she interviewed spoke of the emotional intensity and gratification of movement politics. Statements such as "...the work so far has been far more gratifying than anything I ever anticipated," leaving the movement "would be like living death," or "I go home at night completely exhausted but very happy" were typical. To dismiss this exuberance as romanticism or simply as evidence of youthful idealism would be to seriously misunderstand the life giving aspect of politics outside the party system. It is a way of covering up what Mike Davis has referred to (with respect to workers) as "repeated experiences of disillusionment...and withdrawal from the political system."[51] Perhaps it is time to stop apologizing for the capacity of property owners to become political power brokers and to fragment healthy and nurturing social bonds through the bargaining process.

The point is that movement politics is exactly that, *movement*. The struggle of moving from an "I" to a "we" point of view, from a voting kind of politics to a "We can't sit by any longer" kind of politics is more than an ordinary moment of political existence unavailable in the party system; movement politics is less a means of reaching an end than it is a means of living a life. It is extra-ordinary, at least in our type of society.

* * *

> There's a freedom train a-coming. But you got to be registered to ride. Get on board! Get on board!....We can move from the slave ship to the championship. From the guttermost to the uppermost! From the outhouse to the courthouse! From the statehouse to the White House!
>
> —Jesse Jackson, 1983

> Jesse's campaign is not a political campaign. It is a spiritual, emotional campaign.
>
> —Andrew Young

There is little room in a presidential campaign for the black spirituals of struggle and faith that have been part of black solidarity, of the black river. As Andrew Young points out, spiritualism or emotionalism, so much an accepted feature of movement politics, is not normally considered to be "political." This observation embodies a disturbing moment of truth: what we think of as *political* is separate from what we normally think of as spiritual or emotional.

For example, what would we have to say about the woman who said, "It felt really good to be with so many people who were unified.... We had such feelings of ecstasy, such feelings of being able to make the new world right there"? Or consider the statement, "I couldn't walk down the street, read advertisements, watch TV, without being incensed...at the way women are treated"?[52] Is this the stuff of party politics? Does it belong in presidential campaigns? Is it really *political*.

I think we can get clearer about the broader implications of the separation of emotion and reason that seems to be associated with the traditional notion of politics by examining a statement by Jeremy Brecher regarding the ordinary lives of workers.

> ...workers think, speak and act not as vendors in a market, but as oppressed and exploited human beings in revolt. Their criterion is what they need, not "what the market will bear." Their strikes are not timed to the balance of supply and demand, but to the felt intolerability of their present condition. Their relation to employers and to each other is not expressed in terms of buyers and sellers, but in terms of anger at their oppressors and human solidarity with each other."[53]

Feeling the intolerability of a present condition and speaking and acting as exploited human beings are experiences that are undoubtedly all wrapped up in feelings. And if we live in the memory of these feelings or if the desire to express these intimate sensations becomes the motivation for the battlers of ideas and builders of communities, then won't a party system organized around the needs of people as *buyers and sellers* (or producers and consumers) deny politics as a spiritual development, as a process of finding ourselves and of building communities. Won't a party system designed to support a rationalized way of life give priority to the Thomas Jeffersons and the Andrew Jacksons as it obstructs the Harriet Tubmans and John Browns? As we identify with the party system will we find ways of justifying the exclusion of women, blacks, and workers? And as Democrats and Republicans, as informed voters, will we become the police on each of our blocks, anxious to identify and condemn those who seemingly subvert our cherished way of life, who refuse to accept market relations as human relations?

In spite of the ridicule and repression that movement politics invites, the self-examination of movement politics permits activists to engage in the kind of critical thinking that leads to the transcendance of repressive structures, processes, or shared assumptions. It was, after all, out of the male dominated movement politics of the 1960s that the most recent phase of the woman's movement emerged with renewed vitality. But there is a serious flaw to movement politics. Motivation, for many activists, seems to flow primarily out of simple gut feelings. As healthy as these feelings may be, feelings in and of themselves do not permit the clarification of the felt resistance to mainstream politics or enjoyment of movement politics. The understanding of each is largely implicit. Rarely does one find, within the activities that make up movement politics, an appetite for disciplined intellectual work, the kind of work that could transform such valuable implicit understandings into explicit political forces.

Joan Cocks' exploration of the strengths and weaknesses of radical or cultural feminists sheds a great deal of light on this flaw. Cocks suggests that the women's culture of radical feminism, because it "understands the hegemonic culture in the same terms in which that culture understands itself" and because it completely condemns the dominant order, is "pressed to present itself as all the established society is not...showing itself an unwitting prisoner of the established conceptual schema, which delineates for it definition and counterdefinition, image and counterimage." Of primary concern to Cocks is the tendency among feminists to unreflectively accept the assumption that reason and emotion "mark off actual qualities and experiences that are hostile opposites of one another." In contrast to the hegemony marked by "precepts of domination, performance, hierarchy, abstraction, and rationality" radical feminists understand themselves almost exclusively as "naturally nurturant, receptive, cooperative, intimate, and exulting in the emotions."[54]

A more general application of this thesis, I believe, is appropriate to contemporary movement politics. Having attributed the rationalization of public life and, to a lesser degree, private life to a host of antagonists—men, the ruling class, scientists, professionals, positivists, and various agents of various churches, we completely condemn the dominant order. We are then compelled to present ourselves and our activities as the opposites of the dominant order. Our tendency, also, is to unknowingly become prisoner of the established conceptual schema. In the face of public double-speak, techo-military abstractions, and private manipulation, we stress the honesty of feelings. But in so doing, we also tend to resist the rigorous discipline of abstract thought. We refuse to attend to the complexities of the unconscious mind. We wish to play the music without learning the notes. Our knowledge of Robert Henri's insight that "the drudgery that kills is not half the work joy is," is often too shadowy, too unclear, to become an effective principle of political activity. Might not a clarification of the dangers and rewards of both the rationalized politics of the two party system and the more transformative politics of movement activity help us to get beyond the established conceptual schema of doing politics? If so, then might we, in the context of politics, give creativity, discipline, joy, and reason their best purchase?

This glimpse of the two party system and movement politics suggests that modern democracy has the potential of melting the divisions between control over political processes *and* nurturance from participation within political processes. It appears quite possible to shift the concept of modern democracy, which now seems stuck within the concept of accountability, toward such concepts as self-creativity. Indeed, given the growing concentration of political and economic power, we must transcend the notion which suggests that a democratic state is one in which its citizens are well informed and move to one which suggests that a democratic state is one in which *space is made available for its citizens to engage in and understand creative activity.* Modern democracy, therefore, is unthinkable save in terms not of the two party system but in terms which also celebrate the kind of politics that takes place outside it. In an attempt to fill out those terms, we shall organize the remainder of this book around six sets of questions:

1. What are the philosophical foundations of our political institutions? Might there be defects in the assumptions upon which our political institutions rest? If so, do such defective assumptions contribute to dynamics which structure the activity of the two party system?

2. What is the relationship between the state and the economy generally and party activity and economic activity specifically? Does this relationship structure our political agenda? Does it help explain the formation of governing coalitions?

3. Expansion, growth, conquest, discipline, individual achievement and the work ethic are cherished backround concepts which situate our political and economic freedoms. Is domination (with regard to nature, gender, race, or class) internal to these ideas? As cherished concepts, what is their role in the mobilization of popular

support within the two party system? Is domination a necessary feature of our popular government?

4. Do we acquire a sense of dignity by identifying with our political institutions? If so, do we then persist in organizing party processes around the individual when space for social interaction is required?

5. What is happening in the party system today? Which way is the political wind blowing? Who is benefiting? Who is vulnerable? Who is in a strategic position to effect social change?

6. What are the prospects for progressive change if we work within the two party system? What might an alternative party system look like? How do we get there?

Let us turn now to the philosophical foundation of our political institutions. Our purpose shall be to historically locate some of the political ideas which we celebrate and accept as given. By situating these ideas in the controversies out of which they arose we will be better able to appreciate their purpose and their impact upon our lives today.

2

OUR POLITICAL HERITAGE

Democrats are racing to devise plausible alternatives to Reaganomics, and to package them with attractive slogans that will
captivate the voters in 1984 as the Republican's supply-side
proclamations did in 1980.[1]
—Samuel Bowles, David M. Gordon, and Thomas E. Weisskopf

Most electoral campaigns are indeed struggles over the packaging
of "plausible alternatives." Plausible alternatives are those which do
not challenge the assumptions shared by both Democrats and Republicans. For example, Adlai Stevenson, two-time Democratic nominee for
president, told Smith College (female) graduates in 1955 that marriage
and motherhood gave women a special political duty. A women could
"inspire in her home a vision of the meaning of life and freedom...help
her husband find values that will give purpose to his specialized daily
chores...teach her children the uniqueness of each individual human
being."[2] As the attention of Smith students was drawn to ways of
helping male family members succeed in the public world, their
attention was diverted from considering ways in which they too might
succeed in the public world. The assumption that a woman's place was
exclusively in the home was left unchallenged. Today, of course,
anyone who delivered Stevenson's lines at a commencement ceremony
before all female graduates would run the risk of severe embarassment.
Since 1955, assumptions about the role of women have been challenged
through movement politics. In this case, an assumption once shared by
Democrats and Republicans may be said to have been *politicized*.

I shall argue in this chapter that it is in the consideration of
"implausible" alternatives and in the examination of widely shared
assumptions that political activity is most fruitful and fulfilling.
Unfortunately, the two party system tends to filter out this kind of
political activity. Within the party system, for example, welfare

proposals are debated but not the causes of massive inequality. Massive inequality is assumed by many to be functional, the stimulus of individual achievement. Environmental policy is debated but the assumption that nature is a resource to be used is not challenged. Each party suggests ways in which to "get the economy moving." But no one politicizes the assumption that endless economic growth is in our best interest. Such assumptions may be said to be *tacitly* accepted by most citizens.[3] They constitute the background to our political discourse.

Because our shared assumptions lie hidden below the surface of clear, conscious, and explicit political discourse, they establish limits to our political agenda. Once we explore the ways in which our shared assumptions focus and limit political discussions, we acquire knowledge of the boundaries of our own political thought. We are able then to see beyond the horizon. And by inspecting alternative ways of thinking up close and not from afar, we are encouraged not to accept as complete the given range of political discourse.

While reflective politics of this sort may be viewed as dangerous by some—it could invite relentless criticism of all that is cherished—it is, unmistakeably, a feature of critical and creative thought. Those alarmed by critical thought might find solace in Robert Henri's characterization of the creative experience:

> When the artist is alive in any person, whatever (her or his) kind of work may be, (s/he) becomes an inventive, searching, daring, self-expressing creature. (S/he) becomes interesting to other people. (S/he) distrubs, upsets, enlightens, and (s/he) opens ways for a better understanding. Where those who are not artists are trying to close the book, (s/he opens it, shows there are still more pages possible.[4]

With the sense of being able to turn a page of history, let us briefly probe the assumptions that circumscribe our political thought.

The Rise of Property Relations

All of us have heard friends or relatives discussing the merits of *working for* one company or another. "IBM has terrific benefits," someone might point out. "They don't need a union." Because the idea of working for someone has become part of our background of shared ideas, it is rarely seriously contested. Rather, the contestable issues, working conditions, benefits, and the like, become those that flow from, and therefore accommodate, the assumption that working for someone is an inevitable aspect of everyday life. Let us begin the exploration of our background assumptions by asking why working for someone seems so natural today. In order to do this, we must go back to a point in history when our revolutionary ancestors were actively engaged in the conscious questioning of the tacit dimensions of their own lives.

R. H. Tawney has written that the class hierarchy ("class oppression, exploitation, serfdom") of the Middle Ages was, in part, created by shared ideas that were rooted in religious beliefs. These beliefs suggested that social orders were divinely structured to reflect the form of the human body:

> Society, like the human body, is an organism composed of different members...[each with] its own function...[and] the means suited to its own station...Within classes there must be equality [among men].... Between classes there must be inequality; for otherwise a class cannot perform its function, or—a strange thought to us—enjoy its rights. Peasants must not encroach on those above them. Lords must not despoil peasants. Craftsmen and merchants must receive what will maintain them in their calling, *and no more* (emphasis mine).[5]

This shared sense of mutual obligation, therefore, meant that rigid class inequality was understood quite differently than it is today. It held a different meaning. It was understood as something that was good. Consider John of Salisbury's rather idealized account:

> The health of the whole commonwealth will be assured and vigorous, if the higher members consider the lower and the lower answer in like manner the higher, so that each is in turn a member of every other.[6]

Tawney's insight that the gospel was read according to the "marks of silver" as much as to St. Mark suggests that the notions of mutual obligation and responsibility may have been used by those on top to manipulate those on the bottom. But it is important to note: 1) that the norms and standards of any given age that seem so "natural" are social conventions subject to change; and 2) that in contrast to our own, the norms and standards of the Middle Ages were unusually *social* in nature. Individual needs were subordinant to the perceived needs of the community. Consequently, the social relationships that grew out of the shared belief in equality within each class (among men) and mutual responsibility between classes acted as a barrier to economic egotism or the kind of economic individualism which we celebrate today. The search for wealth beyond the needs commensurate with one's station was avarice. The sharing of good fortunes, standing by one's neighbor in a time of need, and resisting the encroachments of a conscienceless money-power helped insure that professional standards of training and "craftsmanship" would not deteriorate. The exchange relations of the marketplace we now know as impersonal and contractual were then intimate and direct. Trade, although intended by Providence, was observed closely: the public must benefit and the profits that one took must not exceed the wages of one's labor.

The thread of this particular social ethic ran throughout the fabric of feudal life. But as leaders of the Roman Church violated their own religious standards by attempting to maximize their financial gain, their interpretations of divine purpose began to lack credibility. Notes Tawney, their "teaching was violated in practice and violated grossly ....The abuses which were a trickle in the thirteenth century were a torrent in the fifteenth." Protestant reform, in effect, was invited. And the motivation which sustained the self-discipline and the commitment of traders and moneylenders to a social ethic began to wither. Indeed, the much vaunted set of social ethics that had emerged from the ecclesiastic authority became, at every turn, a set of social constraints.[7]

The decline in Catholic orthodoxy and the rise of the Protestant Reformation began what we now refer to as the bourgeois revolution. Difficulties surround the choice of events to mark the ascendency of the bourgeoisie; perhaps identifying the places and institutions where protest took hold better illustrates the manner and direction in which feudal life was being moved. It was along the routes of commerce, throughout the medieval market towns or burgs, and within the larger centers of trade that the demand for credit and capital resonated with the apparent need for norms and standards which would support *individual freedom from social authority.* "No one can deny," asserted the foreign merchants at Antwerp angered by the restrictions placed on trade, "that the cause of the prosperity of this city is the freedom granted to those who trade here."[8] Note the change: the meaning of freedom no longer was linked to the capacity to act out one's particular religious function, as a hardworking serf or responsible King, for example. Freedom was beginning to mean the capacity of an individual to engage in and prosper from trade, or elementary accumulation. Yet the success of the bourgeoisie to eventually make their altogether new conception of freedom one that would be uncontested or tacitly accepted, depended, in part, upon the outcome of struggles quite distinct from the set of class struggles in which they were engaged.

One such struggle was the struggle within the Church. In an effort to rescue the gospel from the corruption of the Church as financial institution, papal authority was repudiated by a stream of criticism that had the effect of exposing to criticism many of the background assumptions that helped to make up the social relationships of feudal life. The major voices within this stream were those of Luther, who helped to give fresh vitality to individualism by claiming that everyone possessed the capacity to individually interpret the gospel without the intervention of the Church ("each man his own priest"), and Calvin, who linked salvation to each individual's worldly deeds. While these religious reformers inveighed against the emerging commercialism within the secular world as within the Church, their emphasis upon individual will and the association made by their followers, such as the Puritans, of individual will with economic independence, helped clear the way for the bourgeois revolution by undermining the social authority of institutions in general. Of course there were other major sources of critical thought that brought the hidden dimension of shared assumptions out into sharp and contestable relief. Copernicus, by placing the Sun at the center of the solar system, not only helped place much of the Church's teaching in doubt but by contrast helped make the methods of science appear as *the* source of knowledge. And Descartes, by emphasizing the certainty of self-knowledge ("I think therefore I am"), placed in doubt the knowledge of God and set in motion for philosophy questions about the veracity of knowledge, thus ending its domination by religious thinkers.

Toward the end of the 17th century, the struggle within the Church was at an end. The magnitude and breath of the transformation of shared assumptions that moved us from the Age of Faith to what we now, perhaps unreflectively, identify as the Age of Reason is astonishing. The ideas supporting a community of unequal classes with varied functions organized around a common end were pushed aside in favor of the idea of society as mechanism, adjusting itself through the play of economic motives. The assumption that religious standards should serve, in part, to repress economic appetites in order to insure the stability of a class hierarchy gave way to the assumption that the satisfaction of economic appetite served religious ends —that "man's self-love is god's providence." Where economics was assumed to be an activity guided by moral consideration, it became an activity impeded by moral consideration that functioned best when left to impersonal market forces.[9]

At the center of these tumultuous shifts in ideas was the epic reversal of what it meant to be a person. Whereas a person was once defined in relation to a larger divine order, after papal authority had been eroded by the attacks upon the Church, the advancements in science, and the turn in philosophy, people began to establish their own notions of who and what they were. In a word, we have since thought of ourselves as self-defining.[10] Freedom no longer meant putting oneself in tune with the larger religious order. No longer did it mean the presence of restraint or the bond of mutual obligation. Rather freedom came to mean the opportunity to act as a creature capable of self-definition and individual expression. The confirmation of this freedom would be sought through the exercise of individual will, through the technological and later administrative domination of objects or nature. No longer invested with spiritual significance, nature as object was felt to be, using Max Weber's term, "disenchanted."

Certain of the most basic features of American political life, features that establish the limits and direction of our own political institutions, can now be identified. We can see our own ideology unfolding in the context of the broad transformation of ideas during the transition from medieval to modern history. Second only to our own self-conception was the recognition of the function and significance of *private* property. The concept of private property is internal to all our political concepts and relationships. Because it represents the most basic means through which an individual can engage in trade and accumulation, it is the stuff essentially which confirmed a person's autonomy as an individual following the bourgeos revolution. Freedom is considered empty without it. The individual right to own property stands in the forefront of characterizations of modern society as they are contrasted with our feudal past. So central to our political ideas is the right to own property that the term "human right" is often substituted in its place. Or as Justice Story noted early in the 19th century, "the fundamental rights of personal liberty and private property should be held sacred." Thus at the center of our ideas about *society* is the *individual* with full liberty to acquire or dispose of property.

An equally important corollary follows: obstacles to the enjoyment of this individual (human) right are social ethics (constraints), imposed by institutions such as the Church or state, and placed upon the acquisition and disposal of property and thus upon the individual. And as the relation between the church and the state was severed by drawing religion into private life, the secular state as a central authority became the institution most capable and likely to promulgate a social ethic.[11] The state within our political vision is the ever present threat to individual freedom. "Smash the state," demand some Leftists. "Get the state off our backs," implore those on the Right. We are all captured by this Liberal notion of freedom. Freedom, then, in one important respect means *freedom from* the state. And in another important respect, the right of the individual as against the state means the *freedom to* acquire and dispose of property.

It is in relation to these assumptions that our notion of equality emerges. Each of us is equal in the sense that we are free from social authority to use (the right of) property as a means of expression and accumulation. We are equal also in that our capacities, especially the capacity to labor, is our property. Whether we are "industrious" and acquire property "in things" or choose to sell our capacity to labor is consistent with our freedom from a social authority. Therefore, the dependence of people (without property in things) for their very livelihood on those with property simply reflects the *natural rights* equally enjoyed by all; rights, that is, which are protected by but not created by the state. Similarly, the jurisdiction of owners to which wage-earners are subject, is, "like the revolution of the stars," not political. To contest the practice of working for someone would not only challenge the meaning of freedom, human rights, and equality. It would be to contest something that cannot be changed (except by coercion). Political demands of this sort are without reason, irrational.

Yet, such political demands are remarkably persistent. That the inequality of condition of so many citizens throughout U.S. history has been an unmistakable fact is a position adopted by those who implicitly reject the concept of equality that allows all citizens, in a formal sense, to be considered equal. This formal sense of equality, as we have just made explicit, is the formal right to property, or as is commonly said, to *opportunity*. Ironically, the sort of equality demanded by such critics is often precisely that of "equal opportunity" or equality with respect to property rights. The point is that it is quite difficult to obtain critical distance from the assumptions we share particularly when both major parties accept them as given. It is difficult for us to understand how the indignities suffered by people dependent upon owners of property might be *the basis or consumation of equal rights.* It is difficult for us to understand, given our assumptions, how formal (abstract) property rights, or equality as we know it, might embody the notion that the distribution of property must be highly unequal.

As was pointed out above, policies which implicity challenge or call into question dearly held and widely shared assumptions are often labled implausible. Our way of thinking is biased. It is nothing to get alarmed about, however. Every way of thinking rests upon pillars of assumptions which help to make up our reality. What is alarming is that our two party system does not provide the space for self-examination, for us to make these assumptions clear and become self-conscious. If our way of thinking is skewed, however, it is possible that we, as well intentioned citizens, might be unaware of the ways in which our shared ideas impact negatively upon the health of the social order. But how do we know? Simple political opposition within the context of these ideas is inadequate as a check. One way out of this morass is to examine our most cherished concepts from a perspective that rests on different assumptions.

The Bias of Plausible Alternatives

With the conquest of nature or the control over things viewed as the expression of individual human freedom, solutions to the problems of conquest and industrial development drew the attention of modern thinkers. But solutions to these sorts of problems were necessarily confined to technical solutions, given the widely shared assumption that human activity was, to some significant degree, governed by the "laws of nature." Consequently, setting one's purpose in accord with nature's laws became the structure of *rational* behavior.

Moreover, with the eclipse of the social authority of the Church, divine revelation as a guide to right and wrong became irrelevant. Irrelevant as well was the analog of a social order as a human body. Taking its place was the idea that the social order was analagous to the machine. Often the image of a clock was invoked. Today, social scientists continue to accept the notion that social reality is governed to a significant degree by scientific law. Thomas Hobbes who pioneered the study of the "laws of civil life" and others who followed have been characterized by Hannah Arendt as attempting to find a theory:

> ...by which one can produce, with scientific precision, political institutions which will regulate the affairs of men with the reliability with which a clock regulates the motions of time or creation understood in terms of a clock regulates the processes of nature.[12]

The scientific, precise, and reliable regulation of public affairs, both political and economic, is the *rationalization* of public life.

We can see why a social order governed by mutual responsibility no longer made sense. With respect to the systematic domination of material things (the domination of nature for example) it was unreliable. Order that was bound up with the *unity and harmony of reason and emotion* often impeded production. Notes Joan Cocks, the application of scientific knowledge for the purpose of increasing productivity, the idea of cost-efficiency, the limited contract and a disciplined workforce did not honor the spiritual taboos, the community's relation to nature, the respect for for natural rhythms and seasons of feudal life.[13] They did not, therefore, possess inherent reasons or have their own objective reasons for arousing particular emotions. It made more sense to create a social order that echoed the technical rhythms of machinery. Social orders of this sort were ones regulated by the enforcement of contracts. The regularity of contractual relations depend less upon the complex discourse of feeling than do relations of mutual obligation. And it was the order of regularity and predictability, as opposed to the spontaneity of emotion or passion, that was understood at first as proof of one's eternal salvation and later as a necessary condition of industrial development, prosperity (accumulation), and individual freedom (opportunities). The concept of the "market" which we celebrate today (despite its marginal existence) stems from these very ideas. We believe that the market is governed by contractual relations, that it exhibits the self-regulating characteristics of a machine, and that it is responsible for making available to all private citizens endless opportunities for individual freedom and prosperity.[14]

There are two important points here. One is that the range of plausible policy options is skewed. That is, as they give expression to assumptions, they also discriminate. This is unavoidable. For example, as financial, industrial, scientific and religious elites rushed to rationalize the public world (primarily the world of craft and industrial production), the private world, preeminently an emotional world inhabited by children and their mothers, became a world that was considered inferior. Although a necessary realm, it was a world that had to be segregated from the public world of rationalized production, exchange and politics. As Christine DiStefano suggests, the world of the helpless and egoless infant was, by contrast to the rationalized public world, a "frightening, chaotic, irrational, emotional, slimy world." Policy initiatives, therefore, if they were to contribute to industrial expansion, individual freedom, and prosperity had to effectively filter out (of the public world) the chaos of spontaneity and the irrationality of emotionalism.

This filtering out process, which continues to this day, need not be conscious. It's just *our* common sense. If women, as Carol Gilligan suggests, employ a language that embodies a "care and concern for others," a sensibility "infused with feeling," such knowledge further confirms that the proper place of women is more than likely to be in the home and surely not in the public sphere of rational discourse. The range of plausible policy alternatives discriminates against women. But as we shall see, discrimination (against women and others) is but one dimension of the bias in question.[15]

Second, this bias is rooted in the acceptance of the scientific method as appropriate to the discovery of social truths and meaning. Modern thinkers, believing that laws of motion could be discovered for political and economic activity (thus rendering public life predictable and manageable), believed that the good life rested upon the repression of certain human drives. The full human personality replete with diverse *passions* had to be exorcised if the certainty and predictive power of scientific reasoning were to advance the material welfare of a given order.[16]

The repression of "disorderly appetites" was accomplished by a simple mechanism called the principle of "countervailing passion." Albert O. Hirschman informs us that 17th century elites believed that "one set of passions, hitherto known variously as greed, avarice, or love of lucre, could be usefully employed to oppose and bridle such other passions as ambition, lust for power, or sexual lust." In other words, useful or productive passion could be pitted against the more dangerous passions. The concept of the market also embodies this idea. Avarice, or the pursuit of private gain, was promoted to the position of the "privileged passion given the job of taming the wild ones...." Locke's belief that "Freedom of Men under Government...not to be subject to the inconstant, uncertain, unknown, Arbitrary Will of another man" further suggests that the celebration of the singleminded pursuit of self-interest was not separate from the general condemnation of the more spontaneous dimensions of our personality, especially sexual ones. In addition, we find that terms such as "national interest," "public interest," or "vital interest" help to carry forward the 17th century image of social orders ruled by (self) interests. Such terms also embody the notion that predictability and control in public affairs is jeopardized by such things as emotional concern for the *interests of others*. For example, we are told it is in the national interest to do business with the Republic of South Africa. The concern among many U.S. citizens that direct investment in South Africa helps maintain apartheid represents the kind of felt responsibility toward others that "gets in the way." Our "vital interests," it is said, may be subverted by such blind passion.[17]

It is important to note that the type of "control" sought by the first modern thinkers had a great deal to do with justifying the extraordinary discipline that was required to set the social order in tune with what was perceived as natural law. Argued Claimed Helvetius in the 18th century, "As the physical world is ruled by the laws of movement so is the moral universe ruled by laws of interest." Such thoughts at first glance seem distant and somewhat amusing. But certainly they are not distant. Rather they might be thought of as a political genetic code which shapes plausible policy options today. Compare the statement of the Duke of Rohan in 1638 with Environmental Protection Agency chief William Ruckelshaus in June 1983:

Duke of Rohan:

> ...in matters of state one must not let oneself be guided by disorderly appetites, which make us often undertake tasks beyond our strength; nor by violent passions, which agitate us in various ways as soon as they possess us;...but by our own interest guided by reason alone, which must be the rule of our actions.

EPA chief Ruckelshaus discussing the problems of controling pollution:

> The public interest is not served by two federal agencies...arguing...in the press. We are now in a troubled and emotional period for pollution control. Many communities are gripped by something approaching panic and the public discussion is dominated by personalities rather than substance. It is no accident that I am raising this subject here in the house of science [before members of the National Academy of Sciences]. I believe that part of the solution to our distress lies with the idea enshrined in this building, the idea that disciplined minds can grapple with ignorance and sometimes win....[the country] must reject the emotionalism that surrounds the current discourse and rescue ourselves from the paralysis of honest public policy it breeds.

We may infer that a plausible policy response to pollution control in part lies with the discouragement of the emotional responses that accompany the toxic contamination of a community. What, then, becomes of the person who has and continues to speak out passionately due to a concern for others, children for example? Is there space in the political world for her? Would Ruckelshaus have found it plausible to allow mothers of a contaminated community to influence policy? Would it be in the public interest to publicize the views of angry citizens?[18]

The bias of plausible policy options, we can see, does more than filter out a particular set of policy initiatives. As feminists have claimed, it filters out particular voices. From Simone de Beauvoir's concern that women have been, in subtle ways, denied access to civilizing arenas[19] to Dorothy Dinnerstein's contention that women are compelled to depend "lopsidedly on love for emotional fulfillment because they are barred from absorbing activity in the public domain,"[20] women have been developing a framework from which the "rationality" of the public world can be viewed directly and assessed from the vantage point of a competing perspective. But there is an important turn here. The bias in question goes beyond filtering out; it invalidates and expunges the experience of so many people who have not practiced calculating the efficiency of various means to an end. The bias in question invalidates the experience of people who have not administered productive property.

For example, some feminists have long suggested that women experience "the social fabric differently, not only because they occupy a life-world populated by babies, housework, and needy husbands, and are second-class citizens in a world dominated by white men, but also because of fundamental psychological experiences and processes that contribute to personal identity."[21] R. Carlson suggests that women are more "socially oriented" than men, that they emphasize "inter-personal" definitions of self whereas men emphasize "individualistic" criteria in defining and assessing their self-worth.[22] Ulrike Prokop is more specific:

> ...we define "need-orientation" as the potential and ability for expressive, non-instrumental behavior which, though not fully developed in every case, is structurally rooted in the female rather than in the male mode of experience....
>
> The process between mother and child consists of a mutual agreement which has a time parameter of its own and which is adversely affected by the requirements of norms [the norms of science?]... In the symbiotic relationship between mother and child there is more at stake than orderly care. The feeding of a baby, for example, is not simply the supplying of food that requires a certain skillful technique.... The relation between mother and child requires of the mother the ability and willingness to build a love relationship. This love relationship, the identification with the baby, enables the mother to recognize and answer adequately numerous pre-verbal signals given by the child as an expression of its needs.... The mother-child relation is a love relationship *a priori* as it were.[23]

A good deal of the contrasts, then, drawn between men and women may, in part, be due to the contrasting spheres of experience: the rational calculating process internal to the public world as opposed to the nurturing and other-directedness internal to the family. It is no accident that affective relationships are generally contained by categorizing them as *kinship* relations. Affective relationships among men, for example, are safely dubbed as "fraternal bonds." Notes Cocks, "The kinship assigned to values, emotions, and intimacy is crucial for the established order in a democratic age, as it helps keep potentially emancipatory interests enclosed in small, inward-looking settings."[24] Affective ties, in other words, tend to subvert the *public* order. Such relationships, if allowed to influence public policy, might undermine freedom as we know it and prosperity as we experience it. Or to put it another way, could the relationships that characterize public life ever resemble the relationship between mother and child? If not, and if women do indeed experience the world differently than men, the plausibility of policy options relies upon the filtering out of the voice of women *as women*. That is, women must be silenced or they must speak as men.

* * *

The bias of plausible policy options impacts upon people of color in a similar fashion. In a pioneering work, Robert Higgins argues that the "subordination of sensuality in a patriarchal setting was...interwoven at the earliest point with the personal disciplines of emerging market society, and with the decision of the English to exploit nonwhite labor." African slavery satisfied the (self) interests of plantation owners (as would have the enslavement of the Irish or Native Americans) by providing these property owners with an inexpensive source of very valuable labor. But African slavery also satisfied the specific sensual motives that, as we have seen, are a part of property relations.[25]

Others have pointed to the linkage of blackness, beastliness, and sexuality within the pre-colonization assumptions of the English. Winthrop Jordan, for example, has written that "it is scarcely surprising that Englishmen should have used people overseas as social mirrors and that they were especially inclined to discover attributes in savages which they found first but could not speak of in themselves."[26] George Rawick goes further by connecting the Puritan/Dissent movement, as an important social base of market society, to the diffusion of repressive attitudes throughout England. These repressive attitudes provided space for the transition from traditional to 'modern' habits of work and family which required "a more disciplined, less spontaneous personality."[27] Writes Rawick:

> In order to ensure that he will not slip back into the old ways or act out his half-suppressed fantasies, he must see a tremendous difference between his reformed self and those whom he

formerly resembled. But because he still has fantasies which he cannot accept, he must impute these fantasies to the realities of someone else.[28]

Higgins makes a broader claim. The English perception of Africans as essentially sexual creatures can be best explained when we understand that economic imperatives are but a facet of deeper, unconscious motivations. Higgins refers to the English economy as a *sexual economy*. Racial slavery can be linked to the demands of a specific labor market but it was also linked to patriarchal and Protestant-ascetic barriers which rest on the denial of self, on the denial that we feel emotion for particular reasons. The concept of a sexual-economy also helps to explain the influencial role which Christianity has played in U.S. politics, particularly in the context of reform movements. Christian clergy, by disciplining all desires attached to sensuous experience helped the state to repress various "disorderly appetites." Christian clergy, as we know today, are once again structurally positioned to legitimize the discipline required of renewed global-industrial expansion. Understanding the central role of the concept of self-denial within the context of the larger economy helps us to grasp these connections. Writes Higgins:

> The ethic of self-denial developing among men of property in England and the colonies was not a simple repression of sexual needs. What was at issue was a complex of belief, a way of acting, which undermined the validity and value of the body except for labor. Physical needs (sex, the enjoyment of food, the need to eliminate, etc.) were *shameful* things to the Puritans, who embodied these attitudes in the extreme.... It was an internal discipline that denied the authority of the physical self...which accepted...external disciplines...first of the parents, then of the worldly calling, work. In Max Weber's words, "...the same prescription is given [in the context of the sexual asceticism of Puritanism] for all sexual temptations as is used against religious doubts and a sense of moral unworthiness: 'Work hard in your calling.'"[29]

Evidence that the sexual economy impacts as negatively upon people of color as it does upon women has been dramatic. Throughout the early 19th century black freedom was associated with the deep-seated and widespread fear of interracial marriage and sexual crimes such as rape and prostitution. The abolitionist movement, as George Frederickson points out, "forced [these] previously unarticulated assumptions to the level of defensive ideological consciousness." Efforts to remove blacks from the Midwest during the 1840s and 1850s (in 1851, for example, Indiana and later Illinois in 1853 prevented blacks from entering their states) can be viewed against the general fear that voting rights for blacks, if not their general proximity, would encourage blacks "to marry our sisters and daughters." Both the

Democrats and the Republicans prior to the Civil War used the issue of interracial marriage to attack each other. Lincoln felt compelled to state categorically that he was not in favor of making voters of blacks "nor of qualifying them to hold office, nor to intermarry with white people."[30]

Following the Civil War, the pattern of associating blacks with sexual crimes seems to have escalated, setting off community retribution through lynching, pogrom, or bombing. The commercial press, during the 1860s, as well as the the Copperhead (dissident Democrats) press was rife with lurid accounts of black men sexually assaulting children. Jacquelyn Hall points out as late as the 1930s it was popularly assumed that in the absence of the discipline and control of slavery "black women were lapsing into prostitution and illegitimacy; above all, black men were acting upon the innate lasciviousness of the savage beast." A Columbia University scholar of the twentieth century, John Burgess, argued that "A black skin means membership in a race of men which has never of itself succeeded in subjecting *passion to reason*; has never, therefore, created civilization of any kind." (my emphasis)[31] In 1939, Hall adds, 65 percent of whites in a national survey were in favor of *lynchings* for sexual assaults. Higgins also interprets residential segregation and racial housing conflict in the context of sexual concerns among whites. Representing a sensuality that was culturally taboo, blacks were kept at arms length through segregation practices. These practices also functioned economically to insure a reserve supply of inexpensive labor and high real estate profits.[32]

* * *

Is our conception of civilization so severe and formal, so much about calculating a means to increase production that we regard people of color who are capable of expressing the sensuality of a pre-rationalized culture as uncivilized and lacking discipline? And in order for the voice of black people to be heard in the public arena, must it first sound like the voice of whites? The sexual economy, let us keep in mind, is still very much an economy. The subordination of women and of people of color means that a majority of the people in our social order will live their lives serving others, either directly or through the performance of the most undignified and mindless tasks. And they will be poorly compensated.

The ethic of self-denial, then, is ultimately bound up with the justification of the accumulation process. The situation of the white male wage earner best illustrates this relationship. How could it be that in a social order rooted in patriarchy and white supremacy, many white men, perhaps even a majority, spend most of their waking hours working under conditions very often unsafe and lacking in skill and dignity. The answer of course is that even white males are fodder for industrial cannons. But although the dynamics of capital accumulation may be the central dynamic of our age, Marxian analyses are incomplete to the degree that they do not connect the subjugation of women and people of color to this specific sense of self-denial. The need to deny the internal connections between reason and emotion is a dynamic that in turn is internal to class domination.

The political situation of the white male wage earner, therefore, is somewhat complex. His essential source of dignity in a rather undignified life situation has been his identity as white male. Aligning with women and/or people of color generally has meant jeopardizing that bit of dignity. Consequently, most of the radical efforts by white male workers to socialize production have left out women and blacks. But, on the other hand, the structure of property relationships insure that the social esteem accorded to white male elites in the public world will always be beyond the white male worker's reach. He has virtually no chance of transcending his class. In an order in which white male authority is something of a principle, union men are thought of as unworthy. Caught in this psychological bind, white male wage earners at best can choose simply to persevere. In the exercise of discipline and self-denial there is respect. In upholding the standards which help to subordinate women and people of color there is respect. And those who are unemployed or unskilled, potentially a politically volatile subclass, feel the pressure to accept these norms for they face the same condemnation that the underemployed faced three hundred years ago: your situation is due to the "relaxation of discipline and the corruption of manners."[33]

From the vantage point of the white male wage earner, "liberation" groups flock only to those who receive welfare and who do not persevere as he does. Liberal intellectuals who prescribe welfare as well as the subordinate constituencies who receive it, mock his self-denial. So do radicals that inveigh against the rationalized processes of public life. But the white male worker has little to say and no place to say it in this democracy. Much like women and people of color, he is taught throughout his educational experience to remain mute and is often unskilled at turning into words what he knows and feels. While the two party system encourages his participation as a voter and solicits his support as a Democrat, it does not encourage him, by way of providing political space, to learn speaking and writing skills, the skills of expression. Independent, reflective, and spontaneous political expression is filtered out or, in the case of strikes, is ridiculed. His tendency to express simple anger and his disdain toward "experts" and intellectuals acts to permit his political allies and opponents to see him not as a white male but as an *ignorant* white male.

And so, despite his acceptance of self-denial, he too is victimized by the sexual economy. His physical strength and muscularity acquired by the daily routine of physical labor make him appear brutish or even sexual to those people captured by the notion that physical strength is without value except for labor. And also, like women and people of color, he must betray his personality if his voice is to be heard. He must try, in his manner of speech and style of dress, to assume the posture and presence of confident authority, of his more "educated," self-possessed white brother.

The Boundaries of Two Party Politics

Thus far we have discussed the roots of our political concepts as well as the biases built into our assumptions about political freedom, opportunity, and prosperity in an industrial setting. Before we conclude this chapter we need to point out the importance of the relationship between the state and the economy. As an institution which permits control of the state and which helps to formulate public policy, the two party system is very much circumscribed by this relation. In addition, an examination of this relation will help us to clarify the ways in which our political heritiage impacts upon our political lives today.

Charles Schultze, who has been an economic adviser to recent liberal administrations, has written about the virtues of a social order organized around the contractual relationships of the market. In his following statement, notice how the assumption of a depersonalized, machine-like order regulated by the calculations of contractual relationships is understood as the basis of individual freedom:

> ...the buyer-seller relationships of the marketplace have substantial advantages as a form of social organization.... When dealing with each other in a buy-sell transaction, individuals can act voluntarily on the basis of mutual advantage...market transactions [however] cannot take place at all without a prior stipulation by political means of property rights and definitions.... Market-like arrangements [furthermore] not only minimize the need for coercion as a means of organizing society; they also reduce the need for compassion, patriotism, brotherly love, and cultural solidarity as motivating forces behind social improvements...the "emotional" forces...harnessing the "base" motive of material self-interest to promote the common good is perhaps *the* most important social invention mankind has yet achieved.[34]

Emotional considerations such as brotherly love may be okay in the private world of personal relationships or in the context of kinship but not when it's time to get serious. Therefore, when it comes to the public world of managing the state and the economy, emotional forces are dangerous. For example, the state often invokes the need for compassion when it forces individuals, by means of fiscal policy, to redistribute income. But such action flirts with coercion. The suggestion is that the state should not act on the basis of moral considerations. The state which preserves the sanctity of individual freedom can help the private economy achieve functional efficiency, help increase productivity, but cannot lament the cruel distribution of its goods. Disembodied reason cannot comment on the validity of moral ends. Notes Cocks, "...competing calculations about the efficiency of means to an end have no resonance in the heart." But there is virtue in this. Only a disembodied order, like the physical order that is ruled by laws of movement, can be ruled by the laws of interest, and according to this viewpoint, the laws of freedom.[35]

Notice that these conditions of freedom cannot take place at all without a prior stipulation by political means of property rights and definitions. And what institution shall make such stipulations and definitions? The answer of course is the state (and by extention institutions closely related to the state such as the two party system). The state is our social authority. It is through the state that we identify with each other as citizens. Consequently our shared ideas as citizens rests upon a social identity even though the ideas with which we identity support the practice of individualism.

The seeds of a social ethic, therefore, are strewn throughout our individualized order. And the tension is most evident within the relationship between the state and the economy. The state must be omni-present, defining the conditions of property rights or the right of individuals to be free from the state. Evidence of this antagonism is all about us. Our self-regulating system is not supposed to invoke brotherly love or patriotism but public officials in the name of sacrifice, austerity, or traditional America consistently ask us to pull together and to be unreflectively and fervently patriotic. John Kennedy's dictum about doing what you can for your country is repeated by the same people who vow to get government off our backs. And in spite of our "popular" government, in spite of the fact that public officials are held accountable to "the people" through competitive elections, government is committed, in order that those same people be free, to do everything in its power to help develop the relationships of property. As Kenneth M. Dolbeare has pointed out:

> From the earliest days of the Republic, the national government has played a significant role in supporting the "private" economy. During Washington's first administration, Secretary of the Treasury Alexander Hamilton initiated a comprehensive program for stabilizing the value of money, establishing a national market, and promoting the growth of manufacturing. As capitalism and industrialization took hold in the 19th century, however, the official ideology of *laissez faire*...developed as a rationale for non-intervention in what was taken to be the naturally self-regulating economic market. In fact, the

federal government was still promoting various nascent industries by elaborate tariff protections, giving lands to the railroads, and vigorously helping to put down strkes. And the
national Supreme Court developed new doctrines in the 1880s
and 1890s to enforce laissez faire principles against state
governments which sought to limit business practices in what
they thought to be the public interest.[36]

The simple fact of the matter is that political institutions such as
the two party system are dependent upon the impassioned interests of
private elites. There are two reasons for this. The first is that the
freedom enjoyed by individual owners of productive property is the
organizing principle of the social order. And the second is that
regardless of what the state may do, even when it seeks to redistribute
income, its revenues depend upon economic expansion; its policies,
therefore, must accommodate the captains of finance and industry.
There is no way of getting around the fact that our political institutions
are not independent, and cannot, without severe stress, support ways of
thinking and relating which collide with Liberal/capitalist dogma.

What does this mean for the two party system? James O'Connor
provides a clue. He says that the "state must involve itself in the
accumulation process but it must either mystify its policies by calling
them something that they are not or it must conceal them (e.g. by
making them into administrative, not political issues)."[37] I believe that
the two party system contributes to the vital function of mystification.
In part, the task of mystification is made easy by the fact that we live in
an "expressively dead" society. As Charles Taylor suggests, our
expressive fulfillment has been stifled "through the all-pervasive
demands of utility, of producing a world in which all acts, objects,
institutions have a use, but none express what men are or could be."
Moreover, the nuances of an expressively dead society are known only
to those skilled in knowing the nuances of language. The injuries
experienced by the disadvantaged constituencies are injuries deeply felt
but often left unspecified. And without validation in the public world,
without independent political parties of major party status, the
expression of these unarticulated feelings through protest would do
more than invite public ridicule, it would deplete limited sources of
public respect. The repression of these feelings, from above and
through self-denial, are, therefore, not only inherent in the structure of
work, it is inherent in the structure of our politics.

But the times are changing. Since the mid-1960s a crisis has been
unfolding that has more omnious implications than have previous
post-war economic downturns. The promise of economic growth and
of individual prosperity no longer seems to possess the meaning it once
had. Environmental degradation, the threat of nuclear war or the
proliferation of Vietnam style interventions, the feminization of
poverty, and the inability of minorities to throw off the yoke of racism

have moved some political activists to explore, from a critical perspective, the roots of their oppression. Women, for example, as they link the militarization of everyday life to male domination are going beyond the traditional demands of individual rights and equal opportunity. They are beginning to ask, at least implicity, whether or not the conditions of what we call freedom might themselves be the conditions of male domination.

Progressive political activists, then, both inside and outside the party system, are tampering with its boundaries. Their tendency is to push implausible policy alternatives into the range of what is considered plausible. But can activists really call into question such things as the validity of endless economic expansion, international market conquest and control, or the acceptance of domination, without challenging the principles upon which the social order rests?

I shall argue that they cannot. In order to call into question the dependency of our political institutions, we need to challenge the two party system. Only by changing the rules of the game to permit more than two major parities can fundamental criticism be given a public airing. Only when minor parties are given the same opportunities to mobilize their support and voice their concerns as Democrats and Republicans will there be space for fundamental political opposition. This means that we must begin to move in the direction of a multi-party system. But more does not necessarily mean better. There must be a turn in the form and purpose of political parties.

We are getting ahead of our analysis. But this much can be said about the vision of an alternative party system. The first is that it must have as one of its essential goals the process of self-creativity and discovery. And politics must be reflective if it is to be self-creative. Isaiah Berlin's belief that societies must probe the assumptions upon which they rest captures this idea. In an interview with Bryan Magee, Berlin notes:

> ...if presuppositions are not examined, and left to lie fallow, societies may become ossified; beliefs harden into dogma, the imagination is warped, the intellect becomes sterile. Societies can decay as a result of going to sleep on some comfortable bed of unquestioned dogma. If the imagination is to be stirred, if the intellect is to work, if mental life is not to sink to a low ebb, and the pursuit of truth (or justice, or self-fulfillment) is not to cease, assumptions must be questioned, presuppositions must be challenged—sufficiently, at any rate, to keep society moving.[38]

Second, the artificial split between reason and emotion must also be challenged and transcended. The structure and the rules internal to the two party system are, to a significant degree, based upon the fear that people at the bottom will challenge the privilege of the people at the top. In other words, the two party system is rooted in a way of thinking that excludes. Politics, therefore, does not address the needs of vast segments of the population, particularly those on the bottom. Its practice is in a word, painful. Unless the creative challenge of our political institutions becomes an organizing theme, it is quite likely that those of us who seek to recapture the concept of politics, however critically we move, will have no option but to preserve within the existing boundaries; and politics ought not to be a record of dull perseverance. In an important respect we are very much like the teacher of the French Impressionist Renoir who scolded the expressiveness of his young student by saying, "One doesn't paint for amusement." Renoir's response embodied what must be the attitude of so many of the inspired activists today who understand politics as a disciplined *and* an enriching experience, as an opportunity to come to know oneself *and* learn from and listen to one another. Said Renoir, "But if it didn't amuse me I shouldn't paint."

We shall probe the implications for the party system of the need to recognize the unity of reason and emotion further on. But our next task is to become more familiar with the history of the two party system and a history of its dynamics. Let us turn first to the relation between the state and the economy and outline its tendency to structure and constrain politics with the two party system.

PART II

Dynamics of
the Two Party
System

How can they fence rivers?
Only dry rivers can be fenced
as only dead people can be quieted.
They can fence the access,
the way in,
the way out,
but water flows through the tiniest crevices
filters through the hardest ground
like the thoughts of imprisoned
people.

                              Angel Nieto

3

GOVERNING COALITIONS AND STRUCTURAL CONSTRAINTS

It is natural for the mind to believe, and for the will to love; so
that for want of true objects they must attach themselves to false.
—Pascal

A working class mother was known to regularly remind her activist
daughter, "But you have to admit, this is a free country." After listening
to a local radio talk show, however, in which the daughter lambasted
President Reagan's Central American policy, the mother became
alarmed. "You better watch out. They will throw you right in jail."

It is a constant refrain. We sing the praise of American freedom and
democracy, yet we know they will throw you right in jail. We live with
that constant tension. At the same time that we are elated with the
unexpected surge of a particular candidate or campaign, we are made
uneasy by the recurring feeling that we are powerless. Voting is the
hallmark of democracy, we say. Voting is a fraud, we feel.

Perhaps for want of a true democracy we attach ourselves to one
that is false. The next three chapters will support this charge in various
ways. In this chapter we shall focus on the role that elites play in the
party system and I shall suggest that owners of considerable amounts of
productive property possess vast political influence. Indeed, for a
democracy, their political power is conspicuously disproportionate to
their numbers.

The analysis presented in this chapter will be a structural analysis.
That is, I shall show that the structural relation between the state and
the economy tends to limit legitimate policy options to those which
contribute to the expansion of property relations. And I shall show how
the two party system has been used by elites to thwart the leftward
march of people with little or no property by linking their protests to
new strategies for expansion.

55

The view of the two party system presented in this chapter is an incomplete view which will be filled out in later chapters. Nevertheless it will help us to think more clearly about how elites set agendas and how governing coalitions are created and recreated. We shall begin by looking at the formation of the two party system. Then we shall examine how various factions of elites, during periods of great social transformation and party reorganization, used the party system to advance and protect the property relationships in which they were implicated. The crisis periods we shall explore will be those of the 1850s, the 1890s and the 1930s.

The Creation of the Federal Government And The Party System

In spite of the distrust of governmental authority shared by most large property owners following the Revolution, elites quickly began to seriously consider ways of centrally co-ordinating the commercial relations of all the states. The unfavorable balance of trade and the growing indebtedness to England explains a good deal of this concern. Jefferson complained that Virginian tobacco planters were becoming the property of mercantile houses in London. In addition, elites were troubled by irregular import duties and practices regarding the circulation of money which varied from state to state. To put it simply, the continued growth of the private economy required central co-ordination, distrust of government or not.[1]

Those who were most adversely affected by the competitive and separate state governments were those who were involved in either inter-state commerce or international trade. The strongest supporters of some kind of legal, central authority, therefore, were among the nation's largest property owners. They were known as *federalists* and were responsible for the adoption of the Constitution of 1787. Marking the creation of a federal government, the Constitution granted powers and functions which had until that time been thought of as too dangerous to assign to any political body above the individual states.[2] Let us survey the primary functions assigned to this newly created institution.

New and diversified sources of revenue could be raised (Article 1, Section 8, para. 1). This meant that the debts of each individual state could be assumed and consolidated thus insuring the validation of the public debt, the creation of interest bearing bonds, the establishment of a national bank, and the attraction of foreign investment. Private property could be protected against the annulment of debts passed by the individual state governments as had happened during the Confederation period when the poor had angrily rebelled against unfair credit policies (Article 1, Section 10, para. 1).[3] The sanctity of contractual relations (Article VI, para. 1) could be federally guaranteed as the "different and unequal properties" were given constitutional protection.[4] A national army was authorized, in part, as a coercive instrument (Article 1, Section 8, para. 12, 15, 16) to enforce contractual relations and, in part, as an element in the authorization of military and diplomatic representation abroad (meaning that firms trading and later investing abroad would have the assistance and backing of the federal government).[5] Broadly speaking the assigned tasks of the federal government may be summarized as "1) safeguarding the validity of the state debt; 2) the protection of private property; and 3) military and diplomatic representation abroad."[6] These assigned tasks help constitute the structural relation between the state and the economy. In other words, these tasks establish, roughly, the boundaries of public policy.

The very first administration of George Washington found, however, that using the federal government as an instrument of economic development created as many problems as it solved. Any given set of policies, in order to be effective in promoting growth or development in the context of a private economy, had to be tailored to meet the needs of specific industries. Therefore, policies which enhanced the market position of one industry foreclosed options and undercut the market position of others.

For example, Alexander Hamilton, as Washington's Secretary of the Treasury, was responsible for specifying the manner in which state debts would be assumed and the revenue or funding sources diversified. His close ties with merchant capital and, undoubtedly, his fondness for the British monarchy moved him to tie his policies to the expansion of trade with Great Britain despite that nation's steadfast refusal to make any commercial treaties with the United States. Speculators, merchants, and shippers of New England as well as many commercial men associated with large scale plantations along the coastal regions and river valleys of the South, who enjoyed their relationship with English commerce, were delighted. Tobacco planters of Virginia, however, were aghast. It was becoming apparent to these slaveowners that the same kind of control over capital markets from which they (as colonists) had sought independence was resurfacing. But this time they were subject not to a king but to the federal government which they had helped to create.

The competition between merchant and slaveowning elites over control of the federal government pushed market competition into the public sphere. Market relations steadily became politicized. This meant two things. First, it meant that political opposition (in this case from tobacco planters) obstructed economic development (of shipping and merchant capital). And because it obstructed the development of a particular economic sector, it obstructed the freedom of elites within that sector. Political opposition, of necessity, would be viewed with the greatest suspicion. Second, elites in opposition, in order to avoid political repression by incumbents, would have to mobilize public sentiment for the agendas they sought to advance.

In this example, after considerable congressional maneuvering over trade relations with Great Britain, the Federalists passed the Sedition Act of 1798, making it a crime to "write, print, utter, or publish...any false, scandalous and malicious writing or writings against the government of the United States, or either house of the Congress of the United States, of the President of the United States with intent...to bring them...into contempt or disrepute."[7] As Howard Zinn points out, it was also an effort to curtail the *public* mobilization of popular support against the government.[8] Tobacco planters of Virginia[9] were compelled, therefore, to formalize the process of mobilizing public support for an opposition agenda. Their strategy for challenging the Federalists rested upon organizing delegate conventions (in the mid-1790s). This attempt to *publicly* enlist support under a party banner, the Jefferson Republican party, was not like the direct public appeals with which we are familiar. Direct appeals to people without property would begin with Andrew Jackson's direct appeal to wage earners in 1832. Nevertheless, the party system, very much underdeveloped, had been born.

The context of the development of the party system deserves emphasis. We notice that the need to involve non-elites in the political process did not stem from a desire to make the political process more democratic. Federalists, as might be expected, thoroughly condemned the new development. John Marshall, troubled by the participation of non-elites on the public stage, complained that "nothing debases or pollutes the human mind more than a political party." Others worried that parties or "combinations of men" inappropriately decided "who should and who should not be voted" for by the people. This particular charge, that political parties interfered with honest and independent thinking, would be repeated so often that a number of anti-party reforms would be enacted during the first two decades of the 20th century. And still others simply swallowed hard and called themselves Federalist Republicans.[10]

And what of the leaders of the Jeffersonian Republicans? What did this first opening of the political process mean to them? Their attitudes are best revealed by the role that Allegheny farmers played in Jefferson and Madison's early opposition party. In 1791, the Federalists passed an excise tax on distilleries as one of several funding measures. Jefferson and Madison (who were both land speculators, trade agents and investors in government bonds) understood the necessity for a central public authority to guarantee the validity of the "public debt." "The worst of all "calamities," stated Jefferson, would be "the total extinction of our credit in Europe."[11] Therefore, when President Washington used 15,000 militiamen in the summer of 1794 to put down an armed rebellion of farmers in western Pennsylvania who felt that the excise tax was tyrannical (for many, whiskey was used as currency), leaders of the Jeffersonian Republicans were silent.[12] Yet in the campaign of 1800, the Jeffersonian Republicans would appeal to Allegheny farmers by invoking the "Federalist Reign of Terror."[13]

True enough, both the Allegheny farmers and the leaders of the Jeffersonian Republicans (from the Sedition Act of 1798) had felt the sting of Federalist tyranny. But there was a world of difference between the two. One was a squabble over which set of elites was to influence economic policy. The other was the crushing of a rebellion in which military force was used and in which the Jeffersonians, by virtue of their silence, were complicit. In both instances of "tyranny" the private interests of various elites were advanced. And in neither instance of tyranny did small farmers or other groups of people with little or no property have a voice equal to that of larger property owners *despite their numbers.*

This example of initial party conflict reveals several aspects of the two party system that will appear again. First, the two party system is an institution which facilitates the creation of coalitions among elites in order to control the government and establish political agendas which advance the development of the private economy. In other words, the two party system facilitates the creation of coalitions which govern. Second, it helps to mobilize popular support around these ends. But it succeeds in doing this by withholding or reinterpreting some considerations which if examined critically would weaken the strength of that coalition's popular support. In the example just cited, a critical examination of the concept "Federalist Reign of Terror" may have jeopardized the popular support which the Jeffersonian Republicans enjoyed among the enfranchised. In other words, the two party system helps to mystify the use of the state as an instrument to advance the private interests of elites by filtering out competing perspectives.

Early Party Competition

> In the aggregate, the varieties of business conflict generate complex patterns of corporate alliance and political coalition.... Whole political systems can be defined with reference to such core coalitions, which are the system's chief beneficiaries and most important sources of stability.
>
> —Ferguson and Rogers[14]

Are political party and economic history woven together? Are the leading personalities found in the private world of exchange and production, their private concerns, their interpretation of the national interest, and the alliances and rivalries in which they are implicated the leading personalities, alliances, and attendant world views that are found in the party system? In other words, are the two public spheres structurally connected? The rise and fall of early parties suggests that they are. The eclipse of shipping and tobacco production curtailed the political domination of those parties, the Federalists and the Jefferson Republicans respectively, that had been associated with these industries. And they gave way to parties which sponsored new growth industries, parties which organized elite coalitions around new and specific strategies to use the federal government as a "developmental" instrument. Are political parties first and foremost the political arm of specific industries or economic sectors? Let us take a closer look at the roots of party competition.

With the tobacco planters of Virginia in control of the federal government in 1801, commercial relations between Great Britain and the United States deteriorated and shipping declined. The Embargo of 1807 under Jefferson and the Non-Intercourse acts of 1810 under Madison crippled many of the smaller merchant shippers of New England.[15] The interruption of foreign trade again during the War of 1812 left the shipping trade in acute depression.[16] A number of merchants who had amassed significant amounts of capital prior to 1807 were persuaded by manufacturing pioneers such as Francis Cabot Lowell that the most profitable form of investment was the direct employment of labor. Therefore, during the decade between 1806 and 1816 manufacturing activity, from cotton and woolen factories to sealing wax and paper mills, began to appear. The mercantile/shipping base of the Federalist Party was eroding.

The political economic situation in the South was also changing significantly. Tobacco exports, which had been the base of the Virginia dynasty, peaked in 1816. The production of cotton, in part spurred on by the invention of the cotton gin in 1793, soon began to account for the nation's economic expansion, in the value of domestic exports, during the first decade of the 19th century. Just before the panic of 1819, cotton production accounted for nearly 39% of total exports. The domination of the federal government by a party run by cotton plantation owners was not far away.

With the collapse of the Federalists, the new sources of economic strength found political backing within the Jeffersonian Republican party. The diversity of the economy, in addition to the decline of tobacco exports, was fragmenting the party. One coalition consisted of speculators, manufacturers, and market-oriented farmers who continued to avoid dependent relations with Great Britain and who were inspired by ideas such as Henry Clay's "American System." Clay envisioned a domestic market that would link the expansion of manufacturing and large scale farming. The idea and the party built around it, for a time, enjoyed national support. Factory owners not only in New England but also in the Carolinas (where experimental mills were struggling to get established),[17] together with iron producers in the Lehigh Valley and Pittsburgh, agreed that credit was needed to finance production and that protective tariffs were needed to lessen foreign competition. Hemp producers in Kentucky, wool farmers in Ohio and Vermont and New York grain producers believed that tariff revenue could then be used to build canals and highways (or internal improvements). Elites with money to lend hoped that the government would provide them with cheap public land that they could then develop. These *National*, as opposed to Jeffersonian or regional, Republicans succeeded in having John Quincy Adams elected president in 1824.

The second major faction was led by cotton plantation owners. They were opposed to protective tariffs, internal improvements, and a commercial economy in general, and like the shippers, supported free trade. Little did they want to sell cotton in a competitive market and buy finished commodities in a protected one. In addition, the magnificent river system of the South provided an adequate transportation system for cotton exporters. Therefore, cotton plantation owners, particularly those that were moving into the Southwest, sought control of the federal government in order to prevent its active support of a burgeoning capitalism. Broadening the suffrage to include workers so that the militant resistance to wage labor could be used as a political weapon against the rising class of manufactory owners, these southwest slaveowners, or *Democratic* Republicans, were able to have Andrew Jackson elected president in 1828.

It can be said, particularly when one notes that it was the intention of the Framers that public institutions serve private interests, that *political parties are, in part, economic forms.* The routine stuff of party competition is, precisely, this sort of rolling competition, the unfolding of private economic development and public subsidy (passive or active). At times, however, such competition unfolds into bitter and divisive conflict. This occurs when the advancement of property relations precipitates instability which in turn threatens the social order. Notice how the development of the commercial economy organized principally around wage labor conflicted at every turn with the needs of the cotton economy organized principally around slave labor. Movement beyond these periods of instability requires some fundamental alteration, reconception, or rejection of a principle rooted within the social order. Such movement requires that the legitimacy and authority of the federal government, or national interest, be placed squarely behind one of the opposing sides. It is not surprising that we find in the platforms of the Democratic Party after 1840 the repeated admonition by slaveowners that "justice and sound policy forbid the federal government to foster one branch of industry to the detriment of any other...."[18]

Social change of this nature has taken place in the 1860s, the 1890s, and the 1930s. In each case the movement of the conflict was marked in the party system by the dramatic reorganization of governing coalitions or what has been commonly referred to as a *party realignment*. And in each case, the reorganized coalition corresponded to the promulgation of new public purposes and new strategies for growth. Let us turn then to these periods of crisis in order to further clarify the process of organizing governing coalitions.

Crisis: The 1850s

Let us sketch the development of property relations during the early part of U.S. history. As we do this, note the close relation between the imperatives of this development and issues which political parties established as *the* political issues of the period. In the 18th century two distinct forms of agriculture existed in the South. Large scale commercial agriculture, based upon slave labor, existed along the Southeast coast, the coast of the Gulf states and the rivers. Small independent farmers and tenant farmers (at least 25% of southern farmers) worked on the hinterlands in the more upland and westward regions. Many of these farmers were the descendants of indentured servants who had migrated from Europe and who were, ironically, set free by the institutionalization of slave labor.[19]

A characteristic of tobacco and cotton production (for profit) was the rapid exhaustion of the soil and the inexorable movement westward. Following the War of 1812, "several hundreds of thousands of people were shifted to the trans-Allegheny region, leading to formation of two territories, the admission of three states, the merciless clearing of Indians to beyond the Mississippi, and indirectly, the 'purchase' of Florida."[20] The effect of this movement was to bring Tennessee, Louisiana, Mississippi, Alabama, Florida, and Arkansas into the "Cotton Kingdom." Therefore, many of the small farmers became actively involved in cotton production. And as we have seen, it was the southwestern slaveowners, disconnected as they were from the commercial economy of the Northeast, who led the Democratic Republicans (referred to only as Democrats after 1828) and who became the "intransigents and 'fire-eaters'" of the 1850s.[21]

Not all cotton plantation owners were as immediately threatened by the expansion of manufacturing and finance capital as were Jacksonian Democrats, however. Most plantation owners within the coastal states of South Carolina, Georgia, Virginia, and North Carolina would eventually take their stand with the Democrats, but only after their long and deep involvement first with financiers and shippers and then with textile manufacturers crumbled during the 1850s. This north/south axis, often referred to as the New York-Virginia axis, was based upon New York City's function as "pivot" on the "great cotton triangle"—the route of goods exported between Europe, the South, and New York.[22]

Political opposition to the Democratic Party was rooted in the alliance among elites that grew out of these north/south commercial ties. Leadership of the coalition, first organized within the National Republican Party, fell to textile factory owners (such as Nathan Appleton, Abbott Lawrence, and Francis Cabot Lowell) known as the Boston Associates. The Boston Associates controlled 1/5 of all cotton spindleage in the U.S. and controlled all the banks of Boston, save one, which failed once they refused credit to it during the panic of 1837.[23] Slaveowners within the National Republicans, however, resisted any suggestion of national or federal power that might interfere with the mode of slave labor and urged that the party's name be changed. The Boston Associates graciously understood these concerns and agreed to change the name of the party. The term "national" had to go. Thus the National Republicans became the Whig Party and the incongruous and unstable alliance was made.

For thirty-two years, beginning with the election of Andrew Jackson in 1828 and ending with the election of Abraham Lincoln in 1860, cotton plantation owners dominated federal policy making. Cotton production, for a time, was the base of stability and source of expansion for each major party. The commitment to the preservation of a cotton monoculture, however, eventually led to severe political-economic antagonisms.

First of all, the slave economy was a primitive economy. There was little diversity, little interregional movement of capital, and a great deal of dependency upon commercial economies for manufactured goods. Its tremendous expansion turned on simple, brutal exploitation of slave labor and the steady acquisition of more land. Therefore, the use of the federal government as an instrument of economic development was also primitive. Its primary function was, predictably, to help acquire land (as was the case in the acquisition of Texas when the federal government precipitated a war with Mexico)[24] and to help enslave labor (through such measures as fugitive slave laws).

Elites implicated in sectors of the commercial economy not directly linked to the production of cotton were as frustrated as were the bourgeoisie of medieval market towns centuries earlier. Their demands for credit and capital and trade were also pushed aside.[25] The general denial of these demands was termed "southern aggression" by burgeoning capitalists. It would become the rallying cry within the party system among those angry with the plantation owners' tight grip on the machinery of the federal government.

Let us take a look at how plantation owners blocked expansion of the commercial economy. During the 1830s Andrew Jackson's (Democratic) three step attack on the northern commercial economy consisted of his veto to recharter the Bank of the United States, the subsequent withdrawal of federal revenue and its redistribution to "pet" state banks, and an act (the Specie Circular) which limited the amount of paper money in circulation. These actions, in addition to his veto of the Maysville Road project and other internal improvements, reflected the desire to contain capital markets, speculation, and the growth of transportation systems which were drawing northern states together under one economy and isolating southerners politically. By the mid-1840s, James Polk (Democrat) managed to retard northern economic expansion by accepting a compromise with Great Britain instead of pushing for the expansion of territory to the northernmost boundary of Oregon (as had been demanded by the *national* Democratic platform of 1844). Polk also effectively increased transportation costs in the Great Lakes area by vetoing river and harbor bills.[26] Also vetoing river and harbor bills (in 1854 and 1855) in addition to land grants was Franklin Pierce (Democrat) much to the dismay of entrepreneurs in Ohio, Michigan, Illinois, Wisconsin, and Iowa who had expressed a desire for these measures, particularly those that would stimulate railroad construction and western settlement.[27]

"Southern aggression" was carried out under the aegis of the Whig Party as well. Succeeding to the presidency upon the death of William Henry Harrison (Whig) in 1841 was John Tyler. Prior to his unexpected elevation to the presidency, Tyler had toyed with the idea of switching parties and of seeking the Democratic Party's nomination for the presidency in 1844. Anxious to support what was being acknowledged as an intentionally provocative or "disunionist" posture by slaveowners, Tyler quickly became an obstacle to the implementation of the Whig Party's *national* economic program which included a high protective tariff, a new charter for a national bank, federal support for internal improvements, and the distribution to the states of revenue from federal land sales. Ten times Tyler used the veto to prevent parts of that program from being enacted.[28]

The severity of the conflict between the imperatives of the two economies generated political polarization along regional lines. The distrust of Democrats in the North was clearly in evidence in Pennsylvania where every Democratic Congressperson from Pennsylvania had been defeated by 1858.[29] Northern Congresspersons, for the first time as a bloc, were voting for a protective tariff—which was derailed, however, by a more unified body of plantation representatives, in retreat though they may have been. The Whig Party, which had been organized around the north/south alliances of textile manufacturers and southeastern cotton producers, was torn apart. By 1856, the Whigs no longer existed as a national organization. Meanwhile, the Democratic Party was fast becoming the regional fortress to which slaveowners were retreating.

Owners of cotton and woolen mills and iron furnaces, together with "small enterprisers" anxious to promote western migration and settlement and western farmers looking for broader markets, were poised to capture control of the federal government. Specifically they were forging a program which would permit the federal government to encourage protective tarriffs, subsidize railroad construction, make it easy to exploit nature or the rich resources of the public domain, create a national bank, and opt for a uniform currency.[30]

But politics is greater than the two party system. It consists of more than the struggle among elites over control of the state. In addition to deciding which industry promised greater horizons of production, elites had to confront the destabilizing protests of the majority of those who in a variety of ways were objects of property themselves. Prior to the Civil War, the entire base of the social edifice was awash with dissent. Outside the party system, space was being created for an alternative kind of politics, a politics based less on growth than upon change.

The most relentless protests were voiced by those who had found themselves made slaves. Herbert Aptheker has found roughly 250 instances where ten or more slaves organized revolts. The instances of sabotage and arson, self-education, co-operation with white workers, Mexicans, and Indians (such as the Seminoles of Florida), and escape numbered in the tens of thousands. This underground movement did more than terrify white rulers. Many escaped slaves such as David Walker, Harriet Tubman, and Frederick Douglass energized the abolitionist movement which threatened to push dissident parties far beyond their call for the containment of slavery.

Threading its way into and away from the abolitionist movement was the protest of women. White working class women had successfully established female unions such as the Lowell Female Labor Reform Association (1845). But with the increase in immigration and the decline in female operatives, the center of the struggle by women shifted.

In 1838 Kentucky had given women the right to vote in school elections under certain conditions. This success was an isolated event, however. But as women, drawn into anti-slavery societies, began to consciously explore and organize around the conditions of their own inequality, the call for women's rights gained momentum. Out of the first Women's Rights Convention at Seneca Falls, New York, in 1848, came a demand for the vote. And as women petitioned state after state to pass legislation which would enable married women to hold property, it was becoming evident that women were moving toward the establishment of an independent political base.

Elites felt the greatest pressure, however, from wage earners. This was due, in part, to the fact that women and most blacks, who were not allowed to vote, remained electorally invisible. The fraternal bonds among white men insured the electoral visibility of most white wage earners. This in addition to the direct investment in wage labor, which

was the crux of the anti-slavery crusade among elites, compelled owners
to appreciate the value and acceptability of bargaining with organized
labor. But during the first few decades of the factory system, many
workers indicated little interest in bargaining. Repeatedly they attempted to form producer and consumer co-operatives and even entire
co-operative communities.[31] Although the co-operative movement
suffered dearly from an inability to secure sufficient capital, it helped
sustain the spirit of mutuality that was central to the union movement
that followed. Indeed, once it became clear (by the 1840s) that many
farmers had no choice but to seek permanent employment in the factory
system, the call of workers changed from a warning—stay away from
the "factory prisons"—to an exhortation, "Organize" and "Union is
Strength."

By 1843, strikes reached "epidemic" proportions, moving one
editor to exclaim, "There are symptoms of rebellion among operatives
in all quarters." And given the history of labor's independent political
activity (such as the Workingmen's Party of 1828) and the expressed
desire among trade unionists as late as 1857 to create a labor party once
again, elites opposed to the expansion of the slave system into the
territories[32] understood that their agenda would, in some way, have to
come to grips with the demands of labor.[33]

Elites Set the Agenda

What might have been our history if our party system had been
designed to encourage and develop the political aspirations of slaves,
women, white male wage earners, and Native Americans? Would
expansion, conquest, and control have been considered less virtuous?
Would our competitive institutions have been tempered by the urge to
co-operate? Would the subjugation of people of color have become a
social taboo? It is more likely that the political voices of such marginal
constituencies, were they able to secure sound political footing, would
have been ruthlessly purged. Indeed, the Civil War itself may be
thought of in this context; the political power of slaveowners was an
obstacle to early capitalist development that had to be removed. It is
important to keep in mind that by the 1850s the singleminded pursuit
of self-interest was aglow with righteousness. It was the harbinger of
freedom and prosperity and the bulwark against slavery. The point of
all this is that the two party system was not neutral *and to the extent that
it gave everyone an equal say* it was still not democratic. The agendas
which it spewed forth, whether they advanced the cause of the slave
economy or the wage economy were, in general, the agendas of
expansion and conquest. The two party system, therefore, largely
ignored the aspirations of those locked out as it helped articulate the
agendas of competing elites.

The problem for the political opponents of the "slaveocracy" since 1820, when debates in Congress revealed for the first time the depth and fury of the political and economic divisions that would follow,[34] was that there was no basis for an agenda capable of uniting those opposed to the extension of slavery. Strong and profitable north/south trade fragmented political opposition to "southern aggression." Only when the decline of cotton production and the ascendancy of the commercial economy each showed signs of irreversibility during the 1840s did political forces opposed to the expansion of slavery demonstrate a potential for unity.[35]

In spite of the unfolding of these productive forces, the major parties were slow to respond. Slowed by the inertia of dependent institutions, the major parties remained deeply enmeshed within the structure of cotton production. Fundamental opposition to the rights of slaveowners, therefore, had to await the formation of sharp internal divisions within the major parties. And even then, this opposition by dissident elites was forced to find expression through minor parties. Let us briefly illustrate the movement of these economic forces and the political changes that followed.

Democratic support in the Northwest grew out of the trade between the suppliers of cheap foodstuffs there and the early southwestern planters. This northwest/southwest trade enabled southwestern planters to reduce production costs, relative to coastal plantations, and keep their best lands in cotton.[36] However, the demand for western foodstuffs generated higher prices and contributed to the tide of western migration which in turn led to "large scale investment in a variety of economic activities. The development of towns, warehousing facilities, and a wide variety of residentiary industry was the typical pattern."[37] Southern Democrats saw the handwriting on the wall. With the West demanding greater amounts of labor and capital from the East and with the Northeast becoming a food deficit area (as agriculture became subordinate to manufacturing), the East displaced the South, in 1843, in relative terms as the primary market for western foodstuffs.[38] In other words, the South risked becoming politically isolated as east/west political ties grew. In 1844, the Democrats declared in their platform, the "Federal Government is one of limited powers...the Constitution does not confer upon the General government the power...to carry on a general system of internal improvements." But with the price of wheat rising, massive railroad construction between 1849 and 1854 moved forward and opened trunklines between the east coast and the midwest.

The development of the northern economy was itself creating political pressure. Farmers of relatively isolated and homogeneous communities were suddenly brought into contact with speculators, bankers, and manufacturers. Urban environments facilitated the exchange between labor and capital, provided a market for manufactured goods as well as foodstuffs, and lowered transportation costs. Most important, urban areas became a reservoir of surplus labor during periods when the development of a wage labor market was critical. The space for northern political unity was being created as disparate groups found mutuality in self-interest. Political parties were needed by this emerging coalition to demand free homesteads, protective tariffs, and a sound capital market.[39] But because the Whigs, as the major party in a position to challenge slaveowners, were committed to protecting their fragile alliance with southeastern cotton suppliers, the programmatic expression of an alternative agenda was stalled.

Eventually the capitalist agenda would find expression through the Republican Party. The story of its rise from the ashes of minor parties has had the unfortunate effect of lending credibility to the claim that third parties are able to permit the triumph of alternative agendas. But notice that: 1) the Republican alternative was simply an alternative to slavery, not to property relations in general; and, 2) the success of the Republicans hinged upon the total collapse of a major (Whig) party. In other words, the situation was unique.

The over-production of cotton coincided with a diminished demand for cotton from Great Britain. The price of cotton fell dramatically.[40] Many alarmed Whig slaveowners abandoned the north/south alliance and joined with their fellow slaveowners in the Democratic Party. Whig textile manufacturers of the North, whose influence depended on the strength of the north/south alliance, became increasingly isolated. In Massachusetts, Ohio, and New York, these "cotton Whigs" were challenged by capitalists who were not dependent upon cotton production. Instead they were implicated in the lumber and boots and shoe industries, iron production, the manufacture of small machinery, and the marketing of leather goods, flour, meal, and liquors. In Massachusetts it was the money of these traders (called Conscience Whigs) and not of the textile manufacturers, that represented the Bostonian investment in railroads in western New England and the West.

Northern Democrats were also feeling the pressure of polarization. New York Democrats were concerned that the southern Democratic push for the admission of Texas as one or more slave states would forever end their influence within the party. They eventually bolted the party in 1848 and created the Barnburners. The Liberty Party, rooted in the abolitionist movement as we have seen, was given a more pragmatic bent by farmers in the Ohio valley, upset with the unwillingness of slaveowners to work for the repeal of British Corn Laws (which had created a glutted grain market, to their advantage), and by merchants and manufacturers, who were protesting the default of payments by slaveowners. In its 1844 platform, for example, "Libertymen" insisted that the "duty of the Government...to exert its utmost energies to extend the markets for the products of free labor." In the Northwest, both

Whigs and Democrats, frustrated with the vetoes of Tyler and Polk, convened in 1847 in Chicago and joined with Libertymen.

In 1848, Libertymen, Barnburners, Conscience Whigs, and other dissident Whigs and Democrats met in Buffalo to create the Free Soil Party. Declaring that they were opposed to "Slavery-extension," Free Soilers in their platform demanded "river and harbor improvements," "reasonable portions of the public lands" to actual settlers, and "tariff of duties as will raise revenue adequate to defray the necessary expenses of the Federal Government." This process of fragmentation and regrouping continued for a decade before the Republicans emerged with an agenda that united a sufficient number of elites and mobilized a sufficient amount of popular support to capture control of the federal government. Noting that the nation's "surprising development of material resources" and "rapid augmentation of wealth" were due to the "Union of the States," the Republican platform of 1860 went on to list other vital principles of unity: "the right of each state to order and control its own domestic institutions." Slavery, Republicans conceded, would be a part of America's future.

But the agenda or the "principles of unity" of the Republican Party was an agenda that precluded the growth of the slave system. The Republican platform continued: "sound policy...(would require that) "duties upon imports...(be adjusted) to encourage the development of the industrial interests of the whole country"; that Congress pass "the complete and satisfactory homestead measure which has already passed the House"; "that appropriations by Congress for river and harbor improvements of a national character, required for...the security of an existing commerce, are authorized by the Constitution"; and "that a railroad to the Pacific Ocean is imperatively demanded by the interests of the whole country; that the federal government ought to render immediate and efficient aid in its construction...." This platform prevented expansion of slavery into the territories, forced plantation owners to sell in a competitive market and buy in a protected one (as cotton prices fell), and insured their dependency upon capital markets as well as their political isolation. The agenda was equivalent to a declaration of war.

Could it have been otherwise? Compromises which the two party system supports are compromises between private individuals pursuing self-interest. But the individual pursuit of self-interest, or freedom, is a principle the two party system protects. Because there are only two major parties, no alternative concept to freedom and prosperity is made available. When structural antagonisms, such as the one between slavery and capitalism, present themselves, the two party system can, at best, provide space for the organization of popular support behind one of the two sides. That the two party system under these circumstances *encourages conflict* is a point worth noting. But let us turn to the organization of popular support. What happened to all the protest?

Linking Protest to Strategies of Expansion

During the 1850s, the acquisition and disposition of lands seem to have been the major concern among elites. Land represented political power. The control of new territory meant additional representation in Congress. And land represented economic power: for slaveowners, some of whom contemplated establishing plantations as far south as Cuba and Brazil, it was a safety valve; for capitalists, it was an expanded and more diversified market and seemingly an unlimited supply of natural resources.

The disposition of newly acquired territory had become the issue around which elites had organized their respective coalitions. The Missouri Compromise of 1820 and the Compromise of 1850 were attempts to balance the coalitions that had lined up behind slave and capitalist states, respectively. The Kansas-Nebraska Act of 1854, however, which allowed capitalists to expand railroad construction and slaveowners to repeal the Missouri Compromise, revealed the degree to which continued compromise only preserved the political power of slaveowners. The election of 1854, therefore, produced a massive proliferation of Anti-Nebraska dissidents or "the Republican Party in embryo." And because capitalist development depended upon favorable land policy and not upon abolition, Alfred Binkley correctly points out that the Republican coalition's opposition to the extension of slavery was rooted firmly in the desire for land.[41]

Prior to the Civil War land was not the primary interest of slaves and free blacks, who sought abolition and equal rights, or of women, who were beginning to work for suffrage reform. With the exception of the Liberty Party, which was supported by black delegates and which nominated blacks for office, and the Workingmen's Party, which worked closely with Francis Wright,[42] political parties generally forbade the participation of blacks and women.[43]

Many white male workers, however, could participate and Republicans needed their support. But like women and blacks, the primary concern of workers was not land reform. It was instead the erosion of craft production and their status as dignified members of the community. They protested the imposition of new labor disciplines, the growing gap between masters and journeymen, and the general stratification of the social order. As we have seen, the establishment of co-operatives was one form of redress. By 1851, 400 consumers' co-operatives were listed in New England alone. Perhaps more ominous to elites was the establishment of unions and the willingness of workers to strike in order to improve working conditions, obtain fair compensation, and shorten the work day. The ten-hour movement was, without doubt, labor's chief concern between 1840 and 1860.[44]

Unwilling to alter the relations of production between owner and wage earner, Republicans used land reform, and to a lesser degree high tariffs, to attract workers to their coalition. Notice also that high tariffs and land reform were well within the range of what the federal government was allowed to do to protect property relations. But how could the notion of land reform be used to deflect the mounting attacks upon the wage system itself? Reformers such as England's George Henry Evans and Republican Horace Greeley had long suggested that land reform, the "free distribution of homesteads to settlers on the public lands," would eradicate the suffering of the worker. One reformer's assertion that "nothing short of an entire revolution in society (can) remove the evils which the laboring people suffer" was typical of their posturing. It was the kind of rhetoric which appealed to and created a common bond among many workers and reformers. Yet, it was also typical of the way in which reformers avoided the delineation of immediate objectives, such as the ten hour day, which might have better strengthened the political position of labor by creating a broader constituency regarding issues of substance.[45]

Land reform, then, was suited to the aspirations of elites within the Republican Party. By ostensibly offering the worker an opportunity to escape the discipline of factory life[46] Republican elites were able to channel worker militancy into support of a land policy that was the political lynchpin of capitalist development at that time. Immigrant workers had been driven, for the most part, into the Democratic Party, and some workers refused to join the Republicans because they believed it would become the political means which would "enable the few to govern the many." The bulk of white native (born) workers, however, saw their class interests as being advanced by Republican success, that is, by the halt to the spread of slavery, by high tariffs and free land.

The first Homestead Act was passed in 1860 and, as we have seen, was largely fraudulent. Speculators moved in and bought up most of the 50 million acres that were made available to the public. As Henry Nash Smith points out, the Homestead Act did nothing to alter the relationships of power. The three decades after its passage were "marked by the most bitter and widespread labor trouble that had yet been seen in the United States."[47] Richard Hofstader has written that the "Homestead Act was a triumph for speculative and capitalistic forces.... [it] was a lure for over-rapid settlement in regions where most settlers found, instead of the agrarian utopia, a wilderness of high costs, low returns, and mortgages."[48]

But legislation of this kind had more far reaching effects. It created the appearance of workers joining with elites in a political coalition, of neutral, unstructured bargaining, of democratic compromise, and of pluralism. Each group gets something but not everything. There is the appearance of democracy and the appearance helps constitute the reality. Republicans were able to make broader appeals to the property-less citizen because the propertyless citizen believed. "Farmers, Workingmen, it is for you to save the country from the combination which threatens to exclude white laborers from the Territories and hand them over to the sole occupancy of slaves and slave-breeders."[49]

To be sure, most white male workers who viewed the wage system as "wage slavery" were still very much in favor of private property. For the most part, workers were content to be members of "a party of small enterprisers" who embodied the "passionate desire of the American bourgeois mind, the unlimited opportunity to rise." The point is not that workers were duped by the two party system. Rather it is that the two party system filtered out critical ideas which in turn insured the withering of leftward tendencies. The filtering out or derailment of processes of self-examination, urged by blacks, women, and workers, also increased the probability that protest would be channeled into policies of capitalist expansion. For example, connections between private ownership and "wage slavery" remained unclear and un-politicized within the party system despite repeated attempts for over 30 years, from Francis Wright, Thomas Skidmore, followers of Robert Owen and Charles Fourier, to numerous unions and workingmen's clubs (particularly among German-American workers), to advance a critical analysis of property relations. In addition, the interests of elites and the role of the state with regard to these interests were mystified despite the insights of the workers themselves. In 1858, workers in New Jersey demanded-that government lands should be withheld from the hands of speculators and sold only to actual settlers in limited quantities and at cost.[50] The ideas of workers were not given the same play as the ideas of elites. Although they were allowed to participate, their status was similar to women and people of color in that their voice was not heard. In short, elites set the agenda.[51]

Crisis: The 1890s

The post-Civil War economy was beset with problems the con-temporary reader might find hard to imagine. Composed of essentially small entrepreneurial firms, the economy was troubled by "unparal-leled and largely uncontrolled growth." *Deflation*, not inflation, was a serious problem. Prices steadily declined. But the upshot was similar to the general post-1965 crisis with which we are familiar: the "general trend of profitability in industry was gradually and inexorably downward."[52] Andrew Carnegie confessed that capitalists needed relief from competition. It behooves neo-classical economists on the Right to note Carnegie's lament.

The solution groped for by capitalists was to insulate themselves from short run market pressures and bring under control important aspects of their operation that were once external to it.[53] This could be achieved, in part, through the combining or centralization of capital which in turn required the creation of regulatory institutions.[54] Much like the creation of the federal government and the Republican agenda following the Civil War, the desire for regulatory mechanisms was but another attempt to further rationalize economic activity. In this case, centralization would allow large capitalists to move away from highly *personalized* capital markets toward a more specialized and regular capital market which would afford investors a more secure vantage point from which to judge their array of investment opportunities.[55]

The concentration of capital, then, was part of the closer bonding of manufacturers and financiers, the owners of factories in need of money and those who had money to lend. The relationship between manufacturing and finance capital had grown closer following the Panic of 1873 (precipitated by the failure of Northern Pacific bonds and the investment house of Jay Cooke). The result was a general shift of investments from railroads to manufacturing. For example, the growth in institutions that functioned as intermediaries in the mobilization of capital (stock exchanges, investment and savings banks, and insurance companies which invested heavily) supported an "aristocracy of finance," which collectively owned some 17% percent of the nation's physical assets by 1890. Many of these financiers had experience in managing railroad investments and had also acquired insights into the special requirements of managing large scale capital commitments. Consequently, many investment bankers, such as J.P. Morgan (in addition to European investors), took an interest in the new issues of industrial stocks and bonds that were being made available. With the purchase of these new issues, financiers were in the strategic position of being able to orchestrate the reorganization of the nation's leading manufacturing combinations.[56]

By the end of the 19th century, the economy of the United States could no longer be thought of as one essentially characterized by a free competitive market. Although still in its early stages of development, a *monopoly sector* was emerging.

Figure 1
Evidence of an Emerging Monopoly Sector

Industry	Percent of 1885-1904 National Market Controlled By Each Industry's Largest Firm
Copper refining	30 (64 for 4 firms)
Cigarettes	75 to 90
Gypsum Products	80
Typewriters	75
Metal Containers	65 to 75
Distilled Liquor	80 to 95
Steel	61

The rise of the monopoly sector triggered unprecedented *resentment* and dissent among workers in the monopoly sector and among elites and non-elites alike within the competitive sector, especially farmers, small manufacturers and mine owners. The protection of large scale manufacturing had resulted in increased costs for many manufactured goods, increased railroad rates, higher priced farm products and increased interest rates. For example, in one short four year period in Kansas during the late 1880s, 11,000 farm mortgages were foreclosed. The control over the worklives of small farmers that flowed out of the credit structure of the economy was " so pervasive...shaping in demeaning detail the daily options of millions" that it constituted, according to Lawrence Goodwyn, "a system that ordered life itself."[57]

For labor, concentrated capital meant layoffs, further elimination of skilled work, wage cuts, arbitrary authority, and a system of external rewards and intimidation.[58] The resulting protest of labor during this period is perhaps best described by John R. Commons, who called it "an elemental protest...a social war."

The impact upon blacks as an economic class and as a political class was just as severe. Blacks came to freedom without cash or land, a major failure of Reconstruction, and 95% were illiterate. Most black families found[59] themselves locked into a cycle of perpetual poverty as sharecroppers. Moreover, because the South was left devoid of capital following the war, blacks were especially vulnerable politically. The South, in order to industrialize, required northern capital and Republican support. Part of the deal in which southern elites permitted the Republicans to win the disputed presidential election of 1876 was that Republicans would support the financing of industrial investments in the South. And, as has been noted, Republicans also agreed not to protect the civil rights of southern blacks. Therefore, as industrialization took hold, unemployment among black cotton sharecroppers soared (at a greater rate than for whites). And by 1900, each southern state had written into law the disenfranchisement and segregation of blacks. Yet in the face of what could be called state-sponsored terror (petty brutality, lynchings at the rate of one hundred a year, and pogroms against the black sections of many towns were frequent), blacks defiantly organized—in Baltimore, Louisiana, the Carolinas, Virginia, Georgia, Florida, Texas, and Kansas.[60]

The political effect of this "new capitalism," as W.E.B. Du Bois called it, was growing disenchantment with each of the major parties. Carl N. Degler has noted that of the "three Republican presidents between 1877 and 1892 only one was elected by a plurality of popular votes and he (Garfield in 1880) received the smallest plurality in the history of the country.... two other Republican presidents (Hayes and Harrison) actually obtained fewer popular votes than their Democratic opponents, gaining the presidency only through victory in the Electoral College."[61] Meanwhile, years of co-operative struggle among poor farmers in the West and South had undercut the popular base of the Democratic Party as "outside the party system" alliances penetrated the party system in the guise of the People's Party. Everywhere there was talk of the "coming revolution." Therefore, the Democratic Party, which held a majority in the House of Representatives in eight of the ten Congresses elected between 1874 and 1892, had all but "disappeared from the plains states westward to the Pacific Coast, and it was tottering toward collapse across the South" by the early 1890s.[62]

Perhaps more frightening to elites than the erosion of their popular support was the leftward tilt of the popular movements. The People's Party in their platform of 1892 argued that "the people must own the railroads." And although many leaders of the People's Party, particularly in the South, were land owners committed to white supremacy, the necessity of breaking away from the Democrats forced them to flirt with black enfranchisement, as in North Carolina and Georgia, and take stands against lynch laws and anti-black terrorism.[63]

Meanwhile, with the economy in a state of severe depression in 1893, the Socialist-dominated AFL convention in Chicago passed the "Political Programme" calling for the collective ownership by all the people of all means of production and consumption. And women suffragists, whose political activism went beyond the relationships of property and struck at patriarchy itself, were gaining ground as they continued to seek planks in state party platforms. Using such tactics as voting illegally (which resulted in 150 arrests in 1872), women took a giant stride in 1869 as Wyoming became the first state granting full suffrage.[64]

Elites Set 1869 Agenda

The concern of party elites, however, was not drawn to the unconsoled voices of protest and despair, but to the boom in American trade. With exports soaring (roughly tripling in current dollar value between the late 1860s and the late 1890s), the negative balance of trade was dramatically turned around by the late 1870s. Pushing the export sector and growing faster than agricultural exports were manufactured goods.[65] And by 1890, as Degler points out, the production of manufactured goods had surpassed in value those from farms as 57% of the workforce was now engaged in non-agricultural activity.[66]

This sharp increase in the export of manufactured goods was due to the increase in capital concentration. In other words, it was due to the creation of monopolies. Greater amounts of capital under unified direction permitted elites to broaden their sphere of discipline and control and helped them to centralize administration, mechanize product distribution and the flow of information. Notice, however, that while the new monopolies meant increased productivity for owners, they meant less autonomy and increased discipline for workers.

The situation with regard to the non-manufacturing sector was parallel given the influence of lending institutions. The credit structure, described by Goodwyn, that impoverished small farmers was for financiers the means to keep prices low. In the context of these relationships of control, the two party system provided a valuable service to elites. It enabled them to deflect creative alternatives to these economic relationships by linking the public interest, promises of a good life, and public debate to ways of expanding international trade. It was around this issue that coalitions would be formed and sides taken.

Lest this sort of elite hegemony seems improbable in a democratic society, keep in mind that most people without property were not allowed to participate and those that could were not part of the agenda-setting mechanism. Goodwyn reminds us that following the Civil War the party system was controlled by "business and financial entre-preneurs to the degree" that by 1892 both major parties were "in thrall to the whims of the money power, and concentrated capital." Walter Dean Burnham has also pointed to the "penetration and control of the cadres of both major parties by the heavily concentrated power of our industrializing elites" as an essential feature of the party system "prior to the closing years of the nineteenth century." Perhaps the salient feature of each major party, then, was the establishment of a dominant northeastern sectional wing that spoke for monopoly (finance and manufacturing) capital. All the Democratic nominees for president from 1868 to 1892 were from the East. And although the Republican leadership included elites from the West, James Sundquist has characterized these western leaders (Senators John Sherman of Ohio, William B. Allison of Iowa, Shelby M. Cullom of Illinois, and President Benjamin Harrison of Indiana) as Republican "dough faces"—that is, "western men with eastern principles."[67]

The major parties equivocated "about the regulation of labor and business, the exclusion of the Chinese, control of immigration, the grant of public lands to railroads, and the control of public utilities" and instead focused upon what the government could do to improve exports. In other words, the range of public debate—conceivably as broad and as revolutionary as farmers and workers were attempting to make it—was narrowed to tariff and monetary policy. *This was a tremendous accomplishment. During the period in our history that comes closest to a revolutionary moment, the two party system managed to contain dissent by casting the hot blooded issues of the day into the dreary molds of tariff and monetary policy.* And Leon Friedman informs us that not even on "important economic issues of the time were the two parties significantly divided."[68]

For example, the Republican approach to protecting the manufacturing sector was by means of high tariff walls. The needs of their agrarian constituency, the vast legacy of the free soil movement stretching from New England through the Northwest, would be met, so it was argued, as the growing industrial sector created adequate demand for agrarian produce. The fear of small farmers, of course, was that they would be forced to sell in a competitive market and buy in a protected one. The Democratic strategy and reasoning were essentially the same. However, because the relentless agrarian protests had arisen from within their base of popular support, Democrats adopted a more conciliatory posture toward tariff reform and free trade.

The monetary policy of the major parties, which would directly affect the nation's money supply or the volume of money available for economic exchange at any given time, was also quite similar. The need among farmers and small manufacturers (in the competitive sector) was for an expansion of the money supply or easy credit. The raising of farm prices and the easing of debt through inflation were first desired through greenbacks (as advocated by the Greenback-Labor parties of the late 1870s) and later silver. Promoters of manufacturing exports, on the other hand, had always argued against any currency but gold, largely because most of U.S. trade was with European nations whose currency was tied to the gold standard. Therefore, a devaluation of U.S. currency, relative to gold (which would have been brought about by either the issuing of greenbacks or the monetization of silver), in the eyes of monopoly capitalists, would have risked "ruinous indebtedness to Europe." President Grant's Secretary of the Treasury had declared, "What we want is a restoration of industry, a diminution of importation and an increase of export. These we are not likely to have as long as a volume of irredeemable currency is kept in circulation." Later, Republican John Sherman of Ohio argued that the policy of coining silver, even on a limited basis, would "detach ourselves from the great commercial nations of the world and join the inferior nations." Republican James G. Blaine went a step further: "Give us the same basis of currency that our competitors of the British Empire enjoy and we will...float a larger tonnage under the American flag."[69]

As early as 1868, divisions between the competitive and monopoly sectors had appeared within each party over monetary policy. The division was more acute within the Democratic Party, which was playing the role of opposition party. Democratic Representative George H. Pendleton of Ohio, for example, advanced the notion of paying off the Civil War debt in depreciated greenbacks rather than gold. This "Ohio Idea" received greatest Democratic support from the West but only marginal support within the East. The "Inflation Bill" of 1873, designed to expand the money supply by $18 million and legalize earlier action by the Grant administration which had released $26 million in greenbacks from the treasury reserve, produced similar results. Supported broadly within each party but opposed within each party by a minority "monopoly" wing, the bill was eventually vetoed by Grant. Throughout the 1870s and 1880s this struggle between the competitive and monopoly sectors ("battle of the farmer versus the bond holder") over the amount of currency in circulation, especially with regard to silver, wore on.

By the early 1890s, it looked as though elites were unable to build the expansionist coalition they had wanted. As farmer alliances grew in number, the People's Party sapped the strength of the Democratic Party, bringing it near collapse in Kansas, Nebraska, Minnesota, the Dakotas, Colorado, Montana, and Oregon.[70] In 1892 a series of violent strikes, involving skilled and unskilled and black and white labor, threatened to topple industrial giants.[71] But these militant actions were met head on by what has been called "a magnificent police state" and "Republican-employer sponsored intimidation." Less militant but just as leftward leaning was the creative agitation by blacks, women, small farmers, and wage earners that kept bubbling through minor party activity to grab the attention and the imagination of the common citizen. These political movements directly threatened elite control of the party system and thus the state. Moreover, impassioned police state tactics, in addition to violating the spirit of republicanism and asceticism, were primitive and unpredictable. What was needed was a political strategy or a series of reforms that would lessen the space which the party system provided for collective agitation. What was needed was the rekindling of the notion of social responsibility as efficiency and independent thought as individualism. Reforms during the Progressive Era partially accomplished these ends, and we shall examine the impact of these reforms more closely in Chapter 5. For now, we shall round out this section by limiting our discussion to the bargaining and co-optive tactics used during the latter part of the 19th century.[72]

Linking Protest to Strategies of Expansion

Elites were in a bind. On the one hand, many believed that "people everywhere appeared to have become absorbed by a realization that the internal development of this country has reached a point where an external commerce is necessary for its prosperity...and that the markets must somewhere be found for the disposition of the surplus."[73] On the other they believed that the market for their surplus would have to be part of the market of the "great commercial nations." Northeastern "goldbugs," lodged within each major party, insisted that the currency be based on gold alone. Therefore, monopolists were locked in a struggle with the competitive sector, which sought not only an expanded or inflationary currency but also expanded trade with Asia and Latin America where many of the currencies were based on silver.

Developments were unfolding, however, that lessened the conflict of interest between certain farmers and monopolists. The change taking place was the slow but significant shift in trade away from near exclusive interaction with the gold-based economies of Europe. Described by Gabriel Kolko as the "most fundamental new development in its the U.S. economic structure at the turn of this century," the growth of imports of raw materials from Asia and the expansion of exports to Canada, Mexico, and other non-European countries (or silver-based currencies) moved elites to consider seriously the need to monetize silver to some degree.[74] In addition, the depression of 1893 had placed severe pressure on the nation's gold reserves.[75] It appeared as though silver, of necessity, would have to become a base of the nation's currency.

The "silver" lobby, which had strength in both major parties, now had an opportunity to mobilize broader support. It had long included Republicans representing mining industries and western business in general (such as Senator William Morris of Nevada and N. Moore Teller of Colorado), Democrats representing southern cotton growers and textile mill manufacturers (such as Representative Bland of Missouri), and large farmers such as Cyrus McCormick who believed that the coinage of silver was needed to penetrate Latin American and Asian markets. Thus, when President Cleveland in the face of the 1893 economic crisis stubbornly insisted on preserving the gold standard, the silver lobby grew dramatically. The American Bimetallic League formed by silver mineowners in 1889 was reinforced by the "National Bimetallic Union" and the "Pan-American Bimetallic Association," and by the emergence of scores of local and regional silver "clubs," silver "unions," and silver "leagues."[76]

The real need for the monetization of silver, however, severely weakened the Populist cause. As Robert Allen points out, "Populism was a revolt within the Democratic Party and it had long been the goal of that party to frighten or cajole the dissidents back into its ranks." The diversification in trade and the depression provided the perfect opportunity. The silver issue did not address the new despotism within the monopoly sector, the evils of the crop lien system, or the second-class citizenship of blacks, women, and immigrants. But to Populists in the South and in Kansas, Nebraska, and the two Dakotas whose discontent was rooted in the declining price of cotton or wheat (and of course the silverite Populists of the mountain states), the promise of increased exports via the remonetization of silver did rekindle the hope that maybe this time the pursuit of self-interest would bring individual freedom and prosperity.[77] These more conservative Populists set out to unite Democrats and Populists (under the Democratic banner). These "fusionists" called for unity around the demand of "free and unlimited coinage of silver."

Populists who believed that the good life lay in government control of credit or ownership of despotic factories were left stranded. With both major parties emphasizing the importance of working within the accepted institutional framework, there was no political alternative. And, in the context of a two party system, they were immobilized. They feared that by challenging the silverite fusionists, especially within the South, they would permanently divide and destroy the People's Party.[78]

But the identification with the norms and standards of any society, which is always a conservative force, might not have been sufficient to stymie the more radical Populists and strengthen the hand of fusionists had it not been for the very structure of the two party system. Both at the national level (because of the electoral college) and at the congressional level (because of single-member districts and plurality elections), it is imperative that candidates build broadly based coalitions. That is, ideologically distinct parties have little chance of winning.[79] Goodwyn has described the People's Party fusionists as those who "held office, had once held office, or sought to hold office.... All wanted to win—and at the next election." The Democrats had suffered badly in 1892 in the West and defections in the South reached "tidal proportions" in 1894, largely due to the Populist strength, as we have mentioned. And although the People's Party had won 25 to 45 percent of the electorate in twenty-odd states, they would do little more than win a few votes in the electoral college—at best. Given the structure of electoral competition, 25 to 45 percent support could not add up to representation unless there was some coalition building or, in this case, fusion. Silverites within the People's Party (often referred to as "millionaire Populist mineowners" and wealthy farmers[80]), therefore, succeeded in not only purging the movement of organized labor and socialist elements, but jettisoned the basic goals of the People's Party (1892) platform as well.[81]

The bargaining process did more than sidestep the crucial issues raised by the propertyless class. By trading the distinctive alternatives of Populists for major party status, fusionists also eliminated the need for the People's Party to reach out to socialists, blacks, and women. The disenfranchisement of blacks accelerated and suffragists were pushed to the side as the party struggled for middle ground.[82] This strategy was made clear in 1895 by the *National Watchman*, the official Populist organ. This time the threat posed was from the left: "The time for Populism and Socialism to part has come.... Let us be conservative, in order to secure the support of the businessmen, the professional men, and the well to do. These are elements we must use if ever success comes to our party."[83]

With the People's Party absorbed into the Democrat's campaign (each party nominated William Jennings Bryan in 1896) for silver, the Republicans were free to creatively link elements within the competitive sector to the imperial quest of monopoly capital in the underdeveloped world. Represented by William McKinley, the Republicans emphasized the remonetization of silver through international agreement (as opposed to the Democrat's unilateral approach). They also moved away from a strict high tariff position by employing reciprocity agreements (as opposed to the Democrat's lower tariff reform) which elites within the railroad industry (Stuyvesant Fish), manufacturing (Andrew Carnegie), and agriculture (Charles W. Marsh) acknowledged as a flexible approach to market expansion. The strength of iron, steel, copper, lumber manufacturers and wool producers (who were left unprotected without reciprocity agreements) in crucial midwestern swing states such as Ohio, Indiana, and Illinois, as well as in Michigan and Wisconsin, transformed those areas into a high tariff region. Senator Lodge and other Republicans, by exploring the possibilities of creating an international bimetallic standard, demonstrated the degree to which the "contest for final peaceful supremacy in the affairs of the world" was no longer cast in "gold."

The election of 1896 destroyed the northern Democratic Party. Represented by William McKinley, the Republicans stressed protective tariffs (which appealed to workers promised higher wages), reciprocal trade agreements and the remonetization of silver through international agreement (which, in keeping with an export economy, appealed to western farmers) while the Democrats, represented by William Jennings Bryan, emphasized unilateral remonetization of silver and tariff reform. In sweeping the North, Republicans received 7,035,000 votes to the Democrats' 6,467,000. The Midwest, which Cleveland had carried in 1892, went Republican. Even the progressive governor of Illinois, John Altgeld, was defeated.

In what Goodwyn describes as the "most self-consciously exclusive party the nation had ever experienced," the white, Protestant, Yankee Republicans set an agenda that transcended the period when economies of scale necessitated instability and when forms of consolidation were tentatively being explored. Elements within monopoly capital found in Third World expansion, as outlined in Republican policies, an opportunity to achieve public support. A coalition built around the establishment and protection of foreign markets and the political-economic control of foreign territory had emerged.

The 1930s Crisis: "Industrial Self Government"

The distribution of income recorded prior to the stock market crash of 1929 reveals that the prosperity of the 1920s was not widely based. Indeed, it appears that the situation *prior to* the Great Depression was one of massive poverty. The richest fifth of the population, for example, received over one half of the personal income. And a 1929 Brookings Institution study indicates that 42 percent of the consumer units lived at or below a "subsistence-and-poverty" level while another 36 percent lived at the "minimum-comfort" level.[84]

The calamitous drop in production, income, and employment between 1929 and 1933, therefore, spawned a broad range of militant left-leaning responses that can only be described as a crisis in legitimacy. Sundquist seems to have captured the urgency of the protests:

> Complete breakdown is imminent," warned *Survey*, the journal of the private charity field, in April 1932, on the basis of reports from thirty-seven cities. New York City's relief bureau closed its doors early in April, leaving the unemployed nowhere even to apply for aid. "Starvation is wide-spread," declared Republican Governor Gifford Pinchot of Pennsylvania, although other governors disagreed. On a single day in April, one-fourth (in acreage) of the state of Mississippi—39,699 farms and 12 to 15 percent of all town property was auctioned in sheriffs' sales. Men talked of violence. "Unless something is done," seven railroad brotherhoods warned the President, "we cannot be responsible for the orderly operation of the railroads...disorder...is sure to arise if conditions continue.... The unemployed citizen whom we represent will not accept starvation." A Methodist minister wrote Senator Royal S. Copeland of New York: "The entire north country is seething with communism.... Expect revolution."[85]

Indeed, Communist Party (CP) membership almost doubled from 1933 to 1935 (albeit from only 14,000 to 27,000). With the CP publishing no less than eight foreign language daily papers and with 60 percent of wage labor either foreign born or second generation "new immigrants," the CP presented a threat to elites far in excess of their numbers. The labor movement, listless since the early 1920s and on the defensive through 1932, struck hard in 1934 with crippling general strikes in Minneapolis and San Francisco. Transportation and municipal services were badly disrupted in Toledo, Milwaukee, Des Moines, Philadelphia, and Kohler (Wisconsin). A wave of violent strikes hit textile industries along the East Coast. Agricultural workers targeted the Imperial and San Joaquin valleys of California as Arkansas tenants organized a socialist union.[86]

These tremors of rebellion were being felt within the party system. The Republican northwest which experienced a severe agricultural depression during the early 1920s, witnessed the transformation of its Nonpartisan Leagues into statewide Farmer-Labor parties. The Republican Party in that region also gave way to transformation, first to Democrats in 1932 and then to Progressives in 1934.[87] In Wisconsin in

1934, the Progressive Party platform called for a government action that went well beyond anything the major parties were willing to offer "guaranteed employment for every able-bodied person, a government-owned central bank, a fair profit for the farmer, the right of labor to organize, and public ownership of the electric power, railroad, and munitions industries."[88]

The Democrats were also feeling the heat in spite of the unprecedented flurry of proposals to halt the continued economic slide following the inauguration of Franklin Roosevelt. The "share our wealth" campaign of Huey Long which demanded free homesteads and education, inexpensive foodstuffs, a cap on private fortunes, and a minimum guaranteed annual income of $5000 was one of several movements that indicated that people at the grassroots were out in front of the Democratic party. Father Coughlin, the popular "radio priest," was able to mobilize the support of millions of listeners for a program of currency inflation, guaranteed wages, and the nationalization of banking and natural resources. By 1936, Francis Townsend was able to garner 25 million signatures on a petition that outlined a way to aid the elderly. All citizens over the age of sixty, according to the Townsend plan, would receive a pension of $200 per month provided that they did not hold a job and provided that the money be spent within 30 days.[89] And in the state of Washington, the Democrats were displaced altogether by a left third party.

Characteristic of the upsurge in critical thinking was the campaign of Upton Sinclair, a life-long socialist, for Governor of California in 1934. Sinclair, borrowing from proposals put forward by Huey Long, Francis Townsend, and others, helped organize an End Poverty League which counted nearly 2000 chapters in 1934. Sinclair proposed to put a half-million of the unemployed to work in idle factories and on unused farmland. He defeated several mainstream candidates to win the Democratic primary. Elites, of course, were alarmed by the popularity of what was then being called "production for use." Earl Warren, then a district attorney, warned that "we must fortify ourselves against a resolute purpose to overwhelm California with Communism." Sinclair's campaign finally succumbed to an unprecedented smear campaign which Arthur Schlesinger Jr. called "the first all-out public relations *Blitzkrieg* in American politics."[90]

The Democrats also were facing a new problem in the black voter. The most dramatic shift of Republicans to Democrats between 1928 and 1936 took place in the industrial cities of the North.[91] In part this was due to the working class reaction to the Republican attempt to restrict immigration as well as the Republican dislike of central European working class Catholics.[92] Much of the new support, however, was coming from blacks who were migrating to northern cities in large numbers and whose disenchantment with the Republican Party was clearly manifested after 1932. But in order for Democrats to maintain the support of blacks, elite backers of Roosevelt would first have to distance themselves from the white supremacist southern wing (especially in light of the black pride and black nationalism stirred by Marcus Garvey and others during the 1920s), for so long a pillar of the party.

The political crisis, from the point of view of elites, therefore, had several dimensions. First, there existed the possibility of revolutionary militance. Second, short of that, organized left opposition could range anywhere from a preliminary challenge of private property to reorganization of coalitions that would preempt the Democrats' fortuitous opportunity to govern. Third, there was confusion. Just as had been the case during the 1850s and 1890s, elites had to thwart the leftward march of the propertyless class by linking protest to new strategies for expansion. But unlike the crisis which precipitated the campaign against the expansion of slavery and the campaign to establish diverse international markets, the political crisis of the 1930s was not due to conflicting strategies for economic growth. There was no strategy for expansion. Elites had thoroughly lost their way.

Elites Set the Agenda

In terms of the development of property relations, the period between World War I and 1929 marked a new phase. For the first time, the expansion of production capacity coincided with an absolute decline in the number of production workers (in farming, manufacturing, and railroads).[93] In other words, fewer workers were producing significantly greater amounts. Yet, in the face of insufficient demand, elites in such industries as petroleum, textiles, coal, banking, chemicals, iron, steel, clothing, paper, and trucking remained faithfully committed to maximizing expansion. The reasoning of property accumulation was moving the social order from a set of antagonistic relationships, where people without property felt the sting of the accumulation process, to one of contradictory relationships, where the act of accumulation itself became self-destructive.[94]

If the elite freedom that comes with the ownership of property were to be preserved, some semblance of co-ordination, or "discipline," was required. That is, some limitations upon the individual prerogatives of property ownership had to be fleshed out, not only to insure economic stability in the abstract, but to insure the kind of economic stability that would help politicians deflect the more radical proposals from below. The direction in which elites reluctantly first moved was simply an extension of the political-economic arrangement worked out during the 1890s. The cooperation of trade associations would again be backed through the legal sanctions of the state and sweetened by generous loans and subsidies from the public treasury.

Hoover's Reconstruction Finance Corporation (RFC) reflected this approach. The idea of using the government to extend credit to the banking system, exemplified by the War Finance Corporation during the agricultural depression following World War I, was again used to back not just banks, but insurance companies, other financial institutions, railroads, and industrial corporations. Democrats, posturing as the opposition, naturally seized the opportunity to make political hay. Stated George Huddleston of Alabama, "To these interests [banks, etc.] he [the President] would open the Treasury, but to starving men, women, and children, he would not give a red cent...."[95]

By late 1931, broad sectors of the property-owning class (larger business speaking through the U.S. Chamber of Commerce and the National Association of Manufacturers, NAM) began to coalesce behind a plan which would permit trade associations, under the guise of federal authority and therefore immune to antitrust laws, to "collectively decide upon production, prices, and investments." They would also be able to make legal, practices that had been considered "unfair." The plan, which originated with big business[96] was ridiculed by President Hoover, despite the parallel design of the RFC. Anxious capitalists were not impressed, particularly when the gross national product was falling sharply (27 percent between 1929 and 1932).[97]

As organized capital began breaking with the Republican administration, the two party system again became their collective board room where time-honored ends were reaffirmed and, this time, vague and sketchy means were put forward. But it was not Franklin Roosevelt (who campaigned on a balanced budget and reduced government spending) who galvanized the hearts and minds of the captains of industry to produce the "welfare state." Rather it was, by default, the Democratic Party. Where were elites to turn?

The one piece of legislation that best illustrates the political-economic turn marked by the New Deal was the National Industrial Recovery Act (NIRA), implemented by the National Recovery Administration (NRA). Broader and more comprehensive than the RFC, the NIRA would seek the cooperation of labor. The heart of the measure was the idea of "industrial self-government." Antitrust laws were relaxed so that elites within "licensed" industries could control prices, restrict output and eliminate "even competition itself when they felt it desirable." In fact, the earliest drafts of the bill focused exclusively upon provisions for codification, licensing, and suspension of the antitrust laws.[98]

Industrial codes were also to be drafted in consultation with consumers and labor (who were never really intended to be consulted, according to Gabriel Kolko).[99] Section 7a legalized collective bargaining and established floors under wage and hour standards in each industry in order that wage variations, and therefore price competition, be reduced. In short, previous voluntary codes of fair practice in each industry, as Edward S. Greenberg points out, became the law of the land.[100]

During the first few months of the Roosevelt administration, emergency meetings among key property owners took place in Washington as several drafts of the NIRA were worked out. Particularly enthusiastic about some kind of "partnership in planning" were trade associations that were seeking legal ways of controlling competition, such as the Cotton Textile Institute, the American Highway Freight Association (and their rival, the American Trucking Association), and the American Petroleum Institute. The NAM and the U.S. Chamber of Commerce, headed by Henry Harriman, lent their support as they had to similar plans before. Enthusiastic as well were elements of big business, such as Gerard Swope (General Electric), Myron Taylor of United States Steel, James Warburg (of the Kuhn, Loeb banking firm), Walter C. Teagle (Standard Oil of New Jersey) and the Rockefeller oil interests, and big business organizations such as the American Iron and Steel Institute, and the National Civic Federation (NCF). Like those who had experience with the 1917-18 War Industries Board (such as Hugh Johnson), many executives of very large corporations understood that stability, predictability, efficiency, and uniformity depended upon the federal government becoming "cooperator, adjuster and friend."[101]

This rather tenuous alliance of self-interested factions was able to move forward with their plan to legally *control* heretofore aspects of "free" market forces, largely because the Democratic Party had the capacity, as had the Republicans before it, to tailor the public perception of what is being done to the public's conception of what the government ought to be doing. It was unlikely that, in the midst of the greatest depression the country had yet seen, popular support could be mobilized to support *a policy that gave large property owners additional political power.*[102] But given that party debate was typically cloaking the issues in moral garb—a Republican senator stressed the need for "the development of sturdy, self-reliant citizenry" while a Democratic senator pointed to the "wan, half-starved children, pale and thin from undernourishment"—the industrial control of government, which NIRA code-making facilitated, would be presented as *government control of industry.* Roosevelt, therefore, told the public that the NIRA was an effort to support a "great cooperative movement throughout all industry in order to obtain wide re-employment, to shorten the working week, to pay a decent wage for the shorter week, and to prevent unfair competition and disastrous overproduction."

The 700 industrial codes that the NIRA ushered in were written in accordance with "the distribution of political power each faction of the industry possessed to impose its will." Kolko has suggested that the NRA "became a tool of big business with only incidental relationship to recovery." Given the domination of big business, consumers and farm organizations soon complained about antitrust law exemptions. And in 1934, Clarence Darrow would be given the job of investigating the extent to which NRA codes were "designed to promote monopolies or to eliminate or oppress small enterprises...."[103]

Midway through FDR's first term, then, it became clear that small business was saying no to "constructive cooperation." Moreover, the situation in cities such as Minneapolis, Toledo, and San Francisco, closed by general strikes, moved Secretary of State Cordell Hull to worry publicly that a "general strike" might topple the government.[104] Attributing the growing militancy of labor to the government's acceptance of collective bargaining, business opposition to the New Deal mushroomed. Alfred P. Sloan and William Knudsen of General Motors, Edward F. Hutton and Colby M. Chester of General Foods, J. Howard Pew of Sun Oil, Sewell L. Avery of Montgomery Ward, and the DuPonts helped form the American Liberty League, an organization committed to protecting property rights from the "radicalism" of the New Deal.[105] And in the summer of 1935, as FDR persisted in precedent-setting relief programs, the NAM and the Chamber of Commerce bailed out as well.

It appeared as though FDR's support from capital was crumbling as he attacked "economic royalists" and moved to advance the cause of the "under privileged." Indeed, party historians have described the transformation of the party system in 1936 (when significant numbers of Republicans began to think of themselves as Democrats) as a "class cleavage." The "masses" (the middle to lower income workers) voted Democratic in 1936 while the "classes" (upper income, business, and professional people) voted Republican.[106] This type of analysis captures a moment of truth. But the structure of the party system is not as flexible as this kind of analysis suggests. Why, after a century and a half of servicing large property owners, should major party elites suddenly reverse direction and open the two party system to the downtrodden?

Linking Protest to Strategies of Expansion

As Otis L. Graham, Jr. points out, the 1936 New Deal coalition combined "the South, the midwestern prairie states, and virtually every city in the country over 250,000 in population." Indeed, it was the transformation of northern urban centers into "the network of Democratic bastions" that marked the party reorganization of the 1936 election. The Democratic grip on the South, among elites that is, requires little explanation. But the South was still a very poor region. Memories of Populism, which New Deal Democrats drew on, were still fresh. Elite southern Democrats were, as Sundquist describes them, "bitterly intransigent anti-New Deal." Carter Glass of Virginia, for example, stated in 1933, that the New Deal was an "utterly dangerous effort of the federal government to transplant Hitlerism to every corner of the nation." Yet more alarming than transplanted Hitlerism to southern Democrats was the loss of political control in the South. And this control in the South depended in no small measure on the national strength of the Democrats, particularly if they obtained a majority status in Congress. Carter Glass, therefore, also was obliged to add, "I'm a Democrat, not a half-way Democrat."[107]

Regional political hegemony also figured in the ability of Roosevelt to deflect his most serious political challenge from the left. In the midwest, under successive titles—the "League for Independent Political Action," the "National Farmer-Labor Party Federation" and the "American Commonwealth Federation"—progressives tried to galvanize the many left farm organizations, trade unions, and statewide third parties in order to launch a national party that would challenge Roosevelt in 1936. This challenge seems to have been turned around when the driving force of the movement, the Farm-Labor Party of Minnesota headed by Governor Floyd B. Olson, lent its support to Roosevelt in 1936 in exchange for a promise by the Democrats not to run a candidate for either governor or senator.[108]

The ability of a major party to divide movement coalitions through the exchange of favors with factions willing to advance their own self-interests again reveals the clout major parties obtain from the two party structure. Were there proportional representation or a multiparty system, the Democrats could not have so easily split the "progressive" vote. The Democrats' ability to engage in this type of bargaining was also enhanced by the government's vast array of programs which its new "partnership" with industry provided. In important respects, the patronage system of the urban machine of the 19th century, decimated by "progressive reforms," was resurfacing at the national level.

For example, the conservative Farm Bureau, representing the larger farmers and often at odds with more militant farm organizations, was lifted to political-economic prominence by supporting and then dominating the administration of the Agricultural Adjustment Act. This act allowed the government to pay certain farmers not to produce and provided emergency mortgage refinancing among other subsidies. As long as organizations such as the Farm Bureau were willing to assist the government in the process of advancing the interests of the wealthier farmers (who received the "lion's share" of farm subsidies) and thereby advance their own cause, people living in the harshest of rural poverty would be squeezed out of the bargaining process. After all, with the cooperation of third party dissidents and with large farmers nailed down, what could impoverished farmers offer the more liberal of the two major parties?

Examination of the gains and losses of organized labor during this period of party reorganization also helps to clarify the limits and possibilities of the two party system. The period may be remembered by workers as the period when unions were finally recognized. Considered as one of labor's greatest achievement, the Wagner National Labor Relations Act of 1935 helped curb unfair labor practices. But more important, it established labor unions as bargaining agents within the corporation system.[109] The Wagner Act instituted a relationship that elites had been trying to develop with labor ever since the creation of the National Civic Federation in 1900: through the NIRA the destabilizing effects of strikes and the adoption of radical ideologies by labor could be minimized, and possibly prevented, by allowing labor leaders to become quasi-junior partners, as it were, through "collective bargaining." Said a NCF spokesperson in 1900, "Our experience has convinced us that the best way to control labor organizations is to lead and not to force them. We are also convinced that the conservative element in all unions will control when properly led and officered."[110]

Collective bargaining illustrates well the way in which politics as bargaining within the party system insures that the terms of exchange rigidly preserve relationships of power based upon property. For example, collective bargaining, while it partially transcended the "class struggle," did not allow workers the greater degree of autonomy in the workplace that had always been a demand of labor. Rather, it allowed labor leaders to share a degree of political power by helping elites stabilize and manage the social order. Notice the tradeoffs: 1) as quasi-junior partners in managing the social order, the political interests of labor leaders and capitalists tend to converge; 2) labor would be able to command a larger piece of the corporate pie, but the acceptance of imperialistic dividends also meant that workers would less likely balk at doing the dirty work (such as enduring the innumerable costs of militarism) that is required to help achieve and maintain U.S. hegemony in an international economy; 3) the exchange permitted labor in general to enjoy the spoils of and identify more closely with white male authority and male domination; and 4) the potential of a revolutionary alliance (among the propertyless class, wage earners, minorities, and women), feared since the creation of "popular government" as evidenced by *Federalist 10*, was virtually ended.[111] In short, the best the two party system could offer was higher wages and the restoration, on a political level, of mutual responsibility which had been sought by labor ever since the demise of craft production and the introduction of unions. But it could not jeopardize property relations by restoring mutual responsibility with respect to ownership. It could not permit labor to either organize an independent political party or obtain workplace autonomy. In the context of a Liberal/capitalist order, then, the bargain struck between organized labor and capital (known as collective bargaining) was as far as labor could go. And in this sense it was the end of the road.

The inability of collective bargaining to address such problems as the lack of community and dignity, hierarchy, and domination flows out of the same limited concept of politics as bargaining that is internal to the two party system. Consider the way in which collective bargaining was first explained to then president of the American Federation of Labor (AFL), Samuel Gompers (as paraphrased by Philip Foner), and notice how the bargaining process, in and of itself, insures that issues such as dignity or power remain off limits:

> The craft unions would win recognition from the leaders of the trustified industries for a small minority of the workers on condition that they would "not make trouble" for the corporations by organizing the mass of the workers in their plants and factories; that they would not challenge the control exercised by the finance capitalist over the American economy; that they would also agree "to keep politics out!" of the unions, and thus avoid challenging the control exercised by the finance capitalists over American government.... If the unions would make no real effort to organize the unskilled workers (especially the foreign-born and Negro workers), the corporations would make certain concessions to the craft unions. Business could afford to pay higher wages to a small number of skilled workers so long as the great body of unskilled workers were unorganized.[112]

Gompers accepted the offer in the early part of the century (as did John Mitchell of the United Mine Workers and other labor leaders) just as William Green, AFL president, accepted organized labor's role in the NIRA in 1933. Green characterized the NIRA as "a very definite step forward in industrial stabilization, rationalization, and economic planning."[113] The political advantages that power brokers could enjoy by recognizing unions were not immediately appreciated by all elites, however. It was not until a more militant urban constituency had pushed Senators to pass the Black-Connery thirty-hour week bill that elites sprang into action. Preventing the bill from coming to a vote in the House, the Democrats then moved quickly on the NIRA, inserting section 7a, ostensibly allowing labor to organize. "Along the line," adds Kolko, "they dropped key words and introduced ambiguity regarding unionism...." The New Deal coalition was in place, or so it seemed.[114]

In competitive industries, such as in garments or coal, where union cooperation was a necessary condition to price stabilization, unions were able to bargain successfully for humanitarian legislation such as decent wage gains and a ban on child labor. In oligopolistic firms, such as auto, collective bargaining posed a threat. And when the AFL acquiesced to pro-employer formulations of the industry's NRA codes, the threat materialized. What Mike Davis describes as an "open revolt of local shop committees" in auto was duplicated throughout the "industrial heartland." The NRA unionization drive had clearly backfired. The rebellion of the unorganized industrial worker not only scared away many elites who were nervous about the NIRA scheme to begin with, but also pulled the rug out from labor leaders such as Teamster leader Daniel Tobin who, worried about the effects of the sudden increase in union ranks, confided, "We do not want to charter the riff-raff or good-for-nothings, or those for whom we cannot make wages or conditions.... We do not want the men today if they are going on strike tomorrow."[115]

It was the political high-water mark for unions. As four million workers surged into the newly created Congress of Industrial Workers (CIO), union doors, for a time, swung open to blacks and women. Moreover, as 1936 approached, FDR's support among elites was fragmented. He needed bases of support within northern urban centers and, therefore, he needed the support of the industrial workers that were pouring into the CIO.[116] Stated New Deal brain-truster Raymond Moley, Roosevelt was devising a strategy to "gather into the Democratic Party many minorities, including the labor unions, through policies calculated to win the urban masses, while he held the farmers in line with cash benefits."[117] The primary tactic FDR had in mind was to reverse his position and support the Wagner Act. Politically, it was a necessary but risky step for Roosevelt. It helped sew up his re-election, enlist organized labor's support in his battle against the Supreme Court (which was bent on invalidating major legislative achievements of the New Deal), and it also helped prevent the further expansion of left controlled sectors of the labor movement. But, as Piven and Cloward suggest, it appeared to some elites as though business had lost control of the state. Such was not the case.[118]

A point often missed but well documented by Davis is that just as FDR needed the CIO, the leaders of the CIO (John L. Lewis and other AFL "secessionist bureaucrats") needed "Roosevelt's backing and the clout of his political-judicial support to bring the rank and file in line." After all, the CIO had drawn upon Lewis' own United Mine Workers, which banned radicals, as the model of industrial unionism. The CIO, much like the UMW, placed emphasis upon "tight central control, limited local autonomy, and minimized rank and file participation."[119] At one level, the bargain may be viewed as the exchange of the Wagner Act and the appointment of pro-CIO liberals in the Labor Department for the CIO endorsement of FDR, along with the help of Sidney Hillman, and the Labor's Nonpartisan League, which in 1936 helped mobilize support for Roosevelt, political as well as financial.[120]

At a more important level, the bargain illustrates the way in which the two party system captures and defeats movement politics. Organized labor was to leaders of the New Deal an instrument to be used first to stabilize key sectors of the economy and second to mobilize political support in key areas of the country. This instrumental use of disadvantaged constituencies was facilitated by the two party system's

denying labor an independent political base or voice. An independent
political base would have permitted workers an opportunity to escape
politics as bargaining. They would have been able to explore the
divergent ideologies, programs, and platforms to which they had been
exposed and which a critical, creative politics requires. Perhaps more
important, the inability to establish an independent political party left
workers extremely vulnerable. Exposed to the corporate strikebreaking
counteroffensive, which by the standards of a democratic society must
stand as corporate terror, they were physically vulnerable.[121] And they
were politically vulnerable, given the need of New Dealers following
FDR's 1936 re-election, to illustrate, for the business community, the
precise limits of organized labor's political influence. In a campaign
against "Little Steel" in 1937, Lewis had counted on New Dealers at the
federal and state levels to put an end to the steel barons' "systematic and
blatant defiance" of the Wagner Act. Troops of the Ohio national
guard sent into the steel towns of Canton, Massillon, and Youngstown
by Democratic Governor Davey were greeted by strikers as liberators.
Much to the strikers' surprise the guards launched what Davis has
characterized as a "reign of terror, reminiscent of the suppression of the
1919 Steel Strike."[122]

Again we find the appearance of party politics at odds with its
reality. With the New Deal coalition leaning heavily upon the support
of labor, the conversion of black Republicans to Democrats, and, to a
lesser degree, on Eleanor Roosevelt's solicitation of women voters, it
appeared as though "the non-owner had come to legislate for the owner
of property." Such appearances, as we have seen, tend to move many
citizens without property to identify with the organizing principles to
which the state is committed: individualism, the pursuit of self-
interest, the expansion and stability of the private economy. And yet it
is these beliefs which gave New Dealers the legitimacy during World
War II, and other administrations afterwards, to establish the kind of
partnership with capital, the "industrial self-government," that had
eluded them with the collapse of the NRA.

The Reality of Party Politics

> The state is primarily in business to promote capital accumula-
> tion and to maintain social harmony and legitimacy.
> —Walter Dean Burnham[125]

In this chapter we have examined the way in which party activity is
structured by the relation of the state to the economy and how structural
constraints assist elites in forming governing coalitions. As I have
noted earlier, the relationship of the state to the economy rests on the
state's obligation to promote freedom. And in the context of property
relations, as Burnham suggests, the promotion of freedom is the

promotion of the process of capital accumulation. Political party activity, then, is, in part, structured by this relationship.

It is clear that the two party system, through the process of competitive elections, facilitates the transfer of the control of the government. But notice, the control of the government is not as open ended as we may have once assumed. The control of the government, in part, is the control of the process of promoting capital accumulation. One important function of the party system, therefore, is to determine who will promote capital accumulation and in what manner that promotion will take place.

This is why dominant factions within political parties that actually run the government (as opposed to mobilizing popular support) can be defined in reference to specific economic interests, strategies, and expectations that correspond to specific agendas. For example, what has been touted as the Reagan "revolution" or Reaganomics was linked to a "supply-side" strategy that entailed tax cuts, cuts in social spending, deregulation, and increased military spending. When the economy was less complex, the linkages between governing coalitions within political parties and specific industries were quite clear. One could point to tobacco planters organizing the Jeffersonian-Republican coalition to contain commercial develop-ment with Great Britain. As the economy became more complex and diversified, governing coalitions could be linked less to the promotion of specific "driving" industries than to sectors of the economy which promised high rates of growth. Thomas Ferguson and Joel Rogers, for instance, argue that the "core of American politics during the Golden Age after World War II may be understood as founded on the alliance of high-technology firms (of which integrated petroleum companies were the most numerous and important) and international finance that first emerged in the 1930s."[124] We shall discuss the linkages between present governing political factions and economic sectors in Chapter 6. But the point here is to note that major parties are, in part, economic forms, that they correspond to specific economic interests, and that the range of policies they promote, the range of voices which are heard, the issues upon which they focus, and the way in which issues are framed are kept safely within the already spun web of shared norms and standards. In other words, party politics is very much structured by the accumulation process.

Attention to the relationship between the state and the economy compels us to re-examine traditional assumptions concerning the dynamics of the two party system. For example, the process which political scientists have termed critical elections can now be understood more fully. A critical election was first defined by V. O. Key, Jr. as "a type of election in which there occurs a sharp and durable electoral realignment between parties." The term "realignment," however, is a bit misleading. It suggests that the *durable* changes in party coalitions which take place during periods of social transformation and which are marked by critical elections are primarily changes in "basic party attachments of the voting citizens," that is, party identification.[125] But party identification is part of what it means to coalesce within a party. In other words, the concept of realignment is circular. It refers to itself and explanations of "realignments" have a tendency to refer only to isolated phenomena internal to party activity proper: charismatic candidates, polarizing issues, and the like. James Sundquist, who has written the most comprehensive explanation of party realignments but who employs traditional assumptions, concludes that "A realignment has its origins in the rise of a new political issue (or cluster of related issues)."[126] Conclusions of this sort are due, largely, to the failure to include inter-connections between public and private institutions as explanatory factors.

A grasp of the structural linkages between the state and the economy enables us to interpret party realignments in a different light. The interpretations presented in this chapter of party change during the periods of the 1850s, 1890s, and 1930s suggest a general explanation of the dynamics internal to "party realignments": the dominant faction within each major party speaks for a coalition of large property owners who share a common strategy for using the government to promote economic development. Competition among elites over control of the government often turns to conflict when the private aspirations of one faction of elites obstruct the economic freedom of another. Often such conflict is rooted in economic antagonisms; that is, when the expansion of one economic sector obstructs the development of another (as was the case during the 1850s and 1890s). During the 1930s, however, the antagonism was partially political. Economic stability required unprecedented governmental intervention and an unusual degree of cooperation of property owners with a segment of the propertyless class (organized labor).

During such periods of economic transformation, party coalitions are reorganized because they have to be. New strategies to use the government to develop property relations require that governing coalitions correspond to the new constellation of leading players in the accumulation process who are creating the conditions of growth and/or stability. Or to put it another way, representatives of one economic sector, say "smoke stack" industries, would have a hard time governing should another group of industries, say "high tech," account for the bulk of the nation's economic growth. The resolution of the conflict among elites with new aspirations and old elites caught in a defensive posture occurs when a reorganized form of production and set of investment opportunities is agreed upon and supported by a sufficient number of constituencies to electorally defeat the old coalition of elites. National elections that signal such a policy shift are termed "critical elections."

But the focus on electoral activity by students of the process tends to obscure and de-legitimize community organizing, strikes, production and consumer cooperatives, and policy proposals which emanate from outside the party system. The electoral focus also suggests that citizens "mandate" policy. This reverses the relationship between voting and policy making. At best, electoral competition allows citizens to approve of certain candidates and, indirectly, certain policies. Ignored is the fact that the range of policy options made available to citizens for their vague approval is terribly narrow and constrained. Voters have a veto power, but only to the degree that major party opposition, within the narrow range of policies which expand the private economy, can provide alternatives. The fixation on electoral activity also creates the illusion that party transformations are "sharp" and "sudden." Overlooked is the fact that transformed party coalitions, generally, are two decades or more in the making. It might be more accurate to say simply that critical elections are a small but important part of the transformation process. They are, in effect, signals to elites to proceed with their new agenda. We may conclude that party realignments are the political component of economic transformations: the party's conception of the public interest, its strategy to further develop property relations, its economic base, and its ideological framework are simultaneously altered.[127] We may conclude also that the historical unfolding of power relations that help constitute party realignments has been made invisible. It would behoove us, for example, to note that following the creation of a centralized federal government in 1789, each of the realignments in question has further centralized and augmented the federal government's intervention into the economy at the same time that they have permitted the federal government to become an instrument in the hands of private elites. In other words, party realignments have marked the steady rationalization of public life and the privatization of political institutions.

Realignments have also marked the resolution of conflict. But notice also that the conflict that is resolved is among elites only. The conflict between elites and non-property owners is displaced. For example, the conflict between factory owners and wage earners, displaced by the triumph of the Republicans during the 1850s, eventually resurfaced in more virulent form in the 1890s and the 1930s. Similarly, anti-discrimination provisos[128] written into many New Deal statutes helped strengthen Democratic support in northern urban areas as it helped legitimize greater private control over productive forces. In this sense such provisos helped stabilize the political order and was thus part of the conflict resolution among elites. But the frank institutional self-examination which is necessary before racial distrust is reduced was avoided. Superficially sanitized within the context of public policy, the inability of the two party system to come to grips with power relationships between races displaced racial conflict out of the spotlight of public inquiry and into the obscure lunch counters, transportation systems, union halls, banks and real estate offices of the social order. Although the violence of the 1960s generated a flurry of much needed legislation and private inquiry, a reflective public discussion of the relation between institutional imperatives and racism still remains outside the range of legitimate party debate.

The reputation of the two party system as an institution which resolves conflict needs to be qualified. The conflict which it is capable of resolving is only that conflict which obstructs the development of property relationships. But it is not always capable of resolving it, witness the Civil War. In other words, despite the resolution of certain conflicts, there will always be large property owners with the capacity to control (politically and economically) the aspirations of those who are not self-sufficient with respect to property. Abstractly, what we refer to as "party realignments" becomes quite clear: *the process is little more than a game of political musical chairs.* When the economy stops, just like when the music stops in the game of children, those with and without comfortable (market) positions must struggle to re-establish or acquire a secure position. Large property owners may lose a degree of political power as their economic fortunes crumble. And if they are willing to push and knock down those who get in the way, it is possible for certain segments of the propertyless class to gain a degree of political security. But when the game of political musical chairs is played out, there are always those left standing and the general relationships of power that flow out of property relations will have been preserved.

Perhaps life ought not to be like a game where winning or losing is an acceptable feature of everyday life. *But as long as politics is understood as bargaining, the game of political musical chairs will be played in earnest.* Bargaining does not permit reflective criticism: "Why don't we create more chairs, or if someone must stand, why don't we take turns?" And it does not permit reflective criticism because if we think "bargaining" we cannot think "caring for others." Working together politically, as in a party, then twists the social experience into an alienating experience: working together politically becomes co-operating in preserving (perhaps not consciously) socially destructive practices. Common interests become the dovetailing of self-interests and the preservation of institutions which foster self-interest because the purpose of doing political work is perceived as part of a developmental process; that is, *development as in accumulation. Growth as in learning from others* and creating the structure to preserve the excitement of learning from others thus becomes the practice of those who do political work outside the party system.

This means that third parties within the context of the two party system cannot be alternative parties which transcend *politics as bargaining*. The two party system itself induces bargaining: dissident parties or a dissident faction within a major party that becomes a third party runs the risk of helping to elect their rivals as they draw electoral support away from the major party with which they are more closely aligned. Also, the realization that alternative agendas cannot be advanced unless alternative parties are represented compels third party leaders to bargain with major party leaders in the hope that a watered-down version of their agenda will be accepted in exchange for their support. The establishment of political independence by disadvantaged constituencies, therefore, is made quite difficult as unexpurgated critical thinking is filtered out. And the opportunity to introduce within the party system the more reflective processes which characterize movement politics is virtually eliminated. For example, the bargaining process, which had made the encouragement of union organizing during the early 1930s a matter of national policy, allowed the Democrats to link the American Federation of Labor (AFL) with big business which in turn prevented labor from acquiring political independence. By 1937 the AFL openly fought the Committee for Industrial Organization (CIO). Left third party movements, city-wide labor tickets, and pressure from the left on the New Deal eroded. President Tobin of the Teamsters could be found obtaining massive federal sedition prosecution of the Trotskyist leadership of Drivers' Local 544—"the nerve centre of labour militancy in the Northwest." And by FDR's third term, labor's role in the government had been reduced to token participation as billions of dollars worth of contracts were awarded to violators of the Wagner Act.[129] The structural reality of a two party system helps to insure that third parties remain minor parties, and bargaining units at that.

As minor parties and as bargaining units, it might be well to think of third parties as *satellites* of the major parties. And as satellites, they function well to co-opt dissent from the propertyless class that could otherwise contribute to a crisis of legitimation. In part, this is due to the fact that dissident elites (Republicans of the 1850s, the "Silverite-Populists" of the 1890s, and although they had captured control of the state, the New Dealers of the 1930s) associated with ascendant economic sectors are perfectly positioned to link protest to new strategies for expansion. The mobilization of protest under expansionist strategies in the context of satellite party activity is a dynamic of the two party system because 1) just as it is quite difficult for dissidents within the propertyless class to form independent political bases, dissident elites are often unable to dislodge ruling elites struggling to preserve dying industries, 2) propertyless dissidents, anxious to have their voice heard within the party system, are in a good bargaining position vis-a-vis dissident elites, and 3) expansionist strategies are what the state is capable of advancing. Consequently, significant third parties are generally cross-class coalitions linking protest to policies of expansion. Dissidents within the People's Party, for example, were largely victims of the crop lien and other credit systems and workers seeking greater autonomy in the workplace and nationalization of transportation and communication systems. The People's Party was led, however, by large farmers and small manufacturers seeking overseas market expansion and mine owners seeking the coinage of silver.

But as we noted at the outset of this chapter, by focusing on the relationship between the state and the economy, we present an incomplete view of party politics. It is incomplete in one respect with which we are familiar. Because economic activity meaningful to us in terms such as individual freedom and achievement *as accumulation*, political strategies to develop property relations *must also be* strategies to encourage perseverance *as self-denial and discipline* and development *as the control and conquest of nature*. This same strategy, then, must discourage (implicitly or explicitly) self-understandings which emphasize the need for sensual relations; that is, social relationships organized around the need to draw nourishment from one another and from nature. A more complete view of the relation between the state and the economy is one that takes into account the political ideas which provide legitimation for the sexual economy.

The discussion presented in this chapter is also incomplete in the respect that we did not address what Burnham suggested at the outset was the function of the state to promote social harmony and legitimation. The promotion of social harmony and legitimation is, however, the legitimation of the sexual economy. And it is with respect to this function that the two party system also plays a key role. One function of the two party system, as we have just seen, is to allow elites to compete publicly for control of the state. A second major function is the mobilization of popular support. It is through the mobilization of popular support for strategies of economic expansion that social harmony and legitimacy are often maintained and established.

We shall now turn to a consideration of this subject. But before we do, two preliminary points are in order. Because legitimation of the private economy requires the encouragement of a kind of sensual/ emotional self-discipline, religion, as a source of moral imperatives regarding sensual activity, plays a key role within the party system in terms of mobilizing popular support. Second, the basic class antagonism within our political-economy turns on property relations. But the Marxian location of this antagonism, between owners of the means of production and wage earners, rests on a narrow conception of economics. If we broaden our conception of economics to include the sexual dimensions we have been discussing, the basic class conflict must be located between owners and non-owners of property generally. This subtle change shifts the point of struggle from the "point of production" to the point of political expression (which includes the point of production). It also helps us to explain why the general struggle between property owners and their representatives and the propertyless class includes women and people of color who are not earning wages in addition to wage earners of all types. The mobilization of popular support within the sexual economy turns as much upon male domination and racial subordination as it does on the division of labor, as much upon the denial that reason cannot be divorced from emotion as it does upon property rights. The political voice of women and people of color, as women and as people of color, undermines the legitimacy of our shared sense of individual achievement and self-denial as much as democracy within the workplace undermines the legitimacy of private ownership and control.

Let us move on, then, to a discussion of the mobilization of popular support. Although our attention is focused on the role of the two party system within the social order, it is the exploration of this function which best allows us to see where the dynamics of class, race, and gender come together.

4

LEGITIMATION AND THE
MOBILIZATION OF POPULAR SUPPORT

> Wherever there are [two] political parties each party will
> attribute every defect of society to the fact that its rival is at the
> helm of the state instead of itself.... Insofar as the state
> acknowledges the evidence of social grievances it locates their
> origin either in the laws of nature over which no human agency
> has control, or in private life which is independent of the state,
> or else in a malfunction of the administration which is
> dependent upon it.
>
> —Karl Marx[1]

Karl Marx's observation of what was then Great Britain's two party
system sheds a great deal of light upon the way in which our own two
party system legitimates state support of the private (sexual) economy.
This legitimation is accomplished as major parties attribute social
grievances to causes which originate outside the private economy. This
function, therefore, enables political parties to mobilize popular
support for strategies to develop the private economy which would
otherwise be quite unpopular.

Marx's observation is relevant to our discussion because the
analysis presented thus far suggests that racial, gender-based, and
political-economic inequality is very much linked to the practice of
protecting individual property rights, that the private economy as a
sexual economy is a major source of social grievances. The legitimation
function mystifies the state's complicity in generating social grievances. Mystification and the mobilization of popular support (a
function traditionally ascribed to the two party system) are very closely
linked. But before we proceed further, let us clarify the observation
made by Marx. We first need to make note of the fact that Great Britain's
two party system, like ours today, was connected to a private economy;
that is, an economy not under public control. We also need to note the
primary assumption underlying the one to which Marx points. Social
grievances, and Marx here is thinking of "pauperism" or inequality, is

entirely due to either natural causes—"John and Mary are lazy"—or to maladministration—"The failure of the present administration to make adjustments in fiscal and monetary policy and thereby compensate for market defects keeps John and Mary out of work." Notice what is missing: neither analysis is capable of suggesting that inequality is exacerbated by the fact that the economy is privately and not publicly, or democratically, controlled. In other words, neither party is capable of linking social grievances to something as fundamental as property rights. And why not? Marx answers: "...no living person believes the defects of his existence to be based on the principle, the essential nature of his own life; they must be grounded in circumstances outside his own life."[2]

We shall explore in this chapter the historical tendency for party elites, when coming to grips with the social grievances of wage earners, people of color, and women, to suggest that such problems are located either in 1) natural causes, defects in character and the like, or in 2) the failure of the previous generation of party leaders to institute proper reforms. And as we locate this oscillation, we shall find that it represents a long cycle in U.S. party history. The attempt to explain inequality by reference to natural causes and character defects was dominant throughout the 19th century. I shall refer to this orientation as the *Police State*. By the turn of the century, a swing away from the Police State and a swing toward the *Welfare State* had begun. Proponents of the Welfare State, noting that massive inequality had become an obstacle to social and economic stability, charged opponents with "maladministration" and suggested that social grievances, particularly the inequality that existed (and still exists) in urban areas, could be tempered through reform. In Chapter 6 I shall argue that since the 1960s, elites have swung back again toward the Police State in which the misery of inequality is more likely to be considered "a crime to be...punished" than a "misfortune to be prevented."[3]

Legitimation and the American Police State

The intimate relation between religious fundamentalists and the rise of the New Right has rekindled debate over the separation of church and state. Unfortunately, an essential aspect of this situation has largely been ignored and that is the assumption that capitalist expansion is divinely inspired, part of "God's plan" as it were.[4] This assumption signals a swing back to the ideology of the Framers, an ideology which suggested that salvation lay in industry and accumulation. President Reagan himself occasionally stresses the fact that his own political-religious values are in line with the conviction of the Framers. What is ominous, however, is that we seem to have forgotten how the values which Mr. Reagan uses to mobilize popular support were at one time the values used to impose discipline on segments of the population. Justified as "moral instruction," the purpose of this discipline was that of indoctrinating potentially subversive groups into the industrial order. They were the values of the American Police State.

By the end of the 18th century, new secular schoolbooks had replaced catechisms and religious tracts in New England. Although secular in nature, they provided a moral training of their own. They were, as Barbara Epstein suggests, intended to "inculcate a certain personality type [for boys]—rational and controlled, competitive, ambitious, and rigidly honest." Individual achievement was to be the measure of individual worth and the measure of achievement was wealth, power, and fame. And wealth, according to the text books, depended upon "industry and frugality."

An essential component of this way of thinking was the notion that "you may be whatever you resolve to be." This belief, of course, much like the "free to choose" motif of today, suggested that the poor were responsible for their plight.[5] Consequently, the poor were held in contempt. But notice that the failure to be industrious was not categorized as simply a misfortune, or an error, or a mistake. Because the industrious personality was the morally sound personality, the apparent failure *to choose* to become industrious was a moral transgression. Poverty, argued the authors of the early schoolbooks, was the result of "intemperance," "sensuality," "vicious indolence and sloth."[6]

The same set of assumptions found in the new textbooks, not coincidentally, were serving to structure public policy. For example, when Hugh Williamson, a North Carolina mathematician, scientist, and delegate to the Constitutional Convention argued for federal support of domestic manufactures and regulation of foreign trade, he linked the decline in industry (and the rise in poverty) following the Revolution to the erosion of temperance and self-denial which he believed had sustained the nation during the struggle for independence.[7] But the danger in all of this was not simply the belief that new commercial ventures had redemptive value. Rather it was that the collaboration among scientists and craftsmen to rationalize industrial activity helped create an extraordinarily productive social order. The promise of wealth and abundance was not only intoxicating, it was proof that a higher order was obstructed only by those who refused to commit themselves to industrial discipline, to divorce reason from emotion. *The property owner's power to manipulate nature and impose discipline over people in order to make them industrious, therefore, was considered to be sanctioned by "Divine Providence."*[8]

Let us probe this power relationship more carefully. I have been suggesting that the spectacular increase in the "Power of Man over Nature" which helped define the Industrial Revolution was also a revolution in the social relationships of power; the newly found excitement of controlling things was, on a personal level, the desire to control spontaneous aspects of the human personality. I have used the term sexual-economy to characterize the linkage between the private economy and the imperative to deny the union of reason and emotion that is internal to it.[9] William Leiss' work also addresses this issue. He argues that the "mastery of external nature is related to mastery of internal nature (human nature)...(in that it is) an instrument for repressing the permanent instinctual threat to social peace." The "permanent instinctual threat to social peace" in the context of an emerging capitalism would be those "passions" which were believed to obstruct the attempt to rationalize production and, therefore, corrupt the attempt to work hard in one's calling: emotion, particularly in the form of social concern for others, a sense of being part of and of being nourished by nature, all forms of sensuality (the fascination with color, the excitement of dance, the enjoyment of alcohol, and of course sex), and pre-industrial attitudes about the rhythms and relationships of work.[10]

The tendency to repress and control the full human personality was evident in early New England factory towns. They were totalitarian in that the towns themselves were virtual institutions of "moral instruction, rehabilitation, and reform...in public education; in support of the fine arts; in Protestant missions; in the treatment of poverty, delinquency, crime, and insanity."[11] The question for our purposes is, were there groups of citizens targetted for moral instruction and if so, how did the targeting of these groups contribute to the legitimation of and the mobilization of popular support for policies of economic expansion? The answer to the first part of the question is yes; women, blacks, and wage earners, more so than other political groupings, were victimized by the desire to control nature and the personality. We shall explore this a bit further and, as we do, we shall see how the legitimation of political repression was part of the process of mobilizing popular support.

Wage Earners as a Target Group

The native journeyman turned wage earner was for a time the focus of moral instruction, as the Sunday School movement illustrates. It was a response to the inability of the new wage earners to let go of traditional customs and morals associated with craft production. Sunday Schools, it was hoped, would inculcate the new moral standards of rational men and curb such habits as tardiness, drinking, cursing, and fornication.[12] However, the primary target among wage earners was the Catholic immigrant, who was considered beyond the reach of the moral instruction provided by evangelists. The waves of Catholic immigrants (largely Irish) that replaced the "Yankee farm girls" in textile mills during the 1830s and 1940s evoked a clear sense of endangerment among ruling Anglo-Saxon Protestants. Like free blacks, they appeared to carry with them more sensual rhythms of the cultures from which they came.[13]

In particular, owners of textile mills who dominated policy formulation within the Whig Party seem to have been most troubled by the Catholic workers. They believed that their industry would provide national economic independence and safeguard moral purity.[14] The way of life of the immigrants seemingly betrayed this ideal. And to add insult to injury, immigrants failed to support their Whig employers politically. Leverett Saltonstall had once predicted that the Whig Party was "doomed" as long as "foreigners could vote." Whigs even blamed the defeat of Henry Clay in 1844 on the "Foreign vote." More important, mill towns showed a tendency to shift from the Whig to the Democratic column. The local political autonomy of textile manufacturers, therefore, was jeopardized by the enfranchisement of immigrants.[15] Let us turn then to the nature of support mobilization under these circumstances.

* * *

Parties connected to a private economy seem to center their appeals upon the self-interest of citizens *as private individuals*: Party X will do Y for *YOU*. It would be unusual, for example, for party leaders to emphasize to white constituents how they could improve the quality of life for people of color unless, that is, such proposals were clearly linked to a particular interest of white voters, such as the lessening of crime, welfare expenditures, and/or taxes. Indeed, the centerpiece of "Reaganomics," lower taxes, is the hallmark of the party appeal. With pinpoint accuracy, it is fastened to an individual's narrow self-interest as a market competitor. During the 19th century, the conceptual framework for this sort of appeal was the teachings of evangelicals which pictured the Irish (and blacks) as given to "Idleness, Frolicking, Drunkenness, and in some few cases to Dishonesty." The party appeal, in this context, therefore, could be used to stimulate base reactive attitudes such as resentment, condescension, and fear.[16] For example:

Resentment: By stressing the virtue of discipline, self-denial, and individual achievement, Whig leaders appealed to the ideals of self-discipline and self-improvement held by white native workers. As part of craft-production relations, they were ideals white native workers were trying to restore. We can see this in the early fraternal orders which in themselves were attempts to restore the cross-class fraternalism of craft production. Orders such as The Independent Order of Good Templars and the Sons of Temperance, for example, were central to the temperance movement of the period that was being organized by evangelist reformers and encouraged by Whigs. Consequently, the resistance to factory discipline and temperance reform by immigrants, at least from the point of view of Anglo-Saxons, mocked the self-restraint of native (born) workers and of the social order. The mobilization of support by Whigs of native workers encouraged the *resentment* which native workers felt toward immigrants. Indeed, the very dignity of white native workers turned on being able to explain the misfortune of those below them, both immigrants and free blacks, as a simple lack of discipline.[17]

Condescension: By connecting the troubled times (loss of jobs and opportunities, lower standards of living and declining pay, the erosion of a simpler way of life, and the destruction of republican traditions) of white native workers to the "uncontrolled" lifestyle of the immigrant, evangelical reformers permitted party elites to cast issues of concern in terms of a *natural* moral hierarchy of Good and Evil in which white Anglo-Saxon males were superior to immigrants, people of color, and women. Native workers were told that they could not compete with foreigners who "feed upon the coarsest, cheapest and roughest fare—stalk about in rags and filth, and are neither fit associates for American laborers and mechanics nor reputable members of any society." Whig mobilization efforts blamed the misfortune of one naturally superior (Good) group upon a naturally inferior (Evil) group. The feeling of superiority engendered in the former was, therefore, justified. *Domination on the basis of race, gender, or ethnicity (which was then considered in racial terms) was natural.*[18]

Fear: By invoking the ascetic religious standards of evangelist reformers, Whig leaders helped to give specific meaning to the concept of republicanism that was central to American Revolutionary ideology. The idea was that republicanism denoted a political and moral condition of rare purity that demanded extraordinary social restraint ("public virtue") by which, as Kasson points out, each individual would repress his or her personal desires for the greater good. By emphasizing intemperance, licentiousness, and idleness as vices, Whig leaders were able to cast immigrants as threats to the republican order and personal liberty. The safe-guarding of public and private institutions, therefore, was felt personally. Moreover, the political repression required to safe-guard the public virtue could be cast in patriotic terms.[19] We get the sense that the members of the Order of United America, the most influential of union/fraternal orders, feared that their personal liberty was threatened by immigrant workers. As a "patriotic society," it worked to protect its members against poverty-stricken old age and immigrant competition not only by supporting state-level prohibition but also more lengthy naturalization processes. "In the name of righteousness," summarizes Paul Kleppner, "evil had to be purged from their society." The self-improvement motif was broadened into a legislative effort to support state-level prohibition and more lengthy naturalization requirements. Notice that the legitimatization of fear justifies, in the name of liberty or freedom, repressive measures.[20]

The space provided within the party system for Protestant "asceticism" (in the name of the repression of passion, passion was encouraged) enabled textile manufacturers within the Whig Party to legitimize and embrace a repressive set of (nativist or anti-immigrant) social standards as they mobilized support among native workers to counter the political influence of immigrants and the poor generally. The Whigs openly formed alliances with nativist parties (American Republicans in Philadelphia and New York City in 1844, for example) and took over the platform of the Native American Party in Massachusetts. In Massachusetts, textile manufacturers (Cotton Whigs) hoped that the encouragement of nativist sentiment might unify the party and forestall the anti-planter wing (Conscience Whigs) from leaving. Similarly, as Whig Party began to collapse nationally during the early 1850's, New York Whigs and businessmen attempted to preserve North-South textile-plantation ties by creating a party based upon nativist sentiment. Their strategy was to foster nativism by taking over the secret Order of the Star Spangled Banner and by rapidly establishing lodges throughout New York and surrounding states. It was out of this scheme that the Know Nothing Party emerged.[21]

For a time the strategy was successful. Even though immigrants were driven into the Democratic Party, the Know Nothing Party had become the fastest growing political movement in the country. They dominated party activity within the wage-economy. By 1855, they controlled all of New England with the exception of Maine and Vermont and they were the major anti-Democratic party in the Middle Atlantic states, California, Maryland, Virginia, Kentucky, Tennessee, Georgia, Alabama, Mississippi, and Louisiana. In direct contests with the nativist party in 1855, the Republicans were defeated in New York, Massachusetts, and Pennsylvania. Even the conscience Whigs made the new party their home for a time.[22]

The Know Nothings, however, were fraught with antagonisms. On the one hand they had become in the Northeast, the major political vehicle for expressing anti-Democratic sentiment. And on the other, their southern wing was constituted primarily by the isolated coastal slaveowners. They were not capable of advancing a programmatic response to "southern aggression." But there was another important reason for tension within the party that deserves our attention. The base of the Know Nothings was composed of native workers, farmers, and poor citizens of small towns who had suffered from the wrenching structural changes and who had found some solace in the rekindling of what to them was republican virtue. Less concerned with north/south unity, they complained that the people had lost control of the political process because of "professional tacticians and wirepullers," "cliques" of corrupt party bosses, and "selfish office-seekers."[23] Citizens who had been encouraged to resent, condescend to, and/or fear Catholic immigrants could turn around and resent the leadership of an unjust social order. By encouraging reactive attitudes, the Know Nothings unwittingly gave citizens space to experience impassioned thought. Emerging out of the ascetic closet, they reassessed prevailing standards and formulated new ones.[24] As division overtook the Know Nothings, the Republicans became the only broadly based vehicle by which anti- and disillusioned-Democrats could reasonably challenge the slave-owning class.[25]

By the late 19th century, immigration was far greater than it had been during the 1840's.[26] The problem of "uncontrolled" lifestyles, therefore, remained. And it was clear, given the Whig/Know Nothing experience, that the encouragement of reactive attitudes was risky business. The problem which James Madison outlined in *Federalist 10*—how to control the effects of political expression and still maintain the appearance of popular government—remained as well.

Blacks as a Target Group

White abolitionists influenced by Protestant evangelism believed that slavery was an evil system. But it was only one of the sins to be fought against to clear the way for the coming Kingdom. Because slavery was simply one of a panoply of social sins, the evangelical fight against slavery carried certain political overtones:

> ...the fight against slavery...was [also]...a positive struggle for America, in which they felt great personal involvement, not only to right the wrongs of the present, but also to vindicate their divinely inspired forefathers—sometimes Puritans and Pilgrims, sometimes the Revolutionary leaders, often all of them. Among white abolitionists, then, the positive aspects of the fight against slavery emerged primarily out of their commitment to a special vision of America, its righteous origins, and its no less righteous destiny.[27]

Evangelists, therefore, struggled not *for* the enslaved as much as they struggled for America and personal salvation. This distinction meant that an abolitionist could still claim that blacks, carrying with them the sensual rhythms of an uncivilized culture, were not capable of subjecting "passion to reason." More important, this distinction suited the purposes of the "anti-slavery" party leaders who were anxious to mobilize sufficient popular support to halt southern aggression *in order* to put capitalists in control of the government.

For example, in 1849, there were 400,000 blacks living in the free states, but most of them were not allowed to vote.[28] In fact, as dislike of "southern aggression" spread throughout the North, the number of states disenfranchising blacks increased.[29] One might have expected

just the reverse, that northern dissident parties, such as the Free Soil
Party would have found free blacks instrumentally significant, just as
Republicans found the enfranchisement of black men following the
Civil War instrumental in their plans for expansion. But the success of
the Free Soil Party as a party which mobilized the anti-slavocracy
sentiment that eventually blossomed into the Republican Party[30]
turned on the ability of its leaders to challenge the use to which
plantation owners put the federal government without challenging the
validity of slavery itself. In other words, their success hinged upon the
acknowledgement of white supremacy. One important example is the
Wilmot Proviso, which prohibited the extension of slavery into the
territory acquired as a result of the Mexican War. It also conspicuously
but silently avoided the question of black civil rights. The Proviso,
more than any other, became the issue which fragmented the major
parties (which were committed to maintaining north/south economic
arrangements) and served to help organize the Free Soil movement.
David Wilmot, author of the proviso, had no objection to its being
referred to as the "Laboring White Man's Proviso."[31]

The eventual legal freedom of blacks, particularly the enfranchisement of black males, added to the perceived sense of vulnerability
on the part of white Anglo-Saxons. To freed slaves, freedom meant
land: "We want...land...to...make it our own," declared Garrison
Frazier as he spoke in 1865 for a black delegation to Secretary of War,
Edwin M. Stanton. But as Vincent Harding suggests, this "new
philosophy and a new politics for the United States," this attempt to
create political space conflicted with the dreams of white citizens. Their
dreams "involved new steel mills and railroad tracks, miles of grain and
loaded ships, and the conquest of nonwhite savages and unbounded
markets across the globe."[32] But conflicts between property owners and
the propertyless in a sexual-economy invite moral recrimination.
During the 1860s the Copperhead Press, a pro-southern faction of the
Democratic Party opposed to Reconstruction, was "rife with reports of
atrocious sexual outrages committed by black men, as well as attention
to the 'tendency' of newly arrived black women in urban areas to
become prostitutes."[33] The encouragement of reactionary attitudes
towards blacks in this case enabled southern states to squelch the
dreams of blacks and set in their place the nightmare of Black Codes.[34]

On a national scale, the casting of blacks as morally inferior
(uncivilized and overly sexual) was necessary if elites were to popularize
the "conquest of non-white savages" and the installation of "unbounded markets across the globe." The analysis of William A.
Williams parallels this theme. Following the exhaustion of the Civil
War, Williams notes that America, as if a phoenix, "burst forth in
evangelical energy and enthusiasm. The glowing feathers, secular as
well as religious, fluttered about in foreign as well as in domestic

affairs. The revived urge to save and reform, if not transform, the world appeared among businessmen, church people, politicians, intellectuals, and even naval officers. Reform at home justified empire abroad."[35]

Perhaps it is more accurate to say that reform at home and empire abroad were policies cut from the same cloth. Empire building was, and still is, viewed as an attempt to save, or to civilize. We need not go to leaders of the Republican and Democratic parties of the era to find supporting evidence. We need only go to leaders of the Populist Party. Ignatius Donnelly spoke for many Populist farmers seeking markets in Asia and Latin America when he explained, "Our form of government is adapted to civilized man everywhere.... [our] destiny is to grasp the commerce of all the seas and sway the scepter of the world." The attempt to save, given the implicit moral imperative, is the attempt to control and repress. The argument here is not simply that racism at home, the lynching of 3,386 blacks between 1882 and 1930, was a pre-condition for the racism abroad, the "orgy of racist slaughter" in which anywhere from 200,000 to 600,000 Filipinos were killed during the conquest of the Philippines at the turn of the century. The argument here concerns the nature of racism, its legitimation, and the mobilization of popular support that flows from it. It is: 1) that the slaughter in the Philippines and other places had to evoke "congratulation and approval from the eminent journals and men of the era who were also much concerned about progress and stability at home" if the restricted debate within the party system over *how* to best secure international markets was to be understood as meaningful and legitimate; and 2) that civilizing people of color around the globe could be made to seem a good thing, part of our divinely structured destiny, if blacks at home were shown to be incapable of manifesting the self-controlled, temperate, calculating, industrialized personality to which white Anglo-Saxons of the period so thoroughly gave expression.[36]

The more spontaneous expression of the human personality by descendants of African culture, of course, was fodder for the cannons of Protestant evangelists and ultimately political elites. For example, African rhythms strongly influenced popular music of the white communities. Ragtime was followed in popularity by the blues and then jazz. Paul Garon has argued that the blues was subversive of bourgeois hegemony in that it represented everything that was repressed by "capitalist morality—desire, imagination, the erotic impulse, community, equality."[37] Defenders of white culture, such as John Philip Sousa, argued that jazz "employs primitive rhythms which excite the baser human instincts." Dr. E. Elliot Rawlings, representing the medical profession concurred: "jazz music causes drunkenness. Reason and reflection are lost and the actions of the person are directed by the stronger animal passions."[38] And given the recurrent expressions of black nationalism which raised implicit and explicit questions concerning the legitimacy of white institutions, from the early 19th century manifestoes of David Walker to the pan-Africanism of W.E.B. Du Bois a century later, the systematic disenfranchisement of blacks from 1890 on within the South appeared, from the point of view of most whites, as morally sound and rational.

In spite of these obstacles, the election of 1892 witnessed the largest participation of blacks since Reconstruction. With black support, the Populists threatened Democratic hegemony in the South and as V.O. Key, Jr. states, the "situation ...in which the plea for white supremacy could be made effectively." And this is the larger point. Religious-political dogma helped the sexual-economy to run more smoothly by effectively eliminating people of color as creative citizens, as subjects. As objects, that one may choose to save, civilize, or reform, their alternative ideas were safely contained.[39]

Women as a Target Group

Barbara Epstein has argued that success in the public world, once production was removed from the home, required that men possess "self-discipline, emotional control, and rational, calculating qualities."[40] This is consistent with the personality requirements of the sexual-economy, as we have seen. But if the industrial personality was the new standard of morally correct human behavior, how were women perceived in the context of these new ruling ideas? One perception was that women were *by nature* "impulsive, irrational, excessively emotional and given to idle and uncontrollable chatter."[41] And it was precisely these "feminine vices" that made women candidates for moral instruction (via wage labor) in the first textile mills. The assumption was:

> ...that girls and young women who were not incessantly occupied were subject to temptation and vicious habits, as well as being a financial drain on their parents and a burden to society.... [B]y offering employment to this "useless" class of the population, [Francis Cabot] Lowell saw that he would not only have docile and tractable workers, but he would overcome much of the opposition to his schemes that might be expected from the agricultural interests.[42]

But the perception by elites of white middle-class women was soon altered. Given their general personal relationship to elites and the fact that their subordination was not structured directly by the labor market (which is not to say that their labor was not exploited) once immigrants replaced them in the textile mills, white middle-class women were gradually enlisted as *guardians* of Anglo-Saxon purity. More troubling to elites than "feminine vices" was the prospect that factory towns would become like the "dark satanic mills" (to use Jefferson's phrase) of Europe. It was believed that certain women could help protect the community from undisciplined immigrants and blacks just as mothers shielded their children from the corrupting influences of the outside world.[43] To this end, white middle-class Protestant women who had infiltrated the temperance and abolitionist movements were eventually permitted membership in female auxiliaries. Auxiliaries would also be creted within fraternal organizations.[44]

Most middle-class women found their new role as moral guardians satisfying. There are several reasons for this. One was status. The labor of women in the home had become less valued as production was separated from the household. A woman's sense of self-worth had diminished as the status of men, as achievers in the public world, had risen. As evangelists called for community reform, the involvement of middle-class women in reform movements earned them social status. They too could become achievers.[45] And in important respects, the role of moral guardian for women was a return to the relationships of the Puritan community where society validated the role of subordinate groups such as women by insisting that the status of subordinates be respected by those in authority. If the desire for conquest and the self-discipline, emotional control, and rational, calculating qualities that conquest demanded eroded family and social bonds, women, so it seemed, were given permission to restore them. But perhaps most important, the role of moral guardian allowed women, as Epstein notes, an opportunity to "drive against the...irresponsibility of men ...the masculine culture that...women saw as supporting such irresponsibility."[46] This is clear within the context of the temperance movement.

Women were frequently the victims of men's drinking. Involvement within the temperance movement allowed them to come to grips with a problem that affected the family as it gave them the opportunity to raise related issues. For example, the question of women's rights was raised, as was dress reform. The *Lily*, the first American periodical dedicated to the improvement of women's status grew out of the temperance movement and featured the work of Elizabeth Cady Stanton.[47] The emergence of women's rights organizations out of the abolitionist movement reflects the same dynamic.

The public platform which reform movements provided women helped create space for an emerging feminism. But the tradeoff was one on which elites depended; because this space was one that was shaped by the concepts of evangelical reform, many white middle-class women identified with and gave expression to the *sexual racism* that was part of the sexual-economy at the end of the 19th century. During this period the temperance movement, which was very much indebted to the concept of Anglo-Saxon purity,[48] was responsible for the largest mass organization of women, the Women's Christian Temperance Union (WCTU). Frances Willard, who headed the WCTU and who called herself a "gospel socialist," castigated the black man for what she perceived was his extraordinary desire for alcohol, a desire which simply fueled his instinctual urge to rape.[49] This was not an uncommon view among reformers. The suffragist movement, unfortunately, serves as an example. In what otherwise must be regarded as a magnificent struggle, the suffragist movement was steeped in Anglo-Saxon supremacy. Time and again the concept of Anglo-Saxon purity was invoked as an argument to convince male elites that woman's suffrage was more than just. It was necessary as Elizabeth Cady Stanton argued in 1867 to "develop the Saxon race into a higher and nobler life..." At the 1901 National American Woman Suffrage Association (NAWSA) convention, Susan B. Anthony argued that it was time for women to fulfill their purpose of becoming saviors of "the Race."

With respect to the direction of the feminist movement, the role which suffragists played, of course, was pivotal. But what needs to be highlighted is the way in which the party system helped to channel the direction of suffragists as women were enlisted in the popular mobilization process. Nowhere in the two party system was there space for critical or reflective thought. That is, nowhere was there space where women could draw out and make explicit what was implicit, namely that their participation in reform movements was, in part, a critique of white male authority and domination. Consequently suffragists did two things: 1) at a conscious level they accepted the standards internal to the masculinized society as human standards (in other words, equality meant becoming more like or having the privileges of men); and 2) they moved right into the space which the party system made available, namely they became allies in the struggle to counter the influence of "undesirable voters"—"the Negro" in the South, the "Democratic machines, the immigrant, and the Negro" in the Northeast, the "prostitutes, frontier riff-raff, and political machines" in the West, and in general the "poor, ignorant and immoral elements in society...."[50] That is, they *insisted* that their enfranchisement would increase the number of "fit" voters.

For fourteen years following the "resolution" of party conflict that preceded the party reorganization of 1896, the suffragists met with "only a dreary succession of defeats." But by 1910, there was a resurgence of interest in the participation of women within the party system. Why? Grimes suggests that the resurgence was due to the same forces giving rise to the "Progressive" movement: "the superiority of native-born, white Americans; the superiority of Protestant...morality; and the superiority of a kind of populism, of some degree of direct control over the state and city machines which, it was alleged, were dominated by the "interests." Grimes adds, "What may generally be defined as woman suffrage supporters consisted mostly of white, middle-class Protestants who were in the main native-born and who sought a purification...of the social and political order." [51]

But we must keep in mind the political-economic ends which the drummed up support for a pure electorate served. The disenfranchisement of vast sectors of the propertyless class which the widespread encouragement of prohibition, the poll tax, and literacy tests brought about insured that elites could use the state more safely as an instrument of economic planning. The emergence of the monopoly sector had brought about a greater need for economic rationalization and centralized control. The Progressive Era was an era of regulation for this reason. In 1912 business executives backed the leading Progressive, Theodore Roosevelt, because they felt the U.S. had to move away from "excessive democracy" toward a more "parental guardianship of the people." The people need, they argued, "the sustaining and guiding hand of the state.... [it was] the work of the state to think for the people and plan for the people—to teach them how to do, what to do, and to sustain them in the doing."[52]

The perceived need among elites to tighten their grip on the state further intensified, as did general political repression following World War I, as the leftward march of "undesirables" continued unabated. In some states, the German language was outlawed from public schools. The pledge of allegiance was institutionalized. The Espionage Act of 1917 made disloyalty a crime. It was followed by the Sedition Act of 1918, which prohibited a person to "...utter, print, write, or publish any disloyal, or profane, scurrilous, or abusive language about the form of government of the United States...intended to ...encourage resistance to the United States." With roughly 1,000 socialists holding office throughout the United States and with the founding of the U.S. Communist Party in 1919, Attorney General Palmer compiled complete case histories of over 60,000 "dangerous radicals." On January 2, 1920, 4,000 suspected radicals were rounded up in thirty-three major cities, covering twenty-three states. Those who were immigrants were incarcerated and reserved for deportation hearings. It was in this political climate that the 19th Amendment calling for the enfranchisement of women was passed by Congress in 1919 and ratified by the thirty-sixth state, Tennessee, in August 1920.[53]

The point is that women, in their long struggle for equality, were allowed to enter upon the public stage only at the direction of men. Their political advancement was conditional on their being used. Indeed, the advancement of the suffragists popularized and lent a progressive tone to political repression of blacks, immigrants, and socialists. "Purity," "civility," and "industry" were terms used to celebrate the filtering out of undesirable ideas and people.[54]

* * *

The Police State achieved mixed results. To be sure, its main accomplishment was to locate the origin of social grievances in the laws of nature, in the character of the dispossessed themselves. And by linking industrial advancement to salvation and freedom, it helped legitimize the political repression which in turn permitted the captains of industry to ignore the industrial carnage as they moved the ship of state ahead full steam. But political repression was also counter-productive at times. It tended to generate among the middle class, as evidenced by the Know Nothings, an unwanted independence. The virulence of the sexual racism it generated spawned a social pathology that moved the social order to the edge of fascist-like self-destruction. And as was the case with women, the maintenance of social purity which encouraged the enfranchisement of women dealt male authority a crushing blow.

But the most serious political failure of the Police State was that it left itself open to charges of ineffectiveness. Social grievances had intensified. The late decades of the 19th century (the "golden age" of American democracy) did not present a pretty picture. It was hardly the picture of the republican, divinely led, essentially just America that had been anticipated by the Lowell mill owners. The Census Bureau in 1892 revealed that 9 percent of the families of the nation owned 71 percent of the wealth. The "new rich, the grandiosely or corruptly rich, the masters of great corporations" were taking over the political and economic reins from the old gentry, the merchants of long standing—in short, "the men of the highest standards."[55] Meanwhile, an estimated 2,250,000 children (under fifteen) were working full time in coal mines, glass factories, textile mills, canning factories, in the cigar industry, and as domestic servants for the rich. Some four-year-olds worked 16 hour days sorting beads or rolling cigars in the tenements of New York City; 5-year-old girls worked the night shift in the cotton mills of the South. Ehrenreich and English comment: "Here was the ultimate 'rationalization' contained in the logic of the Market: all members of the family reduced alike to wage slaves, all human relations, including the most ancient and intimate, dissolved in the cash nexus."[56]

Legitimation and the Welfare State

If the religiosity of Protestant asceticism proved to be an ineffective instrument of legitimation, what would take its place? How would elites rally the troops, so to speak? To answer this question, let us step back from the turn of the century political-economy and get a sense of what was happening with regard to the development of property relations.

As has been pointed out earlier, the transition to monopoly capitalism represented a solution of sorts to the anarchy of competitive capitalism. The centralization of capital allowed elites within the monopoly sector to insulate themselves from short run market pressures, to move away from highly personalized capital markets toward more specialized and regular capital markets which gave investors more space within which to plan. It also allowed owners to move away from the *personalized* conflict and relationships of control of the small factory where production was monitored by the owners themselves. In the larger firm of the monopoly sector, there was now a need for formal mechanisms of coordination that were vertical or top down in nature. Observes Richard Edwards, "However irrational it was from the standpoint of efficiency, hierarchical control constituted a 'rational' framework for the regular and permanent delegation of the capitalist's powers." W. Elliot Brownlee details this more formal, less personalized orchestration of production:

> Rather than trying to drive competitors out of business, they sought to create more orderly flow of the product to the consumer, creating large distribution and purchasing departments, centralizing administration, regularizing the flows of information throughout the bureaucracy, designating responsibility in a clearer fashion, specifying objectives more sharply and, in general, decreasing the reliance on personal relationships in the exercise of authority and the exchange of information.[57]

We can see that in this context the Good-Evil/Self-Denial legitimation of power relationships really did not do the job. One reason was quite simple. As elites found personalized relationships of control less reliable, the encouragement of reactive attitudes (such as resentment, condescension, and fear) in order to legitimate relationships of control got in the way. Two other reasons were more complex. They had to do with basic antagonisms of monopoly capitalism in the United States:

1. The transition to monopoly capital meant that standardization, quality control, and the setting of production standards had to somehow replace the less formally coordinated system of production where many petty producers and worker-entrepreneurs presided over grossly inefficient and poorly supervised networks of contractors and subcontractors. The shared religiosity which linked individual achievement and salvation only fueled the flames of competition and individualism at a time when the regulation of competition and some form of cooperation were required. This tension between the need for individualism and some cohesive social ethic is with us today.

2. The mass consumption industries within the monopoly sector, to be sure, demanded perseverance and discipline of their workers at the point of production. But within the marketplace, insatiable consumers were needed. Therefore, in order to enhance investment opportunities

and reduce investment risk, experiments in advertising were introduced.[58] Religiously motivated self-denial within the context of mass
consumption, however, tended to reduce investment opportunities as it
increased investment risk. The stimulation of, not the denial of,
consumer pleasures was needed. This tension between workplace
perseverance and marketplace abandon also remains with us today.

The clerical allies of elites, then, were slowly pushed aside by the
"experts" and the "professionals." Armed not with the bible, but with
the scientific method, experts, in the name of objectivity, certainty,
precision, and prediction were as capable as clerics in justifying the
repression of the spontaneous personality. Moreover, on a variety of
frontiers (scientific medicine, scientific housekeeping, scientific child
raising, and scientific social work, scientific management, scientific
public administration), professionals qua scientists were capable of
promising a brighter future through the precise administration of
things, and of people as things on a broad scale. For example,
Ehrenreich and English point out that in the interest of creating the
"industrial man—disciplined, efficient, precise," the federal government's pamphlet *Infant Care* carried the following expert advice: "The
rule that parents should not play with the baby may seem hard but it is
no doubt a safe one.... You [the mother] must have the will power, for
the sake of your child, to bring to his service all that has been discovered
for the promotion of human efficiency...."[59]

The need for a more adequate system of legitimation ultimately
provided space for a re-examination of the ruling ideas upon which the
Police State derived a measure of popular support. The first signs that
reformers would locate the source of social grievances not in the
character of the poor but in improper administration came from a
faction within the Republican Party known as the "Mugwumps."[60]
These "mugwump" gentlemen in 1872 and 1884 expressed displeasure
that they were being displaced not only by industrial elites but by
classes from "the bottom of the social heap." Lamenting the "decline of
ethnic homogeneity," the Mugwumps hoped to restore "traditional
democracy" by using civil service reform to slash through the tangle of
personal influence and responsibility that tied public office to the party
system and which shored up immigrant political influence in urban
areas.[61] Note the change: implicitly civil service reform suggested that
exact administration, not proper discipline, was needed. Civil service
reform was the first of a series of reforms which were intended to replace
the "partisanship" of government with "efficient" and "honest"
methods of business: "The government of a city is altogether more a
matter of business, than of statesmanship.... [partisanship led to]
lawlessness, disorganization, pillage and anarchy."[62]

Note also that when government becomes a matter of business, it
attempts more scientifically to achieve a massive coordination of

family, community, and productive relationships in order to reach greater and more stable levels of productivity. This was the promise of better administration, of clock-like or law-like mechanisms of governability and control. And by contrast to the sticky, personalized invectives of evangelists which failed to rid urban areas of graft, corruption, and the misery of slum life, the ideal embedded within this reform tendency seemed *progressive*. Indeed, proponents of this approach, known as Progressives,[63] introduced several such mechanisms, particularly in urban areas where partisanship among the lower classes was especially nasty: the replacement of ward representation with city-wide elections,[64] voter registration, city commission and manager governments. Again the desire was to direct municipal affairs "not by partisans, either Republican or Democratic, but by men who are skilled in business management and social science." This supposed scientific objectivity assured businessmen of a more direct and central role in municipal affairs as it made commitment to social theories, radical or otherwise, seem "biased" and unworthy.[65]

The effort to effect massive coordination of social relations through scientific administration within the public and private spheres, however, seems to have contributed to what Edwards has called "a crisis of control." Within the private workplace, wage earners viewed new scientific systems of management simply as "indiscriminate" use of power.[66] Moreover, immigrants rejected "Americanization" or the attempt to link their citizenship with a commitment to standards of efficiency. As poor workers they were less enthralled by new standards of efficiency than by the reforms prescribed by anarchists and socialists. The revolutionary struggles in Russia, Korea, Egypt, India, and Ireland made the Industrial Workers of the World's attempt to organize the unorganized appear as part of a genuine world-wide movement. In addition, the Socialist Party which had a strong showing (6 percent) in 1912, increased its electoral support in certain areas following WW I.[67] *The Nation* wrote in October 1919 that it had become "clear to discerning men, authority cannot any longer be imposed from above; it comes automatically from below."

We have pointed out that it was during this political climate that party leaders began to give serious attention to the common interests of elites and suffragists. In a similar vein, it was also during this period that party leaders, primarily members of the urban Progressive wing of the Democratic party together with independent Progressives like Robert La Follette and Fiorello La Guardia, began to recognize the importance of the work being done by the National Civic Federation (NCF) in joining labor leaders and owners together in "mutual benefit programs." Representing one third of the 367 corporations with a capitalization of more than $10,000,000 in 1903 and the heads of the major railroad brotherhoods, the NCF initiated numerous welfare programs (which involved 2,500 employers by 1914) in order to establish a cross-class front to curb worker militancy and undermine socialist appeals.[68] The perceived need among Progressive urban Democrats to achieve massive coordination of social relationships moved them, as social engineers, to take class collaboration a step further. They would recognize "industrial unions." This required politically centralized, bureaucratic procedures which not only gave more control to business elites but to union leaders as well. Indeed, Progressives called this new system of labor-capital cooperation "industrial democracy."[69]

In order for "industrial democracy" to get off the ground, however, the Progressive wing of the Democratic Party first had to take control of the party by undermining the popular support for traditional laissez-faire or free market policies developed by smaller and middle-range manufacturers and merchants who themselves were tied into the market and who were simply incapable, given their size, of rising above it.[70] They could do this by enlisting the support of industrial workers in big northern cities. In other words, in order for the new strategy for state-sponsored class collaboration to have any chance of success, industrial workers had to be mobilized to support it. NCF corporate executives had experienced some success in this regard by appealing to the sense of mutual and social responsibility shared by trade unionists. The sense of reciprocal obligation (between master and apprentice) had been an essential feature of pre-industrial craft production. And workers, through unions and fraternal orders, had been struggling to restore the personal and cooperative relations of the trade that had been lost. Although to corporate executives, social responsibility meant the "responsibility of all classes to maintain and increase the efficiency of the existing social order," concepts of mutuality, absent throughout the history of the Police State, suggested to workers that they would receive some form of recognition and a larger piece of an ever expanding economic pie. This appeal, in a word, would become the guts of the New Deal's strategy for mobilizing popular support.

The role that Sidney Hillman played as labor leader bringing discipline to an "outlaw" union composed largely of leftist immigrants (the Amalgamated Clothing Workers or ACW) and as confidante within councils of the Democratic Party illustrates how elites through the party system sought to alter their relationship to members of the propertyless class, particularly wage earners.[71] At the heart of this relationship was the belief that a productive and progressive social order was one that was organized in an authoritarian, highly ration-alized way. Coordination of organized labor, therefore, turned upon the willingness of workers to accept command/obey relationships as part of their social responsibility:

> It depended on the workers' willingness to honor work rules,
> standards of performance, disciplinary procedures, and new

codes of shop-floor behavior which they only indirectly participated in formulating. Most important of all, it depended on work groups relinquishing their right to strike whenever they felt justice or self-interest demanded they exercise it.[72]

Opposition to the Welfare State version of self-discipline and self-denial was strong and it was centered among older skilled workers located in "tiny contract shops, where artisanal skills persisted, and in large inside factories, where archaisms of artisanal solidarity survived."[73] Elites consciously acknowledged the distinction between "artisanal democracy" and "industrial democracy" and they understood that the latter had to be legitimized. Fraser notes that the establishment of industrial democracy required the reorientation of "the behavior of manufacturers and workers" and that "compliance depended on the artful orchestration of psychological behavioral, and cultural currents not absolutely inimical to management and union objects." For example, a sense of class injustice was okay, it "enhanced the credibility of the union.... But such popular sentiments had to be rechanneled, transformed, and encoded in a new rhetoric of workers' demands and perceptions emphasizing economic self-interest and industrial equity." Eventually, concludes Fraser, the millenarian enthusiasm and universalist yearnings that marked the union's founding era were gone, replaced by a "concern for reform modulated by a sense of social responsibility."

There are several points that need to be made here:

1. The shift during the Progressive Era from the Police State to the beginnings of the Welfare State was marked by the emergence of a monopoly sector, regulation of competition, and a greater emphasis placed upon economic stability. The poor may have been understood by elites as a menace to that stability, but unlike the ideologues prior to and including many of the Mugwumps, early architects of the Welfare State, did not accuse the poor of being impure. Personalized invectives were confrontational and theatened social stability. The Progressive turned New Dealer saw the problem as an administrative one. The social instability that contributed to economic instability was due to personalized forms of government and production. What was needed was rationalized organization based on scientific methods, efficiency, or proper administration.

2. The shift from the Police State to the Welfare State appears to have marked an advance in the political freedom of the propertyless class. This appearance seems to be due to our own acceptance of the norms and standards internal to rationalized production and rationalized government as *human standards*; ergo, greater political collaboration within the scheme of things is greater political freedom. We tend to accept the terms of mutuality at a societal level—the shared commitment to a system organized around self-interest—at face value.

Perhaps we need to think back upon the standardization or American-ization of the immigrant:

> At every opportunity the union sought to promote that trans-formation by dissolving foreign language locals into mixed assemblies, merging older craft locals into larger industrial units, encouraging members to take out citizenship papers, and insisting that only English be spoken at union conventions. The union also used a broad program of general education to acquaint the rank and file with the operating assumptions of American life as well as with the particular requirements of the new unionism.... In the long run, this...re-education helped instill in the rank and file a commitment to the principles and policies of social liberalism later effectively mobilized on behalf of the New Deal.[74]

Without opportunities for reflective politics what is often called an American education might very well be indoctrination.

3. The gains which the propertyless class achieved within the context of the Welfare State were essentially economic in character. Urban Democrats sponsored legislative initiatives for unemployment insurance, promised to restore mass purchasing power, and in the spirit of mutuality urged minimum wages, maximum hours, public works, and collective bargaining. But this material progress and the spirit of cooperation that underlay it was less the mark of a democratic government than of the fraternal bonds of the old craft production system. Industrial democracy was primarily a cross-class alliance organized around the productive activities of white men.[75]

The impact of New Deal policies upon blacks helps to illustrate these points. In the style of social engineers, New Dealers created numerous programs intended either to regulate or correct the defects of the market. Viewing society as an administrative system to be run properly, New Dealers, like those before them who viewed the world in terms of moral hierarchies, were incapable of coming to grips with relationships of power. New Deal programs as they rescued and stabilized various sectors of the private economy rescued and stabilized the power relationships internal to those sectors. Consequently, several of the New Deal programs, such as the Agricultural Adjustment administration (AAA) and the Federal Emergency Relief Agency (FERA), actually worsened the situation of blacks.[76] Still other programs, such as the Federal Housing Administration (FHA), the Works Progress Administration (WPA), the Public Works Admin-istration (PWA), and other instruments of the New Deal seem to have contributed directly to racist practices.[77] The point is that the gains which blacks might have made during the New Deal Era seem to have been due primarily to the effect of general economic recovery. Connec-tions between the relationships of power which stability and expansion of the sexual-economy require and the *subordination and domination* of people as a race were not, and have never been, an issue raised by any major political party.[78]

Within the context of the Welfare State, the deflection of critical inspection of issues such as racial or gender subordination is made possible by the use of terms such as "discrimination." Left unclear are the standards to which the term discrimination implicitly refers; or to put it another way, discrimination with respect to what?—obviously with respect to the social norms and standards internal to the Welfare State. In other words, if we are given the opportunity to become a full participant in the effort to obtain massive coordination of social relationships for the purpose of achieving yet even greater horizons of productivity, everything is okay. Much like the concept of social responsibility which nails down one's commitment to standards of efficiency, the term "discrimination" pulls the rug out from under those prepared to launch protests against subordination and domination. The concept of discrimination accepts and therefore protects the shared social norms and standards from criticism. The norms and standards of human conduct implicit in charges of subordination or domination are always those that lie outside the range of shared assumptions. Safe political space is required for their articulation over long periods of time. But the two party system, as it is lodged within the ideology of the Welfare State, denies that space.

For example, by the mid-1930s both parties were unable to ignore black demands; their migration to northern industrial cities increased their political influence considerably.[79] The Democrats, who did worse in the presidential election of 1932 among blacks than they had in 1928, began to make appeals to blacks in the congressional elections of 1934. Two years later *Time* magazine wrote, "In no national election since 1860 have politicians been so Negro-minded as in 1936." Even Republicans sought the black vote. Writes Sitkoff, "Republican publicists pictured nominee Alfred M. Landon as a spiritual descendant of John Brown."[80] The prize of this political recognition is one that is still used to mobilize political support among women and people of color. Congressional Democrats wrote into more than twenty New Deal statutes the proviso: "There shall be no discrimination on account of race, creed or color."

The words "there shall be no discrimination on account of" express well the essence of what a party in the context of the Welfare State can hope to offer women and minorities. It is the fabled formal equality before the law. It is equal opportunity and equal rights. But there is a price to pay when equality is accepted unreflectively. Just as women had been nudged into their proper place, immigrants were Americanized, workers were allowed to help shoulder the responsibility of stabilizing a cyclical economy, and blacks, acknowledged as a political force, were about to be "integrated." Enfranchisement,

Americanization, fraternal collaboration, and integration have all been celebrated as political victories, as signs of greater political freedom. Each has been referred to as a measure of the two party system's capacity to right social wrongs and to cast the net of democracy still further. But in each case, greater political influence (in the established order) obtained meant a partial loss of self. For women, admission to the two party system meant that the campaign against masculine values had to be pushed to the fringe of discredited activism. For workers, the restoration of fraternal bonds within the two party system meant that the struggle for autonomy within the workplace had to be taken up in fragmentary fashion by those who could cling to a belief in collective arrangements. And for blacks, integration within the two party system and within the broader social order meant that they could look forward to assimilation. The dream of creating a *multi-racial* society would have to be left to "extremists" to carry out.

The Reality of the Two Party System

One needs only to monitor the wire services, major news publications, and radio and TV talk shows or survey the history of major party platforms or public debates of leading candidates to understand that the range of political inquiry in the United States is and has been circumscribed. It is as though a Berlin Wall of sorts were implanted within each of our brains. When coming to grips with social problems it is as though each of us were denied access to that part of our brain which might suggest that our social problems might be linked to essential features of our way of life: individualism, the profit motive, the pursuit of self-interest, the repression of sensuality, competition, private property, efficiency, political democracy or republicanism, individual rights, and so on. There seems to be a vast frontier of information, history, data, experience, and competing perspectives that we are forbidden to explore. The one public institution in which as free citizens we should be able to penetrate this wall is the two party system. Instead the two party system is a part of the wall that denies access.

In part, this forbidden zone of politics is due to the fact that we have a popular government as opposed to a democratic state. Within a popular government, as we say in Chapter 3, elites set the agenda of public policy. The two party system supports their authority to do so by facilitating the formation of coalitions that govern, or what political scientists often refer to as the "party in the government." But within the context of popular government, this process must be made popular; that is, support among citizens or "the party in the electorate" must be mobilized. Notice that the purpose of mobilizing popular support is not to consult, listen to, seek advice from, express concern with, or to acknowledge the need to learn from the average citizen. It is to legitimize. The average citizen is considered by party elites as an element to influence. Consequently, like the U.S. general in Vietnam who believed that combat activity would receive public approval by "linking our stated purpose with the emergency conditions created by the flood," party elites understand that sustained government support of an economy which requires inequality must also be legitimized by explaining forms of inequality (which range from simple poverty to alienation, racism, and sexism) in terms that are compatible with the shared assumptions about the distinguishing features of our way of life, such as private property.

In order for charges such as these to move us forward, we first need to get a sense that practices in which we participate every day are, in many respects, temporary features of history which come and go, that history in continual motion. This means that there are many possible ways of life. We are able to get a sense of the way in which a particular way of life embodies points of view which are hard to grasp when we share them by recalling a fragmentary aspect of the way in which certain Native Americans live. Consider the relation of people to nature, for example, when they believed that their territory had been donated by the Great Spirit and that its use must reflect the sacredness of this donation. Children learned that all of nature was infused with a spirit of life.

> There was no such thing as emptiness in the world. Even in the sky there were no vacant places. Everywhere there was life, visible and invisible, and every object possessed something that would be good for us to have also—even the stones.

The concept of possession in a culture based upon human fulfillment as mastery or power over nature is strikingly different.

> ...the Plains tribes had become angry, hostile, but also baffled in their new dependency on this inexplicable people who supplied them with highly desired items but were never satisfied with the simple terms of the exchange. Only when it was all over would they know that the whites had not only wanted beaver, buffalo, rights-of-way, parcels of land for expanding settlements, and military posts to protect the settlers. They had wanted all of it. Everything. And even that would not be enough.[81]

The latter relationship to nature, which marks our private economy, is as decidedly masculine as it is Anglo-Saxon. It derives from the synthesis of scientific and craft knowledge and later took root in the political-economic sphere of productive activity that was divorced from the female experience. Within this public sphere of productive activity the concepts of power, control, conquest, and achievement were linked with the ideas of freedom, individual liberty, independence, and wealth. It was a sphere that was at odds with the more communal,

Puritan sphere of women and the more spontaneous traditional cultures of immigrants and people of color.

At a fundamental level, the two party system helps to legitimize this Anglo-masculine sphere of freedom and conception of politics. In part this is accomplished because there are only two points of view entertained, each corresponding to a major party. Political opposition is reduced, therefore, to a questioning of means and not of ends. That nature, including people, become objects to use or control is assumed and certainly not the basis of political opposition. What is of ultimate importance is that 1) the Anglo-masculine sphere of freedom (or property relations within the sexual-economy) to be universal and eternal, and 2) that human energy be directed toward its expansion. Within this narrow circle of ideas, there is debate. And it is the debate over strategies of expansion that is the stuff of what we call political opposition.

Unreflective participation in the two party system accepts this limited range of political debate and the policy options that flow from it. Unreflective participation, therefore, contributes to the exclusion of genuine alternatives and in a very real sense *contributes to the exclusion of politics.* The result is that the extraordinarily restrained Anglo-masculinity that lies at the center of our public life remains un-examined. And as the norms and standards internal to this masculinity become accepted as human standards, it is emulated. Participation within the two party system, therefore, tends to commit us to a set of ends or a way of life that we cannot really criticize or oppose.

The freezing of political opposition, as it were, has taken two basic forms. We have identified these forms as Police State and the Welfare State. Their commonality is that they legitimize various forms of inequality by grounding evidence of inequality in circumstances outside of the relationships of private property. The Police State did this by suggesting that the disadvantaged had only themselves to blame. The beliefs supporting the repression by the Police State were rooted in evangelical teachings. Party leaders, by weaving these beliefs into their political sermons, were able to mobilize support for the installation and expansion of capitalism. These beliefs also enabled them to effectively block the participation and stifle the voices of Catholic immigrants, blacks, and Leftists and to transform, for a time, the potentially subversive politics of women into a politics of accom-modation, if not complicity.

With the advent of monopoly capitalism and the greater need for social coordination and economic regulation, the source of legitima-tion shifted from religion to science. By invoking standards of mutual responsibility, the cooperation of union leaders was solicited and received. And in the name of social responsibility, organized labor collaborated with capital to achieve a more efficient (with respect to productivity and profits) order. Their reward was a greater piece of the economic pie and greater visibility, perhaps only symbolically, within the Democratic Party. And to a degree commensurate with racial discrimination, black workers in industrial cities made similar gains. Such was the Welfare State.

As I shall argue later, the political-economic crisis of the 1970's marked the end of the effectiveness of the Welfare State. And the triumph, thus far, of the New Right marks the swing back toward evangelistic-like legitimation, political repression, and personalized conflict. But we are still close to the ethos of the Welfare State. It is difficult, therefore, to gain some critical distance from it. Against the backdrop of 19th century repression, anti-discrimination and affirmative action legislation, unemployment compensation, collective bargaining, medical and educational subsidies and other features of the Welfare State appear as features of the good life, particularly to those who are troubled by inequality. To be sure, the tendency within the Welfare State is not to repress undesirables but to enlist them. But against the standards of what politics ought to be—*a process whereby citizens become capable, for purposes of assessment, of seeing relationships of power clearly and transparently*—the Welfare State has not been a step forward. The greater enfranchisement and the greater equality mask our greater inability to feel outrage, to personalize national responsibility, to question, to reflect, to think critically or creatively, and to care about what is done in our name and to whom.

My reading of history suggests that it may have been easier one hundred years ago, within the context of party politics, to reassess prevailing standards critically than it is today. It is in this sense that the politics of the two party system approaches dead politics. The norms and standards internal to our privatized government stand as Authority. The Constitution and principles of Free Enterprise are treated as sacred. Party politics consists, really, of embellishing these Truths. Implicitly, we are left with the absurd proposition that what goes on in the Democratic and Republican parties is all that good citizens, free citizens, and champions of democracy need to nurture their political spirit.

But, one may ask, if our party system and the politics therein is dying, why is it not challenged? Why, if voting approaches something of a sterile ritual, is the act considered a duty? And if within the two party system our greater political equality has cost us our *citizenship*, why have we accepted and, at times, celebrated the exchange? The clue provided in this chapter is that the process of mobilizing popular support for a given public policy appeals to our shared conviction that the principles upon which our political-economy rests are okay, that the various forms of inequality which do exist, in fact, do not suggest that there is a fundamental problem with the way we live. Of course, we realize that if indeed such things as rights of private property, the fascination with manipulating nature, and the perseverance in doing so *are not* connected to our most fundamental social grievances, then each of us, in our daily practices, is more likely to be free from recrimination. Such a position, if we adopt it, provides us with a great deal of comfort. It is to a further discussion of the comforts which such a posture provides that we now turn.

5

ACCEPTING OUR SYSTEM AS OUR OWN

Thus far the limitations of the two party system have been attributed to the structure, purpose, and relations among political-economic institutions. We have also suggested that the norms and standards within the social order itself have been a part of those structures. One implication we may draw from this is that if we accept the norms and standards of our society unreflectively—if we accept the meaning of such terms as freedom without really thinking about their historical specificity for example—we unwittingly help to re-enforce the political limitations in question. This means that victims of political repression may be actively (and unknowingly) supporting those institutions which facilitate the repression from which they suffer.[1] In this chapter, therefore, we shall explore the ways in which each of us actively contributes to the repressive tendencies of the state by accepting as our own the social norms and standards that help to make up what we call free and democratic institutions. In short, this chapter is a discussion of our personal identity as private citizens.

I shall argue that what we tend to accept as free and democratic institutions supports an individualistic kind of politics which in turn collides with the social and collective processes which we, as political activists, generally attempt to construct. In other words, what we accept as free and democratic at a tacit level conflicts with what we often try to establish at a conscious level. First, I shall illustrate what an alternative to individualistic politics is, what it accomplishes, and why it is more meaningful today. Then we shall move on to a discussion of why it is that we identify with the individualistic processes and institutions we receive and why that is a problem. Finally, I shall show how such political reforms such as the direct primary, while appearing to be democratic advances, have actually weakened the prospects of a more genuine democratic politics.

127

Clarification: the Process of Reflective Politics

> Who in the world am I? Ah, that's the great puzzle.
>   —Alice

Democracy, in the United States and in the party system as well, makes no sense save in terms of competitive elections. Competitive elections, for us, embody the meaning of democracy. So important is electoral competition to the legitimacy of our way of life that it takes on a universal quality. That is, we may debate whether or not a given country is democratic, but we do not debate whether or not our electoral process is the mark of a democratic order. A thought experiment may help to illustrate this point. The other day I heard an advertisement on my car radio, part of which said, "...and you will receive the 50 greatest songs of all time." How silly I thought. How could the producers of that ad possibly think that any listener could accept the notion that there is a list of 50 songs which most reasonable people would accept as the greatest of all time—not among the greatest, that is, but *the* greatest? The producer is suggesting that "songs" have an objective character (the number of sales perhaps?) by which the 50 "greatest" could be identified with some degree of certainty.

Now suppose the radio announcer were to say "...and you will receive the names of the 50 greatest democracies of all time." The listener might think, how could anyone determine which democracies "of all time" have been the *greatest*? A reasonable question, I suppose. But would the listener ask, *how could anyone determine which nations have been democratic?* Probably not. Among citizens of the U.S., it seems, it is widely assumed that a democratic order is one that can be observed to be so. That is, the truth of what democracy is or what it means is self-evident and verifiable. Whether or not a nation is democratic is independent of your judgment or mine. Because we assume that democracy has an objective or universal character, we may say that *we use the concept of democracy unreflectively.*

For example, when highly regarded officials within the Reagan administration offered the March 1984 elections in El Salvador as evidence of that nation's democratic character, critics countered with evidence suggesting that the elections *were not really free,* that CIA propaganda influenced the outcome, that Salvadorans were coerced into voting, that threats of reprisal eliminated any genuine opposition, and so on. Government officials countered by pointing to the heavy turn out. Testimony was given that participation was voluntary. Suddenly, what was meant by "democracy" went well beyond the physical act of pulling a lever or placing a marked card in a box. What had been an activity that was to have been validated by international *observers* became an activity that could be validated only by interpretation.

Implicit within the argument of each side was the belief that a genuine competitive election is one where voters make their choices freely. But what about elections where people fail to meet voting qualifications—a slave in Texas in 1850, a woman in Chicago in 1919, or an unemployed person in 1984 who fails to register. Can we speak of these times and places as democracies? In order to answer this question we might wish to know more about the rules governing voting qualifications of each respective time and place. Additional information might then be sought. Why were those rules established and not others? What groups of people were responsible for establishing the rules? Were the disenfranchised allowed to participate in their making, and so on.

Further reflection upon the notion of free choice forces a much wider inquiry. Suppose individuals do not *feel* free to participate in a competitive election—socialists in 1920 or blacks in Mississippi in 1956, for example. The application of our concept of democracy may then await exploration of how individuals within weak political organizations or individuals whose economic standing is marginal feel about their freedom to participate. Consideration of the history of efforts to exclude or manipulate voters may move one to ask, does the admonishment of the non-voter by celebrities on TV or the characterization of the non-voter as "apathetic" by political scientists count as unwarranted pressure?

It soon becomes clear that it is not only difficult to identify the objective criteria of ideas such as democracy, it is impossible. The objective character we search for proves to be illusory because our assumption is invalid. Such objective criteria do not exist. Examples used to clarify one objective application of democracy serve to illustrate how the apparent objectivity is linked to an expanding array of judgments and interpretations. As soon as one illustration is wheeled into place, as soon as our analytic sights are focused, the target, as it were, is transformed before our very eyes. The process of reflection brings into clear view assumptions that had been somewhat shadowy. These assumptions, nevertheless, had made the search for democracy a routine search for competitive elections. Upon reflection, however, the routine search becomes an unsettling journey in which the answers to what had been thought obvious questions begin to reveal themselves only after the researcher examines his or her own personal relationships, aspirations, needs, and interests. Every progressive political activist knows this odyssey well and knows its pain and virtue to be true. We become feminists, labor organizers, peace, Third World and black activists, and environmentalists to learn about specific sets of objective policy considerations. Instead, we learn about what it means to be an "American." We may say that the process whereby we gain new insights into who we are and what our institutions are all about *is a*

process of clarification. It is a process of reflective politics. I shall argue
that without this reflective dimension, without processes of self-
examination, politics loses its life-giving possibilities and becomes
instead dreary and ritualistic.

* * *

> [For the healthy person] the world which is outside him has its
> threads in him to such a degree that it is these threads which
> make him what he really is: he too would become extinct if these
> externalities were to disappear.
>
> —Hegel

If we were citizens of the Soviet Union, it seems probable that we
would accept as our own the principles which lend legitimacy to the
Soviet system. The same could be said of citizens of any system which
did not rely extensively upon overt coercion to achieve political
stability.[2] There is a tendency to identify with the institutions in which
we work, act as family members, or members of a community even
when such institutions may be repressive. Ironically, this may be
especially true when one's position within such institutions provides
limited space for dignity and freedom.

Individuals who sense that their situation is unfree and undignified have few options. They can struggle within or against such
institutions in hopes of changing them. However, when critical view-
points, which would lend support to such a struggle are discouraged,
collective struggle invites repression while individual struggle invites
ridicule. After all, respect for someone who says one thing privately and
another publicly diminishes quickly. The practice of actively creating
multiple personalities or a personality that is not one's own does not
seem to accord with what we think of as a healthy person or a person
whose actions authentically express his or her beliefs. As Hegel suggests, the healthy person is one whose world outside him or her
expresses what he or she really is. Therefore, by identifying with the
institutions in which we live, the tension between who we are and who
we could be dissolves. By meeting social expectations, a sense of dignity
in an otherwise undignified situation can be created. Members of the
propertyless class are rewarded socially when they act out the role of
responsible worker, total women, or docile minority.[3]

It becomes apparent that one's personal identification with
political and economic institutions and with the family as we know it
may obstruct our capacity to *clarify* the purposes of the institutions in
which one lives, one's relationships with others in those institutions, as
well as one's own role within them. One's identity, therefore, may
obstruct the process of reflective politics. It may obstruct the process of
critical thought and the process of developing creative alternatives.

But what about *our* personal identity as "Americans," as members of a free and democratic society? Surely, we do not have to worry. We live in a free country. We have the Bill of Rights. We have competitive elections, a two party system, and "60 Minutes." "Only in America," we say. Perhaps, but to be on the safe side let us clarify what it is that we identify with or accept as our own.

Not infrequently political activists face the sober conditions of their lives when people whom they are most trying to reach respond to their protestations by saying, "If you don't like what's going on write your Congressman, or run for office." Extended conversations sometimes only harden the disparity. Somewhat proudly, our friends declare, "Only in America can a bum one day become a millionaire the next."

There are four aspects to our friend's sentiments I shall assume to be true: 1.) They express his or her identification with political and economic institutions in the United States; 2.) They are widely held sentiments that are often expressed by many citizens of the U.S.; 3.) They are a portrait of freedom: both the public and private sphere are sound as is the relation between the two. The private sphere is the sphere of opportunity. It is protected by the state, the sphere of accountability; and 4.) They seriously misrepresent the opportunities for both freedom and dignity. They are exaggerations.

Both the content (a portrait of freedom) and the form (exaggeration) of this person's interpretation of our political and economic institutions suggest that our friend's opportunity to engage in reflective politics is impaired. Let us first discuss the meaning of exaggeration before moving on to the implication of this particular meaning of freedom, which is more complex.

Exaggerations, because they are attempts to persuade, are often expressions of the public self, not the private self or beliefs held "deep down inside." Much like the woman who admitted to drinking beer occasionally but who protested on a local radio talk show the putting of a can of beer in the town's time capsule, our private thoughts and actions may conflict with perceived social norms and standards. But we need to publicly identify with perceived social norms and standards from time to time in order to replenish the sense of dignity that comes with being a recognized responsible, dependable, and contributing member of a larger community.[4] Again, this need may be greater among those who are held in low esteem to begin with—the underemployed, unemployed, minorities and women, workers, etc. It is they who must struggle for approval and acceptance within the larger community. Their identification with social norms must appear to be unflinching, almost total. Their public affirmations must appear to be clear and loud, if not exaggerated. For example, the public affirmation of U.S. foreign policy during the late 1960s by "hard hats" may have been an attempt to gain the respect of the President and of the nation. Privately, workers had long been out in front of professional classes in terms of opposition to the war.[5] Similarly, when Muslims who happened to be black began training in judo and karate during the early 1960s, leaders of the white community became alarmed in spite of the fact that, as Malcolm X put it, "Even in grammar school classes, little girls, are taught to defend themselves." The tacit *quid pro quo*—publicly affirm social norms and you will earn our respect—had been violated. Blacks were not expected to betray a sense of vulnerability by training in judo and karate. The point here is that the public expectation of what we should be and how we should act is a force that encourages us to identify with social institutions. It is also a force which discourages reflective politics and the identification with alternative institutions.

Let us move on to the meaning of freedom as it was cast in the statements above. What does it mean that a "bum" one day can be a millionaire the next? Notice the suggestions: the private economy is a sphere of freedom. Opportunity for affluence and independence abound. The prospect of upward mobility, of escaping one's plight as a "bum" is real. The image projected is of a sound and just economic system, one that rewards individual ability. It is an echo of J. Olney's 1835 dictum, "My friends, you may be whatever you resolve to be." More contemporary versions are the U.S. Army's commercial slogan, "Be all that you can be." Even VISA credit card commercials implore, "You can do it if you try."

This interpretation does not empower those in subordinate positions. Indeed, the implication is that members of subordinate classes deserve to be where they are. But notice that the interpretation does validate the extraordinary self-restraint required of those who perform endless routinized tasks: workers in and outside the home can take pride in having held up their end under disagreeable conditions. Even the thankless tasks in a free and just economy are contributing elements of freedom and justice. This validation is particularly strong when the worker believes that such work is a *sacrifice* performed for the benefit of another. Richard Sennett and Jonathan Cobb in their study of Boston workers stress the meaning that sacrifice held: "if you feel inadequate and unfulfilled in demonstrating your worth, thinking you are doing it for the good of someone else makes the performance legitimate for you." The interpretation, therefore, becomes not only part of one's personal identity as a member of a larger community but also as a free person who has chosen to sacrifice for others. This particular identification with the economic order reduces the possibility that workers would attempt to create or accept alternative institutional arrangements in spite of their subordination.[6]

Let us consider the meaning of freedom embodied in the notion that our government is accessible and accountable, that we can write our Congresspeople or run for office. William E. Connolly argues that in a social order in which the state is formally held accountable through competitive elections the need to "save" the appearance of dignity under unfavorable circumstances moves citizens to tailor their grievances in a particular way. Writes Connolly, "We can see ourselves as free, free as a people, if the central institution of electoral accountability and public action [the state] is widely believed to have sufficient resources to act with effectiveness in the pursuit of collective ends." However, if what the state can do is limited by the structural imperatives of economic expansion, then the state may not have sufficient resources to act with effectiveness in the pursuit of collective ends. What does a citizen do? Publicly acknowledge that the state cannot respond to our demands as citizens? Unlikely, says Connolly. We do not wish to magnify our disenchantment. Rather, "We define our grievances and policy agendas as falling within the limits of action available to the welfare state so that we can see that state, and ourselves, as free." The need to see ourselves as free citizens living within a free state also weakens the possibility of reflective politics. Although the range of options made available through competitive elections is constrained, *we need to see the electoral process as as valid process, that is, as a distinguishing feature of a democratic order.*[7]

Connolly has illustrated his point elsewhere: "...victims of spiraling inflation, unable to curb the expensive style changes, shoddy products, manufacturing priorities, and price markups in the corporate sector, demand cuts in school budgets and welfare expenditures to ease those sources of high taxes and inflation that are subject to some degree of voter control."[8] The need to see ourselves as free citizens and, correspondingly, the state as unconstrained helps to explain the conservative influence that the two party system has had upon mass movements. The century long efforts by blacks and women to obtain the franchise or of workers to obtain recognition as a partner with capital in a major party expressed the belief that voting and party participation would go a long way toward solving the problems of race, gender, and class. In other words, it expressed the belief that the state was free. It would have been odd, then, for subordinate classes to persist in making demands that the state could not respond to once having gained access to the party system. By exposing the rather severe limitations of the state, subordinate classes would be exposing as well the limitations of their own struggle, that is, the limitations of working within the two party system.

For example, the roles which women, blacks, and workers have played within the context of movement politics have often supported policy objectives which fell outside the orbit of legitimate state action. The persistent demand for land and education by wage earners prior to the Civil War and by blacks following the Civil War embodied the hunger for autonomy and independence that the state could not possibly have satisfied given its prior commitment to the creation of a supply of labor sufficient to meet the needs of an expanding private economy. Consequently, creating space for politics by means of direct action remained the province of movement politics: women within reform movements, who also sought autonomy, at times tackled the "irresponsibility of men" directly. Amelia Bloomer constructed a pant-like skirt to free women from the immobility of traditional dress. The Woman's Crusade assaulted the saloon owners of Ohio, demanding that they close. The multi-racial Knights of Labor explored cooperative arrangements as did many farmers alliances of the Populist era. Yet they also explored and discussed the merits of "greenbackism," the single tax, utopian socialism, and temperance—clear signs of a reflective politics. Many groups even urged public ownership of one type or another. In 1893, the AFL supported the collective ownership of all the means of production and distribution. Nationalism and racial pride was the focus of the campaigns, such as Pan-Africanism, led by Marcus Garvey, W.E.B. DuBois, Henry Sylvester Williams, Martin R. Delaney, and others. But as these movement groups passed over the threshold into the constrained politics of a two party system, the creative and substantive methods of obtaining direct control over one's life had to be given up for some mutation of equality before the law or equal opportunity. Ironically, in order to see oneself as free, one had to abandon programs that may have empowered people directly in favor of guarantees of *legal* equality, which were guarantees of social inequality. Collective bargaining, which abandoned the demand for worker autonomy, and laws which barred discrimination on the basis of race or gender, as we have seen, saved the appearance that the state had sufficient resources to deal with grievances of the most disadvantaged citizens at the same time that they left unexamined the ruling ideas which justified racial and gender subordination.

* * *

We suggested, briefly, that identification with a free economy validates the self-restraint and sacrifice of those in subordinate positions. We have also explored arguments suggesting that identification with a state whose policies are constrained by its support of a private economy moves us to redefine our grievances in a way that preserves the appearance of a free state. Obviously our identification with a free economy and a free state is linked. Our sense of freedom, in part, rests upon the state's accountability, but it also rests upon the opportunity or the right to acquire and dispose of property. The concepts of "private" and of "freedom" here are tightly bound. We need, then, to broaden our scope. To be sure, we think of ourselves as free citizens of a free state but we also think of ourselves as private individuals in a private economy. Moreover, we generally collapse the two; we tend to see ourselves as "private citizens in a free country."

Because we seem to be identifying with the relationship between the state and the economy, it may be useful to suggest that we are identifying with a particular *process*. For example, I happened to overhear a conversation between two women in a cafeteria. They were bitter about the conditions under which they had to work. They were "tired of being told what to do" and of having to "play the game" in order to keep their jobs. Finding work elsewhere was difficult. What counted most was "who you know." The solution to these problems was eventually arrived at: "What we need to do is to start our own business." It is a familiar solution: *become your own boss.*

We might infer that for these women the idea of becoming your own boss is a natural aspiration, something to which most people would aspire. But notice: the features of the accumulation process internal to a privately owned business (hierarchy, competition, individualism, division of labor, etc.), rarely clarified and politicized, are not questioned in spite of the tacit recognition that something is wrong about someone being bossed. The reason for this may be that to explicitly question the process would be to call into question the end to which the process is a part. In other words, it would be to call into question what appears to them as the only possibility of escape from the subordination they resent. Again, reflective politics is made more unlikely.[9]

Similarly, workers in the Sennett and Cobb study, while expressing the desire for community, believed that they had to "earn the right to communal respect by showing others they could totally take care of themselves." Dignity and freedom means demonstrating the ability that one can get along without others, that one does, in fact, have the capacity to be one's own boss. Write Sennett and Cobb:

> That ability is the badge of individual worth, that calculation of ability creates an image of a few individuals standing out from the mass, that to be an individual by virtue of ability is to have the right to transcend one's social origins—these are the basic suppositions of a society that produces feelings of powerlessness and inadequacy in the lives of people....

Our personal identification with our *free* political and economic institutions makes individualism a central element of citizenship. For citizenship to us means *private* citizenship. Here too we must demonstrate the capacity as a citizen to think *independently* of other citizens. Only as *private* citizens is each of us our own boss. Independent thought is a virtue. The processes of clarification and reflection which are collective processes and which entail prolonged discussions as well as critical examination of the essential institutions within the social order are not.

The Failure of Individualistic Politics

Vincent Harding's use of a river as a metaphor to capture the meaning of the collective struggle of black people in North American history also illustrates the process of clarification: "The river is in us, created by us, flowing out of us, surrounding us, re-creating us and this entire nation." Harding's personal identity here is not that of a private citizen whose political ideas are arrived at independently. Rather it is that of a black man with a profound sense of belonging to the black community. His ideas are strongly influenced by the ideas of others; his are a tributary to the river. The emphasis is on "we" not "I," on development in terms of consciousness not achievement, on the need to get along together, not individually. The process of clarification is one of creation and re-creation. It is an end which black people in South Carolina said they sought in 1865: "the right to develop our whole *being*."[10]

Many readers whose personal identity as private citizens was altered during the period of the Vietnam War may be familiar with the process of clarification or reflective politics. The profound social divisions during this period forced many private citizens to reflect upon and clarify what it was that they stood for. Many defenders of U.S. foreign policy were moved to question the role of the United States in Vietnam. But often the movement did not end with a position vis-a-vis a specific policy such as the war issue. Rather, a fuller comprehension of the purpose of U.S. participation often brought into view a fuller comprehension of the purpose, scope, and limitations of a range of institutions that had once been accepted unreflectively. Changed interpretations of the larger order often meant changed interpretations of self. Changed interpretations of self generated changes in living arrangements, family relationships, relationships to nature, one's appearance and style. Such adjustments were necessary. Beliefs expressed in every day activity, at least for the healthy person, are simple extensions of what one really believes deep inside.

Notice the process: defense of a single policy, doubt about that policy, criticism of that policy, questioning the purpose of institutions essential to that policy, grasping the inter-connections of a range of institutions essential to the social order, self-examination, re-creation of self-interpretation and practices which express self. What is of interest to us is that political growth seems to require prolonged periods of discussion, an unconstrained range of positions, and *repeated clarification* in the light of criticism and self-criticism amidst friends, family and co-workers, and especially among complete strangers *at each and every turn.* The process of clarification is quintessentially a *social* process. Notice also it is unlike the process of voting as we know it.

What emerged, rightly or wrongly, was a clarification by large numbers of people of the common purposes to which we had *unreflectively* been committed. The process was one of moving from an identification with vague and shadowy ends such as "freedom" to ends that could be understood clearly in terms of everyday life—the freedom of a few to control the lives of many. The process, therefore, enabled many to create or conceptualize alternative ends, ideals, norms and standards. Like the social bond that unifies the people of Harding's river, this social process of clarification is a self-creative process. It is a process that potentially generates divergent ends from the ones with which we unreflectively identify.

Because political parties bring people together for political purposes, they do harbor the potential to institutionalize this social and developmental process and to facilitate the clarification of a range of divergent purposes. Parties, however, have always been intended to provide a forum only for debate over strategies to expand and strengthen our political-economic order. They were not supposed to become forums for clarifying the meaning and purpose of our political-economic order. Parties were intended to mobilize popular support. They were not intended to popularize critical thought. Political parties, therefore, have posed a serious problem for elites. The possibility that a faction from below will penetrate a major party and usurp its legitimacy for purposes of critical thought has always been feared. Indeed, early in our nation's history many elites seem to have feared that the "Spirit of Party" would give rise to the articulation of alternative social norms and standards.[11]

Austin Ranney has shown that the fear that parties would mobilize support around divergent social ends was pervasive throughout the 19th century. Because elites tended to interpret social political processes in terms of coercion as opposed to development, the word most commonly used to refer to this problem was *partisanship*. A number of proposals were advanced during the 19th century to circumvent the "dangers" of partisanship. Nathan Cree suggested in 1892 that all lawmaking be placed in the hands of the people through the initiative and referendum. James Sayles Brown in 1897 in his *Partisan Politics: The Evil and the Remedy* argued that the final cure would be "a law declaring any candidate nominated by any such political organization ineligible to the office for which he is designated." James Madison who wrestled with the problem before the Constitution was written fully anticipated the most effective solution:

> Extend the sphere, and you take in a greater variety of parties
> and interests; you make it less probable that a majority ("those
> who are without property") of the whole will have a common
> motive to invade the rights of other citizens ("those who
> hold...property"); or if such a common motive exists, *it will be
> more difficult for all who feel it to discover their own strength,
> and to act in unison with each other.*(emphasis added)

The one attempt to lessen the danger of political parties that seems
to have best expressed the Madisonian solution has been the primary
process. The nomination of candidates through primaries as opposed
to conventions or caucuses has had the effect of lessening the probability that the majority within a given party will discover its own
strength. We shall discuss the creation of the primary system and its
effects shortly, but first we need to briefly get a sense of the political
conditions that led elites at the turn of the century to urge the adoption
of what most historians agree were "anti-party" reforms.[12]

* * *

By the end of the 19th century the fear that the legitimacy of
republican institutions might be challenged through the party system
had intensified. These fears were not unwarranted. Stirrings of black
nationalism in addition to the range of socialist oriented proposals
arising from agrarian and labor protests suggested that the "masses"
were, indeed, discovering their own strength.[13] The greatest fear,
however, was of the growing political influence of the lower classes
within urban machines. This at a time when cities were becoming vital
centers of economic life.[14]

Although the emergence of a monopoly sector had helped elites
consolidate political power at the national level, at the local level
political power was considerably less centralized. Samuel P. Hays has
observed that "leaders who reflected a wide variety of community
interests and who represented the views of people of every circumstance
arose to guide and direct municipal affairs."[15] In light of Jim Crow
legislation during the same period and the disenfranchisement of
women, Hays' observation may be overstated. However, we do know
that the urban political "machine" because it was organized within a
context of personal relationships among subordinate groups, many of
whom were immigrants ("it provided quick naturalization, jobs, social
services, personal access to authority, release from the surveillance of
the courts, deference to ethnic pride"),[16] was capable of expressing
norms, standards and priorities that diverged from those upon which
political-economic institutions rested. For example, during the strikes
of the 1870s, city officials often sided with the workers by refusing to use
police to protect strikebreakers, thus forcing corporate elites to rely
upon their own private police, such as the Pinkertons, or state militia.[17]

The criticism most frequently made of urban machines was that they were corrupt. It is important to understand that the term "corruption" held a specific meaning in this context. It was, from the viewpoint of elites, a corruption of the republican political process. It expressed the fear that an individual could not possibly vote *freely* when *he* was influenced by personal relationships and obligations. Richard Hofstadter comments on this particular conception of politics:

> At the core of their conception of politics was a figure quite as old-fashioned as the figure of the little competitive entrepreneur who represented the most commonly accepted economic ideal. This old-fashioned character was the Man of Good Will, the same innocent, bewildered, bespectacled, and mustached figure we see in the cartoons today labeled John Q. Public—a white collar or small business voter-taxpayer with perhaps a modest home in the suburbs.... In years past he had been careless about his civic responsibilities, but now he was rising in righteous wrath and asserting himself. He was at last ready to address himself seriously to the business of government. The problem was to devise such governmental machinery as would empower him to rule.[18]

Robert Wood adds to our understanding of what partisanship meant to elites:

> Finally, and most fundamentally, no-party politics implies some positive assumptions about political behavior that go beyond simple antagonism to partisanship. Inescapably, there is a belief that the individual can and should arrive at his political convictions untutored and unruled; and an expectation that in the formal process of election and decision making a consensus will emerge through the process of right reason and by the higher call to the common good...the citizen, on his own, knows best....[19]

The same process of rationalization that had transformed highly personalized modes of work and exchange into regularized, depersonal and *predictable* practices was being brought into the party system. The right to develop one's whole being through the interaction of expression, criticism, and self criticism, the ongoing movement of collective struggle or social process, changing and yet continuing, as Harding puts it, was squarely at odds with Progressive reformer's conception of individual freedom. From his viewpoint, re-creative collective struggle was not understood as a creative social process but only as a vast tangle of personal relationship that bordered on coercion. It hardly was the measure of an "efficient" political system and given its association with impassioned lower classes, such processes were more than likely "impure."[20] The free person on the other hand was one whose values and ideas had not been distorted by emotional or subjective biases. He was the entrepreneur anxious to compete, bargain, and achieve.

This white collar voter-taxpayer was and remains John Q. Public. *He* is the meaning of private citizen. Of importance to us is to notice that the political process that enables him to rule is the process with which we identify as private citizens. It is not surprising, therefore, that although political campaigns are suppose to be organized around the discussion of issues we do not think of them as processes structured to permit "consciousness raising." Oddly, within the context of our two party system, the public discussion of vital issues is not understood as leading to the creation of alternative social identities and social forms. Perhaps this is because freedom from subjective bias, personal ties, and social bonds filters out collective and prolonged discussion. Politics within the two party system undercuts self-examination.

* * *

Austin Ranney points out that political parties in every "modern democratic polity" with the exception of West Germany "are largely or entirely unknown to the law....In the United States, on the other hand, ever since the last decade of the 19th century our state and local parties have operated under severe restrictions imposed by elaborate legal codes that govern every aspect of their affairs."[21] Walter Dean Burnham explains why.

> Political parties were dangerous anachronisms when it came to giving cities efficient, expert corporatist government. They were to be abolished where possible (especially on the urban level), and were elsewhere to be heavily regulated by the state. In particular, their monopoly over nominations would be stripped from them, so that "the people" (functionally between 5 and 35 percent of the potential electorate, as a rule) could choose candidates in direct primaries.[22]

Madison's outline for eroding the effects of the party proved to be quite effective. The "extended sphere" did, indeed, create a no-party politics, or to put it another way, no-politics parties. The primary system was not the first attempt to extend the sphere of the nominating process. It has long been a "democratic" reform. Initially, candidates for president were named by congressional caucuses. Schemes to involve greater numbers were quickly advanced, however, by splinter factions of the major parties which did not have the strength to win in the congressional caucuses. Disillusioned Federalists, for example, held a secret delegate convention in New York in 1808 in hopes of selecting a candidate that could win. In 1824, after various factional struggles, weaker candidates denounced the caucus system as unrepresentative and unconstitutional.[23]

Slowly, the national convention system replaced the congressional caucus. The extended sphere in this case took in a greater variety of "interests," thus diluting the base of any given dominant interest. The primary system had a similar effect. It was to the national convention system as the national convention system was to the congressional caucus. Each of these changes was sincerely cast in democratic rhetoric. "No longer," stated Robert La Follette in reference to the primary system, "will there stand between the voter and the official a political machine with a complicated system of caucuses and conventions....each citizen shall for himself exercise his choice by direct vote, without the intervention or interference of any political agency." La Follette also spoke of undistorted expression of the people's will and of purifying the parties. What did that mean? On the one hand it expressed the Progressive ideal of individualism. Note Progressive George W. Norris' support of primaries:

> The direct primary will lower party responsibility. In its stead it establishes individual responsibility. It does lessen allegiance to party and increase individual independence, both as to the public official and as to the private citizen. It takes away the power of the party leader or boss and places the responsibility for control upon the individual. It lessens party spirit and decreases partisanship.[24]

Also intended to lessen party spirit and decrease partisanship in addition to the direct primary were the referendum, the initiative and the recall. We have come to think of these reforms as democratic reforms primarily because they have seemingly made the participation of private citizens in party and public affairs more direct. Party nominees, for example, can be chosen directly by party members who have never attended a party meeting or struggled in a group to advance a particular position. V.O. Key, Jr., however, after examining the participation in primaries concludes that the primary system is the "illusion of popular rule."[25] Why is this?

Key's analysis reveals that voters "stay away from the direct primaries in droves." Consequently, the nomination process is controlled by a minority of elites. Nelson Polsby concurs stating that "those voters lower down on the socioeconomic scale are disproportionately missing from primary electorates."[26] Were it not for our tendency to identify with the primary system as a democratic system, we would not be surprised. The reforms in question were intended to make government more efficient not only by empowering businesspeople, but also by undermining the political influence of lower classes. For example, the first state primary, introduced in California in 1866 when expressed hostility toward Chinese immigrants was high, insured that only "reputable" citizens participated. By the end of the century, most primaries had been established in large cities, given the concern with the "purity of elections" and the "evils appearing in urban communities." The primary system, in essence, represented a rules change to insure that parties, while functioning as a mechanism for mobilizing popular support, *not become organizing vehicles for the under classes.*[27]

We need, however, to get beyond the focus on participation. For example, if anti-union reforms had been introduced to insure that workers could participate more directly in contract negotiations with employers *as individuals,* it is unlikely that we would see such reforms as a democratic advance. We seem to appreciate, although we often do not explicitly acknowledge, the educational value that comes only through the kind of social interaction that takes place in group settings.[28] Nelson Polsby, for instance, laments the fact that primaries seem to have helped transform parties into "masses of individual voters who pick among various candidates in primary elections as they would among any alternatives marketed by the mass media." The problem is one of process. But we do not make process a political issue (excepting the feminist breakthrough which we shall discuss in Chapter 6) because we correctly understand that to call into question political and economic processes would be to call into question the end to which the process is a part, namely the relative autonomy which businesspeople seemingly enjoy. And it is this autonomy that we believe we and/or our children have a chance of obtaining. Only by relinquishing that aspiration can we take a look at the processes of our "democratic" reforms. Let us do that by way of an illustrative example.

In October 1984, the United States invaded Grenada. The news of this invasion greeted most solidarity workers (people working in solidarity with the people of the Caribbean and Central America) early on a Tuesday morning. In Northampton, Massachusetts a number of solidarity workers hurriedly contacted each other by phone. A quick response of some kind was necessary. But what, how, with whom? It was decided that in order to answer these questions an open meeting would have to be called. It was further decided that in order to involve as many people as possible the meeting would be held, not in Northampton which is a small town, but in the nearby town of Amherst, at the University of Massachusetts which is much larger.

The meeting which took place that evening was very well attended. The rather large turnout of about 100 people was due to the attendance of many people who were not solidarity workers or political activists in general but who were alarmed by the day's events. Throughout the meeting various proposals were considered in the context of a far ranging discussion of the meaning and purpose of the invasion. Eventually a series of actions was agreed upon. However, the general message that was to be conveyed to the community by these actions was hotly contested. Solidarity workers, who interpreted the invasion in a historical context of U.S. military domination of the region, sought to link the invasion with U.S. military activity in Central America. They also sought to encourage public support of the Sandinistas who were resisting U.S. backed efforts to topple the government in Nicaragua. Those new to the discussion were aghast. They strongly believed that only a protest of the invasion of Grenada itself was called for, that broader claims or support of "enemies" of the United States was inappropriate and counter-productive.

Let us compare the processes internal to the political work of three distinct groups of people regarding this meeting. First, there were the organizers of the meeting. As political organizers, these activists had been meeting regularly to discuss ways of mobilizing the community in support of a particular foreign policy position. This had entailed the development of an understanding of the needs, wants, and purposes of other community activists, such as peace, gay and lesbian activists, and activists organized around issues of concern to women and minorities. It also entailed working with community officials such as members of local governments, the police, and the clergy in order to obtain permits for demonstrations, marches, fundraisers, the showing of films or the organization of forums. Often meetings with the printed and electronic media had been necessary. At each step of the way, the purposes and strategies in question were clarified and reviewed. Conflicting interpretations of the group's purpose and strategy had to be defended, altered, even abandoned at times. The process, much like the experience of those caught up in the debate during the Vietnam period, supported, *but did not require*, the creation of alternative social norms and standards with which to identify.

Consider a second group, the group of alarmed citizens. Unattached to a formal political process, they brought with them to the meeting the traditional respect for our political and economic institutions which one might expect. It was likely that many understood social norms to be self-evident, invariant, and not subject to debate. However, their encounter with competing perspectives forced them to articulate, and therefore clarify to some degree, the beliefs they held. For them, *this was the first time that they had had to publicly clarify a viewpoint that was assumed not to require clarification.* That they themselves had to clarify what until that time had simply been assumed enhanced the possibility that they might revise in some way what they thought social norms *ought* to be. Their understanding of what constituted the range of legitimate debate may have been broadened. The meeting, therefore, encouraged them to engage in a process of self-examination. We can see that this kind of collective process supports the re-creation of social norms and standards even though it may be vulnerable to the kind of "bossism" that reformers generally fear.

Finally, there is the group of people who for whatever reason did not attend the meeting and who do not attend meetings like it. They are the vast majority of private citizens. Their identification with political and economic institutions leads them to accept, as each of us does in varying degrees, the concept of politics as either electoral activity or as "Washington, D.C." This "anti-politics" politics appears to alienate vast numbers of citizens as low voter turnouts suggest. It means having to become interested in a limited range of distant and abstract issues, for the most part, every two or four years. When the celebrated voting day arrives, those private citizens who have been ignored or left out in the decision making process within the community, at work and/or in the home are expected to make a choice. The ballot leaves no room for questioning, qualification, self-examination, or social interaction. The voter as isolate comes and goes. His or her views, in part due to the primary system, remain undistorted by boss rule. But also due to the primary system, his or her self-interpretation and the interpretation of the world he or she inhabits is more likely to remain the same.

The Reality of Self Imposed Constraints

The induced passivity of anti-party reforms has frequently been measured by political scientists. Less than 1 percent of adult private citizens ever seek or hold public office. Less than 5 percent participate in a party, campaign, or attend meetings. Roughly 10 percent contribute to campaigns while 15 percent display buttons or stickers. U.S. electoral participation is easily the lowest among "free democratic countries" or a little more than half of the eligible voting population.[29]

These facts have repeatedly been explained away by the conceptual creation of the "apathetic voter." But the word is getting out. More contemporary students of party politics are beginning to suggest that these facts reflect less the political apathy among the lower classes than it does the sterility which the structure of politics in the United States invites. The sterility is most apparent when we notice what has been an inexorable trend in our political-economy. As property ownership has steadily moved in the direction of greater concentration, the extension of suffrage reform has permitted ever increasing numbers of property-less people the opportunity to participate in the party system. Greater political participation moves in tandem with the steady decline in one's opportunity to control his or her private life. Do these trends signify a revolutionary moment? Hardly. *The potentially greater political participation is at the level of individual voting, and voting, as the "apathetic" citizen knows, is a rather empty experience when it is disconnected from unconstrained and prolonged discussions, when it is disconnected from the real grievances persistently pointed to in the relations of private life, and when it is disconnected from the felt anxiety of having to clarify your thoughts in the face of honest criticism.* If, as has been suggested by others, the reform of consciousness begins with the awareness of consciousness, our individualized forms of political participation freezes our collective point of view. It may be primarily in virtue of politics outside the party system which extends into the broader culture that there is any political development at all.

Yet if we are aware of the emptiness of voting why do we not challenge the electoral process? The answer suggested here is 1) that our awareness is rarely made explicit, and 2) that each of us as private citizens secures dignity by identifying with the very political and economic processes that are the source of indignity. The two party system not only provides us with the opportunity to act out the role of free citizen by allowing us to re-define our grievances, it also provides us with an important forum to publicly affirm our acceptance of the processes that are the human glue of production for profit and market competition, private individualism. Our identification with these processes is a trap. It nourishes the soul by giving us a sense of a collective spirit. It makes the idea of community somewhat real. But once we speak, think and act, our collective spirit becomes yet an another form of individualism, our community an abstract patriotic bond. Our only escape is to pledge allegiance to being No. 1, increased productivity and endless expansion by becoming our own boss.

Two party politics is an essential element in this trap because it does not encourage the social and collective processes which are capable of illuminating the way we live, of making transparent the varied relationships of power. This feature of the two party system has taken on greater significance with the introduction of anti-party reforms such as the direct primary. That we believe such reforms to be democratic in nature is evidence of how our need to identify with the larger order is capable of betraying our real interests. Our opiate is believing that the problems of race, class, and gender can be solved by obtaining yet further degrees of legal or formal equality. The result is that we struggle to secure the fundamental freedom to struggle without struggling to secure fundamental change. The two party system which was not intended to admit real opposition has been reformed in order to eliminate the possibility that broad sectors of the population might identify with views that diverge from social norms.

During the Progressive Era, it may have been more appropriate to criticize the process internal to boss-dominated conventions rather than having dismantled the convention style nominations altogether. That way the potential for reflective politics which a strong programmatic party would have held could have been nourished instead of eliminated. Yet anti-party "democratic" reforms continue to erode the possibility of collective political work. Not only are increasing numbers of convention delegates elected by primaries, but the number of citizens identifying as Independents or expressing "no party preference" is on the rise. Moreover, the establishment of the "open" primaries, where citizens may vote in any party primary regardless of their own personal party identification, is increasingly being touted as a progressive reform.[30]

The situation represents an ominous cycle:

1. The deterioration of the American two party system which has not provided the propertyless class with a meaningful degree of self-determination has not been lamented by most citizens. Greater numbers of citizens seemingly take pride in calling themselves "Independents." Consequently, the substitution of certain party functions, such as the nominating process, by more direct and more individualized political processes has produced "candidate-centered organizations" and single issue campaigns. Analyses which focus upon single issues or candidates implicitly suggest that the system itself is sound. Suggestions that issues are connected or that relationships, particularly those of power, ought to be critically examined, are deflected. Systemic analysis is neatly filtered out while the opportunity to transcend one's personal identity through reflective politics is stifled. This dynamic is strengthened by the increasing role which the media plays in party politics. As campaign managers are able to rely upon the media to package their candidate, there is less need to engage in dialogue and less need to establish party linkages among communities. Working with, listening to, and becoming part of grassroot level political activity increasingly can be avoided.[31]

2. Candidate dominated elections encourage us to believe that the formulation of public policy depends mostly upon who is elected. The identification with individual candidates as opposed to specific and comprehensive positions or frameworks, therefore, makes it more difficult to make the claim that institutional structures and inter-connections or shared ideas and assumptions play as great a role in shaping policy as do elected officials. And as candidate domination personalizes the political process, it further personalizes our identification with the norms, standards, and practices that are internal to it. Our resistance to critical thought is hardened.

3. The belief that direct individualized political participation is the hallmark of democracy has been reinforced through the application of technology. One example is Warner Amex Cable Communications' QUBE in Columbus, Ohio or "interactive television" in which television sets are used to register the "instant" opinions of private citizens. As Jean Elshtain points out, the encouragement of "social atomization" makes it easier to foster the notion that "an electronic transaction is an authentic democratic choice." But as Elshtain argues such electronic transactions (in which "we face our television screens rather than one another") actually contribute to a kind of "authoritarian politics carried out under the guise of, or with the connivance of, majority opinion."[32] The more obvious example has been the proliferation of political action committees or PACs. PACs serve as the quintessential compliment to the packaging of candidates and policies;

they are, in the literal sense, the necessary consumer. PACs further legitimize the buying/renting of candidates/office-holders as political participation. And further considered illegitimate is the creation of space for critical thought.

Most alarming, as we shall find in the outline in the next chapter, the mounting unavailability of deliberative and social processes has been coincident with the resurgence of the Police State. But unlike the 19th century when the encouragement of reactive attitudes could not be controlled, in part due to the greater availability of social interaction (at least among white men) within the party system, the personal identification with lever-pulling as democracy today makes it less likely that citizens would challenge practitioners of the Police State. The political space in which alternative standards can be pressed, at least in the context of party politics, has been fragmented. From where, then, does creative opposition come? And what must be done to make the two party system valid?

Before we answer these questions we must assess the trends of party politics since World War II. It is to that subject that we now turn.

PART III

Moving Beyond the Two Party System

Too often
people are measured
by titles and diplomas,
but achievements
cannot always be certified.

I suppose
that we should honor heroism
and so we build monuments
and name streets
and write bibliographies
of the people that history
chooses to remember.
But let us not forget:
revolutions are in reality
the work of anonymous people.

Perhaps
you will never get a certificate,
nobody will build you a monument,
name a street after you,
or write your story.

So you may ask,
what have we achieved?
Where is the proof of our contribution,
where the result of our struggle?

Look around you.
Your achievements
are reflected in our faces,
the faces of your friends.
In us you can see
your accomplishments.
If in any way
we are today better,
or stronger,
or happier,
it is because of your dedication,
because of your courage,
because of your love.

We are your history.
We are your certificate.
We are the monument
to your heroism.

                              Angel Nieto

6

THE POLICE STATE OF THE 1980s

We have examined the two party system from three levels of analysis. One level of analysis, which was structural, suggested that party activity is constrained by the relation of the state to the economy. The second level rested on an examination of the party system's legitimation function or the mobilization of popular support. From this level we saw that because the two party system is incapable of exploring the relation between inequality and property relations, parties tend to oscillate between positions which suggest either that marginal constituencies are morally irresponsible and require discipline (the Police State) or are victims of maladministration and require public assistance (the Welfare State). Finally the third level of analysis rested on the proposition that as private citizens we personally identify with public institutions and tend to actively resist competing ideas and perspectives. These levels of analysis shall inform our examination of post-war party development as, in this chapter, we bring the analysis up to the present.

We shall find that since 1965 there have been structural changes as significant as those that were central to previous periods of party realignment. In other words, economic structural changes appear to warrant a durable realignment of party coalitions or a redirection of the public purpose. We shall also find that the potential for reorganization of the party system is coincident with the erosion of the New Deal Democratic coalition and the Welfare State. The rise of the New Right and the legitimation which they derive from the corresponding rise in fundamentalist religion, therefore, appears to mark a swing back toward the Police State. But we shall find that the restoration of the Police State may be blocked by the imaginative response which emerges from the political work of movement activists, particularly feminists.

151

The Structural Decline of the Welfare State and the Democratic Coalition

> ...the drawing of a social contract must take precedence over the aspirations of the poor, the minorities, and the environmentalists.
>
> —Business Week, June 1980

One aspect of the post war crisis that has received as much attention, if not more than any other, has been the *fiscal* crisis or the tendency of government expenditures to outrun revenues. James O'Connor, who fully anticipated this crisis, has pointed to the relationship between the state and the economy as the general source of the problem. He has argued that the "general cause" of monopoly sector growth has been the expansion of the state sector and, conversely, that the general "effect" of monopoly sector growth has been the growth of the state sector. Adds O'Connor, "the growth of monopoly and state sectors is a single process."[1] The implication is that we can expect increasing federal expenditures and an increased potential for a debt economy: sustained growth of the monopoly sector has and continues to require massive state subsidies (industrial development-parks, transportation subsidies, technical education, defense contracts which insure U.S. global military authority, research grants, pollution control, unemployment compensation, health insurance, etc.).

The postwar expansion from 1945-1971, driven by multinational industrial and financial sectors, provided sufficient tax revenue for the federal government to pay for the required subsidies. The war ravaged economies of U.S. competitors permitted the international hegemony of U.S. capital.[2] Moreover, the U.S. also dominated other key industries such as international oil, computers, electronics, and both investment and commercial finance.[3] Political dividends fell primarily to Democratic liberals who were able to deliver on the promise that had been formulated during the Progressive Era that had become a distinguishing feature of the Democratic party ever since the New Deal: you give us labor discipline within the monopoly sector and we will give you rising real wages and an "increase in the social autonomy" within the working class. And in addition, the science of Keynesian economics and later of the "New Economics" of the 1960s provided the necessary formal legitimation of the Welfare State: intelligent administration, not inequality, was necessary to generate sufficient savings for economic growth to occur. Democrats became the party of "full employment," health care, and education for all. With the New Frontier and the Great Society, Democrats played a familiar tune: expansion and the defense of freedom abroad was a simple extension of reform at home. Democrats were key players in an international arena.[4]

Yet there was an obvious danger. If the monopoly sector were not able to grow fast enough, there would not be sufficient tax revenues to pay for the social costs of monopoly expansion. Nor would there be sufficient tax revenues to pay for old age benefits, education for the middle-class, and income-maintenance programs (cash, food, health-care, and low-cost housing) or what is often called the *social wage* for low income people.[5] During the early 1970s this danger, or fiscal crisis, did indeed occur. But given the inability of party leaders to call into question relationships of property, in this case the relation between the state and the economy, they retreated from the application of more reform. Instead, they simply called for "sacrifice" and "belt-tightening" on the assumption that the relationship between the state and the economy was sound. *This was clear evidence that the swing back toward the disciplinary approach of the Police State had begun.*

Those most vulnerable to the slow-down in monopoly expansion, those who had been recipients of the social wage, were the central constituency of the popular base of the Democratic party since World War II. Therefore, the relative decline of the monopoly sector imposed the greatest problems for the Democrats, especially liberal Democrats. It was they who continued to promise assistance to those in need at the same time they made public commitments to the implementation of "austerity programs." Space was being created for conservative Republicans. Unlike liberal Democrats, they were not caught in a bind; they could easily castigate welfare recipients and impose austerity programs without breaking stride. And unlike liberals, they were more consistent. In the jargon of American party politics, conservatives appeared not to "flip flop."

* * *

There is good reason to believe that Democrats thought that the social wage could be maintained endlessly as long as they encouraged what some observers have characterized as the "imperialism of free trade." We find, therefore, Democratic spokespersons from Harry S. Truman to Jimmy Carter synthesizing cold war policies with liberal rhetoric where domestic policy was concerned. Truman may have had an advantage in this respect. Not only did his presidency inaugurate *Pax Americana* or the domination of the international economy by U.S. based companies but he also had a Republican controlled Congress. With a Republican controlled Congress, price controls, housing, and tax reform, as Alan Wolfe points out, could be publicly endorsed knowing that the battles over them would be symbolic only, that there was no danger of them actually passing.[6] And because the genuine lynchpin of the Democratic agenda was the support of multi-national overseas expansion, Truman's first concern was providing U.S. assistance to combat internal or external communist threats (defending freedom) anywhere in the world. This "Truman Doctrine," then, has been the foundation of Third World intervention ever since.

As the U.S. empire declined[7], however, Democratic presidents found it increasingly difficult to obtain the necessary imperial dividends to pay for social harmony and legitimacy. Compounding the problems of decreasing revenues and a shrinking empire were the escalating costs of decayed urban centers and eroded neighborhoods, polluted air and water, exhausted and contaminated soil, and increased alienation among blacks and women. The conflict between mobilizing a popular base around the state's perceived capacity to come to grips with social grievances through administrative reform *and* empire building first became manifest under Lyndon Johnson. The war on poverty collapsed under the weight of the war on communism, or as Martin Luther King, Jr. stated, it was lost on the battlefield of Vietnam. By the time Jimmy Carter had reached the White House, liberal rhetoric had been reduced to soft whispers of tax reform, health care, and full employment. And as Carter cut social spending, jobs for the poor, aid to the cities, and introduced voluntary wage-price control program, the Democratic liberal agenda was slipping into the past, overtaken by the imperatives of a new trading order, otherwise known as Trilateralism.[8]

* * *

Post-war imperial free traders, like the "Goldbugs" of a hundred years earlier, dominated both major parties. But stubborn protectionist opposition, fueled by entrepreneurial ideology and Taft isolationism within the Republican party, grew with a vengeance as the fiscal crisis unfolded. Richard Nixon's 1960 victory over Nelson Rockefeller was due to the protectionist wing as was Barry Goldwater's nomination in 1964. Although Goldwater's support among elites was thin, it signified the growing political strength of corporate leaders within national firms such as George Humphrey of National Steel, Roger Milliken of the large textile firm Deering Milliken, and independent oilmen like John Pew and Henry Salvatore. The emergence of Republican protectionists as a national political force encouraged many Republican multinational free traders to join the Democrats. Consequently, the influence of Nelson Rockefeller along with the "eastern establishment" support for foreign aid and the United Nations steadily declined within the Republican party.[9]

The political strength of the Republican protectionist wing has rested on their capacity to mobilize support within what we have come to know as the Sunbelt. Two essential features of the Sunbelt help to explain its political significance. First, it is marked by labor intensive, less concentrated firms that characterize the competitive sector of the economy. Within the competitive sector, the labor movement is underdeveloped and wages are low. Unlike monopoly sector firms, firms in the competitive sector are unable to pass on costs in the form of higher prices. The incentive for manufacturers in this sector is to drive down the social wage (or weaken the "safety net") in order to drive down wages. Therefore, wages are depressed and "workers are condemned to relative material impoverishment."[10]

Second, and very much related to the first feature, the Sunbelt is a region in which the command-obey relationships of fundamentalist religion help to constitute the norms and standards with which Sunbelt citizens personally identify. The relationship of the state to subordinate classes within this area resembles the discipline oriented, evangelical based reform periods of the past. The emphasis on entrepreneurial individualism, self-discipline, and self-denial encourages resentment of the aristocratic/monopolistic Northeastern establishment (both Democratic and Republican), intellectuals and prescriptive liberalism, and welfare in general. And given the need in the 1960s to legitimize "law and order" (or the political repression of civil rights and eventually peace activists) and in the 1970s to legitimize austerity measures, the standards of conservative populists, particularly in the hands of elites opposed to international free trade, gradually became a powerful political instrument. The nomination of Barry Goldwater, in this sense, represented a major failure, unknown at the time, of the legitimation apparatus of the Welfare State. With the movement of firms from the Frostbelt to the Sunbelt[11], the growth of "defense" and high-tech industries, the decline of U.S. global hegemony, and the resurgence of a vibrant feminism, the political significance of protectionists increased. Protectionists, however, did not represent a sector of the economy capable of challenging the control of the government by multinationalists. *Rather it was their perceived ability to mobilize popular support behind cutbacks in the social wage that made them useful to multinationalists whose political success turned upon the legitimation of austerity programs.*

But what are the economic needs of multinationalists? The answer, simply, is to restore global hegemony. Let us first recall the economic "miracles" of Germany and Japan. According to Harrison and Blueston, these miracles were due largely to the direct involvement of U.S. corporations. This involvement took several forms: in order to gain access to overseas markets, licenses were granted to foreigners to enter U.S. industries; U.S. developed technologies were exchanged for royalties; joint production arrangements were implemented; and U.S. firms invested directly in the stock of foreign firms. For example, by 1970 General Electric had licensing agreements with over sixty

Japanese companies. More astonishing, perhaps, is the fact that bankers shifted investments from domestic steel producers (thus closing down the Youngstown Sheet and Tube Company in Ohio) to Japanese steel producers. Even the U.S. Steel Corporation, as it cried foul and charged Japan with unfair competition, was investing "in overseas operations linked directly to that very competition."[12]

There are several implications that follow from this development:

1. Global firms have become extraordinarily *interdependent.* This interdependence has generated efforts to create new global management institutions as we shall see.

2. The increased strength of foreign based corporations has contributed to a decline, as Harrison and Bluestone claim, in inflation-adjusted, after-tax rates of profits of U.S. based corporations.[13]

3. The regulatory guarantees that had restored a sense of mutual responsibility for wage earners when industrial discipline was needed (such as minimum wages, fair labor standards, occupational health and safety provisions, equal employment opportunity, extended unemployment benefits, and improvements in workers' compensation) became burdensome.[14] The transnational scope of corporations in addition to advances in communications and transportations permitted capital to transcend their social contract with labor. By the mid-1970's, owners simply side-stepped the social contract by shifting resources and capital from one location to another.[15]

4. As Alan Wolfe points out, "The interests of the American economy and the interests of American multinational corporations were no longer the same." Whereas Democrats Kennedy and Johnson could facilitate the growth of American investment abroad and obtain sufficient tax returns to pay for the social wage, the new or "hyper" mobility of capital enabled corporate owners *to circumvent the constraints of the nation-state.* Harrison and Bluestone note that "government can no longer coerce the private sector to cooperate in the regulatory process or to provide the necessary revenue for the provisio of public goods and social redistribution." Carter's attempt at sustaining the Welfare State ended in chronic stagflation. Corporate owners, in effect, forced him to cut the social wage. Structural changes such as these have been, as we noted in Chapter 3, essential features of party realignments.[16]

This antagonism between the agenda of the Welfare State and the need upon the part of multinationalists to come to grips with the erosion of global hegemony of U.S. corporations makes it difficult for liberal Democrats to "govern." But it also makes it difficult for any administration to assert social authority. We have seen state governments, for example, lower property taxes in order to attract capital (Proposition 13 in California and Proposition 2 1/2 in Massachusetts). However, the need to create a "good business climate" impacts as well on nation-states. Reagan's cuts in corporate taxes, reductions in the social wage, and "virtual deregulation of the private sector" suggest that the government of the United States is now being held hostage.

The recognition among multinationalists that nation states could no longer be relied upon to successfully assist in the development of property relations appears to have occurred during the administration of Richard Nixon. In 1971, the U.S. experienced its first trade deficit in a century. Nixon's response, the New Economic Policy (NEP), reflected not the politics of Kissinger-Rockefeller multinationalism but rather the protectionism of Sunbelt Treasury Secretary John Connally. The collapse of the Bretton Woods Agreement, which had established the dollar as the capitalist world's principle reserve and therefore the U.S. domination of the international economy, was acknowledged as Nixon unilaterally devalued the dollar. The NEP also consisted of a 10 percent surcharge on imports, requests of Third World competitors that they slow the flood of textiles into the U.S., and pressure on Western Europe and Japan to permit greater U.S. corporate access to their domestic markets.[17]

Stung by these policies and the downturn of 1973, multinationals regrouped. Organizations that had been revitalized (Council on Foreign Relations) or created (International Monetary Fund and the International Bank for Reconstruction and Development or World Bank) during World War II to outline and co-ordinate "political, military, territorial, and economic requirements" of the United States now took on added significance. In other words, *transnational governing mechanisms were required by multinationalists to match their transnational interdependence and power*.[18] Out of a series of articles, conferences, and exchanges of concern of the most important representatives of transnational capital, the Trilateral Commission or the "executive advisory committee to transnational finance capital" emerged.[19] Richard Falk has written that the purpose of trilateralists can be understood in the general context of subordinating "territorial politics to non-territorial economic goals."[20]

Relieved by Watergate and the departure of Richard Nixon[21], Trilateralists were guardedly optimistic with Gerald Ford in the White House and Nelson Rockefeller as Vice-President. Yet, as Jeff Frieden has argued, Trilateralists "felt that the Republican Party was dead." Particularly worrisome in 1976 was the possible nomination of Ronald Reagan who "stood for everything the transnational imperialists had worked to eliminate." The Commission's focus, therefore, was turned to the Democratic nominating process.

Looking for a southern representative in 1973, and perhaps a conservative Democrat, trilateralists recruited Jimmy Carter. Mark Allen has pointed out that David Rockefeller and Zbigniew Brzezinski:

...were considering Carter, Florida's Reuben Askew, and former North Carolina Governor Terry Sanford as their representative of the New South to sit in the White House...Brzezinski was later to tell Peter Pringle of the *London Sunday Times*, 'It was a close call between Carter and Reuben Askew of Florida, but we were impressed that Carter had opened trade offices fo the state of Georgia in Brussels and Tokyo. That seemed to fit perfectly into the concept of the Trilateral.'[22]

But as we have seen, pandering to the Democratic coalition prevented Carter from governing even with Brzezinski in charge of foreign policy and other Commission members in key positions.[23] In 1980, as the campaigns of George Bush and John Anderson, both Trilateral members, fizzled, most trilateralists and multinationalists endorsed Reagan.[24] The Welfare State and the period of Democratic liberalism was at an end.

For Legitimate Reasons

As we have noted, there are two distinct party coalitions, one which governs (by formulating policy required of economic expansion and stability) and one which is mobilized for popular support. Multi-nationalist participation within the protectionist oriented Reagan coalition may appear puzzling until this distinction is made. Within the Reagan administration, multinationalists inconspicuously set the agenda for public policy while protectionist led elements, which are given public visibility, function to mobilize sufficient popular support to win elections. Market sector protectionists seek protection only to re-establish the honest competitive conditions of the free market. Thus, protectionists within the Reagan camp are free market ideologues. There are, of course, common interests between elements of each coalition beyond the making of virtuous noise. One is to protect the mobility of capital. In search of the perfect "business climate," one-half of all the new *Fortune 500* plants, when they have been located within the United States, have located in right-to-work states which are largely found either in the Sunbelt or the Plains States.[25] Another substantive common policy interest is "defense" spending. With the collapse of detente by the late 1970s, international bankers and industrialists, turning their gaze away from the potentially lucrative Soviet market, channeled petrodollars into the Third World. For example, private bank lending to non-OPEC Less Developed Countries increased from $34 billion in 1974 to $120 billion in 1979.[26] This Third World investment strategy, in addition to the increased need among multinationalists to flee regulation, organized labor, and genuine opposition at home, demanded a greater capacity for military intervention in order to impose a greater capacity for military intervention in order to impose appropriate business climates abroad. The systemic need for increased military preparedness also contributed to the political significance of the Sun Belt which, in some respects, might be thought of as the headquarters of aerospace and high tech defense contractors. Consequently, there were reasons for the vast defense industry, which since World War II had been the basis for the coalition among southern conservative Democrats and western conservative Republicans, the powerful anti-communist lobby, and domestic firms concerned about international competition to work more closely with multinationalists. The proliferation of conferences, seminars, lectures, and the massive advertising campaign designed to mobilize support for increased military spending during the late 1970s reveals the degree to which multinationalists and protectionists had found common ground.[27]

There was one important hitch to this momentus political reorganization. This financial community, worried about the inflationary effects of military spending, was hesitant to sign on. Particularly trouble-some in this regard were income-maintenance programs. Although military spending tends to be inflationary, it has been the practice to curb inflation by creating high levels of unemployment; at least that was the case prior to the creation of income-maintenance programs. As Piven and Cloward point out, by the late 1970s it was clear that the "reserve army of labor was no longer performing its historic functio-n....income maintenance programs have weakened capital's ability to depress wages by means of economic insecurity...."[28] In other words, in order to lessen the inflationary impact of increased military spending and thereby gain the confidence of the financial community, income-maintenance programs had to be cut. Carter apparently understood that continued support of traditional Welfare State programs (and maintenance of the Democratic coalition) was as costly politically as it was economically. Indeed, in 1980, most investment bankers supported Carter because he demonstrated his willingness to cut the social wage.[29] In order to prove their worth and earn the support of the nation's financial community for intensified militarism (as well as manufacturing capital's confidence that the social contract would be broken), Republicans, following Reagan's election, had to slash income-maintenance programs with a vengeance.

It may be fruitful to contrast the agency which does the "slashing," the Office of Management and Budget (OMB) with the International Monetary fund (IMF), created in 1944 to protect free trade and investment. While one has an international jurisdiction and the other a domestic one, each is a "policeman" of sorts capable of imposing discipline and austerity. Well placed austerity in turn not only provides a hedge against inflation, it reduces the expectations of politically marginal constituencies and in so doing provides an indispensable measure of social control. Consider the views of trilateralists in this regard:

...the fund must be given more *authority* than it now has in guiding balance of payments adjustments. [My emphasis]

and in a U.S. Senate report of August 1977,

IMF "adjustment" policies may also bring about a low standard of living, higher unemployment, a cutback in social welfare programs...the steps a government has to take to carry out those recommendations can in many instances lead to heightened political tension and greater social unrest. In some countries, governments may have to resort to political repression in order to carry out such policies.[30]

That the U.S. government may also have to resort to repression in imposing its austerity programs is a fear articulated by scholars of both the Left and the Right who see in the "Reagan Revolution" the signs of a fascist state.[31] To trilateralist Samuel Huntington, however, political coercion by the state in the interest of political and economic stability are *consistent with a democratic order*. In the Trilateral Commission's well known publication, *The Crisis of Democracy*, Huntington describes the demands for income-maintenance programs as an "overload" on the state. This overload is directly attributed to "a product of democratic politics." Among Huntington's prescriptions is a restoration of the "legitimacy of hierarchy, coercion, discipline, secrecy, and deception—all of which are, in some measure inescapable attributes of the process of government." In other words, Huntington seeks a "moderation in democracy": "The effective operation of a democratic political system usually requires some measure of apathy and non-involvement on the part of some individuals and groups...marginality on the part of some groups...is...one of the factors which has enabled democracy to function effectively."[32]

Although Stuart Eizenstat, Carter's domestic adviser, insightfully characterized the problem by arguing that the Democratic party had to shed its "historical mission" of helping the poor, multinationalists opted for the popular coalition capable of being mobilized by protectionists under the Republican banner.[33] What was needed was not simply the abandonment of the disenchanted mass base of the Democrats. *Rather the "moderation of democracy" had to be legitimized.* This meant that abandonment of administrative reform, or the abandonment of the mainsprings of Welfare State policies, had to be made popular. In other words, a swing away from the collaborative focus of the Welfare State to the disciplinary focus of the Police State was required. And the Reagan coalition, in spite of its protectionist trappings, provided the right bridge for the transition.

Insights by Kevin Phillips help to expose the function which the New Right as a popular conservative movement provides. He makes clear, when he politely refers to the New Right as "nostalgic conservatism," that the New Right is "trying to restore the role of religion sixty years [and more]—not just in the evangelist's tent but in the country clubs and chambers of commerce."[34] But it is the historical setting, according to Phillips, that makes the restoration of the "Old Morality" or "re-awakening" significant:

> ...the offense many Americans have taken at the perceived excesses of sociologists, egalitarians, drug advocates, sexual liberationists, permissive educators, pornographers, modern artists, media programmers, and such, is disturbingly like the reaction of many Germans of the 1920s to the famous "cabaret culture" of Berlin....[35]

What Phillips is pointing to is the incubation of reactive attitudes which accompanies crises within the Police State. Virtually in unison, members of the New Right insist that administrative reforms of the Welfare State have not simply failed, they have coddled the lazy and have corrupted the enterprising spirit. Harrison and Bluestone's characterization of the conservative point of view is apt:

> If it were not for a plethora of public insurance schemes and "social safety nets," people would presumably work harder, save more, and invest more in productive activity. Public programs ranging from cash assistance for the poor to auto emission standards have destroyed the incentive...for investment, killed entrepreneurial initiative, and devalued the very concept of honest work. High taxes have muted the gains from investment; government regulations have taken the excitement out of entrepreneurial activity; and welfare spending has made it possible—or so these people say—to live comfortably without ever working....As Irving Kristol writes, tends to corrupt and absolute dependency corrupts absolutely."[36]

In the abscence of economic constraints, such as the imposition of "industrial democracy" during the 1930's, resentment toward "permissiveness" (which Phillips claims is central to the frustration of the "middle classes")[38] is apt to flow freely. And if elites can come to grips with the late 20th century crisis only by engineering lop-sided economic expansion in which the propertyless class must be excluded, free flowing resentment may work to their political advantage. Certainly, reactive attitudes toward the "have nots" can be encouraged among the "haves;" after all, if the "have nots" are responsible for their misfortune, likewise the "haves" are responsible for their wealth. But the encouragement of reactive attitudes also impacts upon those whose who become dislocated during social transformations, such as the white male wage earner whose security becomes vulnerable as the Democratic coalition becomes fragmented.

The worker "sees poverty...as depriving men of the capacity to act rationally, to exercise self-control....[for a poor man] dignity means, specifically, moving toward a position in which he deals with the world in some controlled, emotionally restrained way." This struggle for dignity, which has as its object the industrial personality, is in itself an extraordinary exercise in self-discipline. Interpreting his struggle as a sacrifice for others, the white male wage earner in this situation must persevere daily within the context of a routinized, often demeaning job. Notice, however, his attitude towards those whom he perceives as lacking discipline:

> Welfare!....Those lazy sluts having kids like it was a factory....I work for my money....My job is to work for my family....they don't wanna work, they live for nothing but kicks, nothing but good booze and good sex....What kills me are these people that are on welfare and things like that—or like these colored people that're always squakin.[38]

Lazy sluts, kicks, good booze and good sex, welfare, ...colored people always squakin—these sentiments resonate with the protests against permissiveness, homosexuality, and abortion heard on the right. The common denominator is repressed sensuality.[39] Within this narrow range of thought available within the two party system, the white male worker, who has represented a swing constituency during party realignments, drifts toward the Right.

But the capacity of Republicans to trade upon reactive attitudes exists primarily because reflective participation among workers and other constituencies within the party system is unavailable. Consider the interpretation of the needs and wants of the white male worker by William Connolly. Believing that he is accepting the work routines and authoritarian controls in order to find dignity and in order to improve the life chances of his family, he becomes vulnerable to a range of liberal policies that implicitly mock his self-restraint:

> If the welfare recipient claims that unemployment is created by structural causes rather than by the personal defects of the recipient, the worker's very possession of a job may appear to be more a matter of luck than of self-discipline....If the recipient calls for higher levels of support the worker's own sacrifice may begin to look foolish. If radicals [or liberals] claim that common crimes are implicitly acts of rebellion against an order that breeds criminals, they inadvertently condemn the worker for bowing passively to that order. Or: they mock his exercise of self-restraint by relieving the criminal of responsibility for stealing under existing social conditions. If feminists claim that women are imprisoned in the home, the worker's sacrifice is reinterpreted as a restraint on her freedom and dignity....If university students debunk the privileged way of life they are about to enter they ridicule the purpose which informs the worker's life activity.[40]

Unable to engage in reflective politics and unable to clarify his own self-interpretation, the white male worker, like the rest of us is unlikely to reassess his understanding of the social order, and, therefore, unlikely to propose and/or identify with alternatives. He is compelled to exist politically at the level of reaction. Racism and sexism, in effect, are dispensed like drugs to ease his pain.[41]

There is yet a darker side to this. Within the context of a restored Police State, the mobilization support among one set of constituencies is at the same time the attempt to block the participation of the others.

* * *

Since the latter part of the 1960s, the notion that unorthodox political activists deserve to be punished or disciplined has gained currency. Gay and lesbian activist are the latest in a succession of activists that have been tagged as "permissive." Separate from his criminal convictions and removal from office, President Nixon's Vice President, Spiro Agnew, may best be remembered for his bitter denunciation of political activists who chose to express themselves politically outside the two party system. They were "spoiled brats who never had a good spanking." It was the 1968 campaign of George Wallace which linked "permissiveness" to liberal intellectuals and thereby transformed reactive attitudes into a political program that had broad appeal among white male factory workers. His diatribes against relief payments, which were woven into unequivocal ridicule of "bureaucrats with beards and briefcases," resonated, in ways that were described above, with the self-interpretation of the blue collar worker. It is useful to recall that during the same time frame, Ronald Reagan, as Governor of California, was calling activists "mad dogs," charged that "civilization simply cannot afford...politicians who demand that social security be tripled...that negroes need not obey the law...." When Martin Luther King, Jr. was assassinated, Reagan stated that it was the sort of "great tragedy that began when we began compromising with law and order...." Following Robert Kennedy's assassination, Reagan linked the "philosophy of permissiveness" to the killing of policemen in Chicago. Observed three British journalists, "What was obvious irresponsibility in the mouth of George Wallace passed as smooth reason in the low-ky tones of California's Governor." [?]

But the distinguishing feature of the Police State is not simply the betrayal of repressed sensuality or crude denunciations of those on the bottom struggling to keep above water. It is the legitimation of political repression. Signs that the Police State is being reconstructed, then, would be those that combine the reactionary slogans of a Wallace or a Reagan with the need to prevent the uninhibited political expression of particular constituencies. The popular base of the Reagan coalition, whose roots extend back to the Dixiecrat revolt of 1948, does appear to be organized around this end. Seeking to throw the presidential election into the House of Representatives in hopes of being able to trade votes for a commitment by the federal government to protect white (male) supremacy and the disenfrancisement of blacks, Dixiecrats led by Strom ·

Thurmond bolted the Democrats to form the States' Rights Party. Party," in part, no doubt, because Goldwater told the convention that nominated him in 1964 that "Security from domestic violence, no less than from foreign aggression is the most elementary and fundamental purpose of any government." The "black (soil) belt" of the deep South which supported Thurmond in 1948 was in Goldwater's column in 1964. Part of the Sunbelt by 1980, this region stood firmly behind Reagan. The black belt also was the heart of George Wallace's support in 1968 and from there both Keven Phillips and James Sundquist have traced the Wallace vote to Reagan; "...it is fair to say that the New Right is a partial heir of the Wallace movement," states Phillips.[43]

It is also interesting to note that since corporate pre-tax profits peaked in 1965, every elected president has come from the Sunbelt. The relation between the evangelism of the Sunbelt, the resurrection of authority and discipline, and the electibility of Sunbelt candidates is significant. Louis Harris found that Moral Majority-influenced voters accounted for two thirds of Reagan's ten point majority in 1980. In addition, Walter Dean Burnham has found that the defections from Carter "were concentrated among those for whom unemployment was the most important problem." This confirms what Phillips has suggested, that the New Right has a populist base. A populist base, we may add that rests upon the encouragement of reactive attitudes. Needless to say, political scientists do not use the term "reactive attitudes" to describe the marked increased in resentment, condescension, and fear within specific regions or constituencies. Rather we are told in misleadingly "objective" terms that there is increased concern with *social issues*. We ought not be surprised, then, when observors report that "social-issue voters represent the difference between conservatives getting 43-44 percent nationally and climbing to 51-52 percent" or that the "increment of social-and religious-issue voters may well have provided 5-6 percentage points of Reagan's 10-point program [in 1980]."[44]

So whom do conservative elites wish to silence by popularizing reaction within the Sunbelt? Whose political voice would, if given free expression, cast doubt upon the agenda of transnational coroporations: slashing the social wage, busting unions, and deregulation? The answer of course is those who are most apt to campaign for a stronger more socially responsible federal government. The primary target from 1948 to 1968 was blacks. Indeed, the campaign to curb black political expression, particularly given their gains through movement politics, became *"programmatic"* in 1968. At that time Kevin Philips, who coined the term "Sunbelt," submitted to Nixon headquarters an analysis which argued that a Republican victory (and a long term Sunbelt based realignment) turned on a "Southern strategy." This strategy emphasized making "coded" anti-black appeals, such as "law

and order," to blue-collar Democratic constituencies. Right wing
ideologue William Rusher's analysis of new alignment forces, according to Michael Omi and Howard Winant, is typical of "hidden racist
appeals" that have since followed. Note how the distinction between
"producers" and "welfare" recipients again calls attention to the
division between those compelled to exercise self-restraint and those
who seemingly mock such self-restraint :

> A new economic division pits the producers—businessmen,
> hard-hats, manufacturers, bule-collar workers, and farmers—
> against a new and powerful class of non-producers comprised of
> a liberal verbalist elite...and a semi-permanent welfare consti-
> tuency, all coexisting happily in a state of mutually sustaining
> symbosis.[45]

Since the late 1960s, the most formidable political obstacle to
conservative elites has been the political work of women.[46] Indeed, if
the restoration of male authority undergirds the agenda of transnational corporate hegemony and the New Right, the political contest
of the 1980s and beyond will between those who seek to legitimize the
political repression of women and those who seek to permit women full
political expression—not as moral guardians, male helpers, or even as
vice-presidents, but as women.

From Civil Rights to Liberation

The day Rosa Parks refused to relinquish her seat on a Montgomery bus in 1955 deserves greater attention from historians. Although less militant and less bloody than certain previous movements,
the Civil Rights movement following *Brown vs Board of Education* as
well as the movements it spawned are distinctive in that they were not
struggles centered upon *control*—over the government, the means of
production, or anything else. Shifting the focus away from future
ends—who governs, when, and where—the more creative elements
among black activists and later among women focused instead upon
the more immediate, the more personal, the more carnal. Blacks refused
to "wait"; their "passion for justice" demanded freedom *"now."*
Women began to create "free space" and asked: "What is our nature as
women? What are our needs? How shall we live? Is there a place for love
and caring within a masculinist society?"[47] Personal aspirations and
institutional norms, by the late 1950s, seemed to come apart a bit. The
crisis that the arrest of Rosa Parks ushered in was not simply one of
instability, lawlessness, protest, or resistance. It was one of legitimation.

Contrasts are often drawn between the early and later phases of the
Civil Rights movement. The early phase, organized by the Southern
Christian Leadership Conference (SCLC, a group of black church
leaders from ten states), the Student Nonviolent Coordinating Committee (SNCC), and the Congress of Racial Equality (CORE), success-

fully challenged segregation laws across the South. It has been characterized as a middle-class movement led by ministers and college students who thought less in terms of access to jobs and more in terms of access to "social amenities such as restaurants, theaters and hotels." Compared with the later phase of the struggle which extended to nearly all major urban areas outside the South, the organized effort to end segregation is often viewed as having been politically naive. The appeal to the conscience of white America and the emphasis on civil rights, it is said, represented a fundamental misunderstanding of the structural dimensions of white power. From this point of view, the transformation of SNCC into champions of Black Power (Stokely Carmichael and H. "Rap" Brown both emerged from SNCC), the guerrilla-like approach of the Black Panthers, and the emphasis on ownership and community control advanced by black nationalists such as Malcom X is accorded higher marks. Unequivocal celebration of the black identity and systemic critiques that went beyond the legalisms of civil rights have been pointed to as the more appropriate response to racism within a social order that appears to require the subordination of people of color.[48]

The steadily expanding scope of the work of Martin Luther King, Jr., a pioneer of the early phase of the Civil Rights movement, tends to support this view. The Poor People's Campaign, for example, which King was unable to complete before his death, was intended to "cripple the operations of an oppressive society." Although steadfastly committed to non-violence, the belief that social change lay in appeals to conscience alone had vanished. Yet comparisons of this nature often get bogged down in debates over the validity, implications, and meaning of non-violence as compared to paramilitary activity. Strategies based upon moral appeal are separated from the more confrontational struggles for control. Glossed over in these debates, ironically, is what many suggest is an essential feature of the black struggle, the process of re-creation and self-examination. It may be possible to learn new lessons from the movements of the 1950s and 1960s if we keep this essential feature in mind.

There is much evidence to suggest that the aspirations of SCLC leaders were politically mainstream. For example, as King argued that the "central front" of the Civil Rights movement was "that of suffrage," so Attorney General Robert Kennedy would argue that "from participation in the elections, flow all other rights." With the emphasis on electoral politics, SNCC and the CORE were persuaded to concentrate on voter registration in 1961. This Voter Education Project, not surprisingly, was urged by the Justice Department and financed by northern (white) philanthropic organizations. It is this rather "liberal" approach to social change which so many blacks by the late 1960s hoped to transcend. Yet there is an aspect of this liberal approach that deserves our attention.[49]

We may divide protests into two types, internal and external. An internal protest is one where the protest relies upon social norms and standards internal to the political institutions in which protestors are implicated. In the case of Civil Rights protestors, all that was demanded was that which was promised: equality before the law. Civil Rights leaders, therefore, were in a position to argue, "If we are wrong, the Constitution of the United States is wrong." In other words, internal protests reveal what King often referred to as a "monstrous contradiction."

External protests, on the other hand, rely on norms and standards external to the political institutions—that blacks in the United States are a colonized people, or are held in colonial bondage, for example. External protests such as those by the Black Panthers, therefore, are lodged within competing perspectives. The norms and standards upon which they rest are incompatible with those widely held. Within the framework of the dominant view, external protests cannot be fully understood. They appear irrational. And given the inability of the two party system to support competing perspectives, external protests invite repression. The point is that while profound insights may lead one into a competing perspective, it is the internal protest that more effectively creates *political space*. Why? Because conscious contradictory thoughts cannot be sustained. Learning that peaceful black protestors were beaten and arrested conflicted with the racist conception of the savage black, the rapist, or the "uppity nigger." Whites had to check their basic assumptions, go to the limit of their framework in its terms, and then proceed to stand outside of it, to become conscious of it, to become clear as to what it really achieved, and how far these achievements did or did not square with its actual norms and standards.[50] More concisely, internal protests make contradictions quite clear or as King might have said, they make the "invisible visible."[51]

Perhaps more than any previous movement, the Civil Rights movement created the space for collective self-examination and in so doing created the space for *politics*. Omi and Winant believe that the "social movement for racial equality had its greatest success in its ability to create a new racial "subject," in its ability to *redefine the meaning of racial identity*, and consequently of race *itself*, in American society." (Original emphasis.)[52] This change in the meaning of racial identity necessarily impacted upon the meaning of sexual identity as well, especially for southern white women, as Sara Evans explains:

> Within southern society, "white womanhood" provided a potent cultural symbol that also implied little practical power for women. The necessity of policing the boundaries between black and white heightened the symbolic importance of traditional domestic arrangements: white women in their proper place guaranteed the sanctity of the home and the purity of the

white race. As long as they remained "ladies," they represented the domination of white men. Thus the most brutally repressed assault upon white authority became a sexual liaison between a black man and a white woman....And the polar opposition of the "pure white woman," rigidly confined to her domestic sphere, and the animalistic black man, violently pressed into subservience, represented classic elements in the psychosis of southern racism.[53]

Like the situation of the 1820s and 1830s, the struggle by blacks and by women are more than parallel, they are internally connected. Let us draw out the linkages further.

One link was the role model which black women played. Angela Davis points out that under the slave system, compulsory labor overshadowed every other aspect of women's existence. Gender distinctions seem to have been minimal. Much like white women in colonial New England, female slaves played a central role in the slave community. However, because of racial segregation, the introduction of the factory system did not have the effect of domesticating black women. What Daniel Moynihan and others have referred to as black matriarchy may instead have more to do with the fact until recently, production within the black community was not as cleanly separated from the home as it was in white communities. As under the slave system, black women did the work that men did under Jim Crow. Although scholars such as Moynihan have viewed the independence and self-reliance of black women as troublesome (they lack "the spirit of subordination to masculine authority"), the strength and perseverance of black women during the Civil Rights movement struggle, such as the resourcefulness of an Ella Baker, "opened new possibilities in vivid contrast to the tradition of the "southern lady." "For the first time," said one white woman in reference to black activists, "I had role models I could really respect."[54]

If we follow the transformation of the Civil Rights movement and study its impact upon the political activity of women we cross a threshold of sorts. In effect we leave the party system. We could turn back and explore terrain that is located within the party system: for example, we could ask, what can Republicans or Democrats do to win the confidence of women with regard to "women's issues," such as abortion or childcare? But therein lies the problem. Internal explorations of the party system permit us only to know it in terms that are themselves constitutive of party politics. For example, this question is based upon the assumption that women differ from men politically in that they "feel" strongly about distinct sets of specific issues. Absent is the suspicion that women simply experience the world differently than do men. Absent as well is the desire to learn about and from that experience. Perhaps, the best way to grasp this particular limitation of the two party system is simply to cross that threshold. Therefore, let us immerse ourselves in the competing perspective of feminist thought (this is not to suggest that all feminists share the same perspective) so that we may appreciate a different kind of politics and understand more deeply the tension between what the two party system can offer feminists and what feminists want.

* * *

Christine DiStefano argues that in order to understand women *as women* and the implications of their political work we need to explore unconscious levels of human interaction and communication "where childhood memories, infantile needs, overwhelming desires for security and love abound." In our culture, the masculine, although distorted, has become the standard-bearer for the human, the feminine has become ignored or degraded, and exploration of unconscious activity generally has been pushed aside. In particular it is difficult for the "rational, enlightened, and self-interested individual," the ideal (male) citizen, to explore his "repressed underside," the "helpless and egoless infant, at the mercy of his bodily needs and urges...." Notes DiStefano, "It is a frightening, chaotic, irrational, emotional, slimy world. A magnificent edifice of power, control, rationality, objectivity, and planning has been erected over its repressed ruins."[55]

Feminists working in the psychoanalytic tradition have been exploring these ruins in order to better understand the essential features of the female *and* human experience as well as the female identity. One such feminist is Ulrike Prokop who argues that because of the female potential and ability for expressive, non-instrumental behavior, women are less oriented toward the realization of vaguely defined future goals.[56] Instead women are more oriented toward the "structuring the immediate 'current of affective devotion.'" The feeding of a baby illustrates what Prokop means by this:

> The feeding of a baby is only a part...of the relation between two human beings....they rely on each other and understand each other....You will understand what it means when it turns its head away and refuses to drink, or when instead of drinking it goes to sleep in your arms, or when it becomes restless and will not suck steadily. It is only frightened by its own feelings, and that is a situation in which you better than anybody else can help with your great patience by allowing it to play....[57]

Notice how different this relationship is when compared to the relationship between boss and worker, party elites and citizens, or between the human beings in general who fill the slots of public life. There is a marked diminishment of rationalized control. Reason and emotion are bonded. There is no suggestion of manipulation no apparent need for self-denial. The purpose of the activity is not entirely future oriented. Rather the immediate is assigned value as well. The activity becomes an end in itself. But most important, there is an obvious sense of *other-directedness.*

This other-directedness encourages group orientation as opposed to orientation toward individual achievement. States Prokop:

> During experimental games, female subjects behave differently from male subjects, namely in a conciliatory way; they will suggest, for example, that the prizes be distributed before the game has even started (instead of having them conferred on the winner, and they will make altruistic offers where the rules of the game prescribe competitive behavior. Thus they change those games in which the object is to ouwit the others.[58]

We have noted Barbara Ehrenreich and Deirdre English's observation that "Everything that seems uniquely female becomes a challenge to the rational scientific intellect." It is little wonder. The bedrock of the rational scientific intellect, which permeates market and production discipline, is, in a word, control. And control, especially when it is excessive, tends to be a liability for women. Control thwarts the unity of "reflection, judgment, and emotion" that Sara Ruddick calls "maternal thinking." Moreover, control is the antithesis to an understanding of the limits of one's action, or humility, which according to Ruddick, is central to maternal thinking. "Humility which emerges from maternal practices accepts not only the facts of damage and death, but also the facts of the independent and uncontrollable, developing and increasingly separate existences of the lives it seeks to preserve."[59]

Ruddick's account of women as mothers also seems to turn on the quality of other-directedness mentioned above: "A mother, in order to understand her child, must assume the existence of a conscious continuing person whose acts make sense in terms of perceptions and responses to a meaning-filled world." This appreciation and enjoyment of the growth of others permits women to expect change, or as Ruddick says, "to change with change." Psychologist Jean Baker Miller makes the same point, "In a very immediate and day to day way women *live* for change."[60]

We are in a position now to better understand the political space created by the Civil Rights/Black Power movement. Women were able to experience publicly those aspects of the female experience that had been kept private. The humility with respect to and enchantment with another's growth and the desire to become a part of the spontaneous development of a community can be inferred from the expression of women activists who joined the movement.:

> This will be a black baby born in Mississippi, and thus where ever he is born he will be in prison. I believe that if I go to jail now it may help hasten that day when my child and all children will be free—not only on the day of their birth but for all their lives.

I've lost faith or interest in most of the things that a lot of people get absorbed in....About the only thing I really believe in is the ability of people to sometimes get through to one another...to make living easier for one another. I don't know exactly why it is [but] I feel more strongly about [the civil rights movement] than about, say, any other form of social injustice and misery....

...finally it all boils down to human relationship....It is the question of...whether I shall go on living in isolation or whether there shall be a we.[61]

It may be useful to think of the Civil Rights/Black Power movement as simply creating space for politics. That is, space was provided not simply for women to gain equal rights. Space was provided for women to collectively rethink who they were and what they were doing. Space was provided for their *liberation*.

It is not surprising that the transformation of nonviolence to nationalism and the beloved community to black power was coincident with the first stirrings of critical self-examination by women. It appears that the opportunity for reflection permitted the expression of a female personality which Sherry B. Ortner believes has a different psychic structure, one whose language is composed of concrete feelings and thoughts about people and objects rather than with abstract categories. Rae Carlson makes a similar distinction: "males represent experiences of self, other, space, and time in individualistic, objective, and distant ways, while females represent experiences in relatively interpersonal, subjective, immediate ways."[62] Does this mean that politics as space for exploring assumptions, for making the tacit dimensions of everyday life explicit, for making the invisible visible resonates with women to a degree more than men? with blacks more than whites? or perhaps we should say with those given their situation, who are able to experience the world more sensually than those who are pressed to experience the world through the prism of rationalized production? There seems, in any case, a greater potential among women and blacks on the Left, particular those who resist the temptation to completely condemn the dominant order, to consciously create the conditions of a reflective politics.

When we examine the words of SNCC workers Casey Hayden and Mary King, written in 1965 when the re-creative process within the movement seemed to be accelerating, we sense their awareness of politics as a self-creative process:

Women [like blacks] seem to be caught up in a common-law caste system that operates, sometimes subtly, forcing them to work around or outside hierarchical structures of power which may exclude them. Women seem to be placed in the same position of assumed subordination in personal situations too....having learned from the movement to think radically about the personal worth and abilities of people whose role in society had gone unchallenged before, a lot of women in the movement have begun trying to apply those lessons to their own relations with men...[but there is a] lack of community for discussion: Nobody is writing, or organizing or talking publicly about women, in any way that reflects the problems....

In January of 1966, the clarity of purpose and the attention to the creative process is evident. Writes Casey Hayden, "People need institutions that belong to them, that they can experiment with and shape. In that process it's possible to develop new forms of activity which can provide new models for how people can work together so participants can think radically about how society could operate." A year later within a "Women's Liberation Workshop," women stated, "...we find that women are in a colonial relationship to men and we recognize ourselves as part of the Third World." Finally, women then directly located the root of their oppression in "their personal, social, and political relationships." The significance of this step deserves emphasis. Women expressing themselves as women were able to bring into analyses of social activity, of politics, discussions of intimate connections. This is quite unlike analyses of public policy internal to party politics which avoid discussion of initmate connections. The Left prior to the 1970s, in spite of its critical thinking, by concerning itself with the discussion of objective forces and distant objectives (such as "socialism," "revolution," "ownership of the means of production," "control of the community," "collective bargaining," "the subtreasury system," or "free silver") also tended to filter out the intimate connections of personal politics. Not even campaigns to shorten the work day or to bring about anti-discrimination legislation seem to have had the personal *immediacy* as did the campaigns centered upon process.[63]

The point here is not to rank order historic struggles. Rather the point is that the emphasis upon "black is beautiful," conceptual distinctions between black and negro or between girl and woman, the general frontal assault upon sex roles, and the politicization of personal relationships by women marked a new phase in the struggle of subordinate classes. A few blacks and women were giving a new meaning to politics. Legal struggles were unfolding into liberation struggles. The landmarks of masculinity—strength, courage, perseverance, action, absence of emotion, and objectivity.[64] were not just pushed aside, they were dragged out into the light of politics and found wanting. Perhaps more important, the process represented a turn; subordinant classes were doing more than seeking reform, *they were acting out and experiencing an alternative which they were creating*. In other words, they were becoming subjects.

* * *

Is it possible for the two party system to support a kind of politics which embodies the truths feminists established during the 1970s?[65] The response among multinationals and party elites to the resurgence of feminism during the 1970s gives us a clue. Noted *Business Week* in 1974, after they declared that the "whole economic future of the world" depended upon "some people" having to do with less, the idea that income and resources would have to be redistributed upwards toward big business would require a "selling job" beyond anything that any country had attempted in modern times.[66] In other words, because ordinary people had begun to find fulfillment in transformatory politics precisely at the time when it became clear that the American empire was declining, elites understood that expanded and reflective political participation represented a full blown crisis of legitimation.

Trilateralist, for example, expressed concern about the erosion of "the legitimacy of hierarchy, coercion, discipline, secrecy, and deception—all of which are, in some measure inescapable attributes of the process of government....people no longer felt the same compulsion to obey those whom they had previously considered superior to themselves in age, rank, status, expertise, character, or talents." The people who no longer felt the same compulsion to obey were primarily blacks and women. However, the problem may not be framed properly. Blacks and women no longer deferred to whites and men because the self-examination process helped them to create divergent norms and standards with which to personally identify. The self-realization through expressions of nationalism, black power, and black being beautiful, released blacks from the onus of having to be white to feel self-esteem. The proliferation of actions by feminists directed against militarism is but one example which suggests that the female identity is linked to a vision of society that transcends a series of "women's issues" and challenges directly male authority and forcible rule.

Not grasping the essence of the emergence of counter-identities or the meaning of genuine political space, trilateralists have viewed the political activism of blacks and women simply in terms of demands placed on the state or "overload" as has been noted. Suggests Huntington:

> Previously passive or unorganized groups in the population, blacks, Indians, Chicanos, white ethnic groups, students, and women now embarked on concerted efforts to establish their claims to opportunities, positions, rewards, and privileges, which they had not considered themselves entitled before.

Consistent with the tendency toward political repression within the Police State, trilateralists suggest that marginal constituencies need to be made passive, their political involvement minimized:

...The effective operation of a democratic political system usually *requires some measure of apathy and non-involvement on the part of some individuals and groups.* In the past, every democratic society has had a marginal population, of greater or lesser size, which has not actively participated in politics. In itself, this marginality on the part of some groups is inherently undemocratic but it is also one of the factors which has enabled democracy to function effectively. (Emphasis mine.)[67]

The failure of blacks and women to obey has been an irritant for both parties. Zillah Eisenstein has argued that Jimmy Carter, although anxious to mobilize the support of women, was careful not to allow the voice of women *as women* to be heard. For example, his dismissal of Bella Abzug as co-chair of the National Advisory Committee on Women seems to have been to due the the committee's linkage of Carter's anti-inflationary program (the slashing of social programs), military expenditures, and unsatisfied human needs. In other words, not only did women stray from women's issues and enter the male domain, they were expressing, perhaps not consciously, what Ruddick has called the maternal interests of growth, preservation and acceptability. Carter could have been speaking for a great many elites when he told his bible class two years afterwards, "women have gone about as far as they ought to go now...."[68]

It is important to understand that the firing of Abzug was due not simply to the fact that women were making connections between their economic and sexual subordination. Rather it was that a group was coming very close to politicizing the fact that, and again this does not mean that the politicization had to be conscious (it is unlikely that Carter consciously understood the implications), the entire order has a sexual-racial bent to it. Rather Carter's dismissal of Abzug, much like Moynihan's concern that "neither economic necessity nor tradition had imbued [in the black woman] the spirit of subordination to masculine authority," seems to have grown out of a sense that the (white) masculine authority of the economic order and the paternal authority of the state was in jeopardy.

In this context, the politics of "restrengthening" America, as Eisenstein suggests, is implicitly a sexual politics. Much like the evangelists of the 19th century, Reagan evangelists link the "rearming of America" with the rebuilding of a morally strong America. Indeed, the very budgets which shift appropriations from welfare to warfare have been justified in terms of restoring male authority. George Gilder, a "promethean intellectual" to several Reagan administration members, has argued that welfare "destroy(s) the father's key role and authority....male confidence and authority, which determine sexual potency, respect from the wife and children...." Gilder is explicit in the linkage of repressed sexuality, civility, and economic development:

> The lives of the poor, all too often, are governed by the rhythms
> of tension and release that characterize the sexual experience of
> young single men. Because female sexuality...is psychologically
> rooted in the bearing and nurturing of children, women have
> long horizons within their very bodies, glimpses of eternity
> within their wombs. Civilized society is dependent upon the
> submission of the short-term sexuality of young men to the
> extended maternal horizons of women. This is what happens in
> monogamous marriage; the man disciplines his sexuality and
> extends it in to the future through the womb of a woman. The
> woman gives him access to his children...and he gives her the
> product of his labor, otherwise dissipated on temporary plea-
> sures....Sexual energies...[are] directly tied to economic growth.

The independence of women, secured by welfare and/or by jobs,
especially of black women (which "only further expand[s] the appal-
ling percentages of black children raised without fathers") must be
eliminated. "Nothing is so destructive to all these male values as the
growing, imperious recognition that when all is said and done his wife
and children can do better without him." Aid for Families with
Dependent Children (AFDC) seems to unleash the tendency toward
promiscuity: "In a free society a man cannot long be made to work to
pay for children whom he rarely sees, kept by a woman who is living
with someone else."[69] In this context, the Democratic alternative, a
female vice president who chaired the 1984 platform committee which
ratified the party's abandonment of the social wage, neatly derails the
feminist thrust while appearing to embrace it.[70]

Reagan's coalition to mobilize popular support, unlike the
Democratic effort to co-opt feminism, appears to intend to undermine
feminism as a political and social force. The moral foundation of white
male authority that it provides serves to legitimate military expansion
and aggression. But it also provides a formidable weapon to curb
feminism, which it associates with sexual promiscuity. That weapon is
the moral indictment of abortion. As Ellen Willis argues, in demanding unrestricted abortion that "women's liberationists dramatically
rejected the traditional definition of woman as womb, as passive
extension of the fecund earth....the thought of 'liberated' women
pursuing sexual pleasure for its own sake was bad enough, but the
specter of women denying that their purpose in life was to serve others
haunted every institution from family and church to corporation."[71]

In some respects, "pro-life" or anti-abortionists represent the
attack troops of the New Right. Their target is larger than "promis-
cuous" women; their target is feminists who undermine the "traditional family," the traditional state, and the traditional social order
where subordinate groups feel compelled to obey their superiors and
where marginal constituencies remain politically uninvolved. But the
popular base of the Reagan coalition which threatens to legitimate a

return to state sanctioned punishment and discipline must not be viewed as a collection of reactionaries, misguided by yet unexplored racist and sexist assumptions. The growing political divisions are not that clean. There are moments of truth within the New Right that progressive activists need to think through more carefully. We shall examine what some of these truths are but first we need to draw some conclusions.

The Reality of the Two Party System

Ever since V.O. Key, Jr. in 1955 defined "critical elections" as "a type of election in which there occurs a sharp and durable electoral realignment between parties" a plethora of electoral typologies have been presented in an effort to nail down a scientific explanation of party activity. Much like comets that pass through our solar system, party realignments demonstrated "striking periodicity...from 1854 to 1894 is a period of forty years, between 1894 and 1930 thirty-six years."[72] In spite of the fact that there is nothing particularly meaningful about these intervals, political scientists have been searching high and low for the realignment that should have taken place around 1970, give or take a precise number of years. Quasi-scientific concepts such as "dealignment" and "rolling realignment" have been introduced to help explain the absence of the expected phenomenon.

We might do well to leave the scientific approach aside. The essential role that data play within scientific analyses compel political scientists to focus upon election returns—hence the limitation of the party analyses dependent upon electoral activity alone. Focusing upon election returns in hopes of understanding party activity might be analogus to focusing upon a scoreboard at a ball game in hopes of understanding the activity on the playing field. It is an abstraction of the activity itself. It may be more fruitful if we focus instead upon human needs, wants, intentions, and purposes especially as these essential features of politics are expressed through institutions and practices. For example, Paul Sweezy's rather commonsensical interpretation of the purpose of the state provides us with a good starting point:

> The function of the state is to see that the environment, the conditions, the atmosphere, and so on are such that corporations can prosper. But you can't do that all the time. There are fights among the corporations as to who is going to have the most influence over the state....There are fierce struggles within the corporate world. [The question is] Who is going to get on top and knock their heads together and bring out some coherent program for society as a whole?[73]

The arguments presented here tend to share Sweezy's assumptions about the state and the economy. Indeed, one function of the state is to protect and develop property relations. This relationship, assumed to be the lynchpin of individual freedom, economic independence, and national sovereignty goes unquestioned and, therefore, structures or sets limits to the range of policy options that are considered legitimate. Politics, then, becomes the contest among elites representing various economic sectors to gain control of the government. The purpose of the party system, in part, has been to facilitate this competition by formalizing the process: elites, in order to gain control of the government, must organize coalitions within a political party both within the government (which govern) and within the electorate (which legitimize specific investment strategies, strategies for stability and/or expansion). In other words, each party that seeks to govern must present a program which, in effect, outlines why any given combination of private interests ought to become the national interest.

As Sweezy suggests, there are conflicts among elites over whose private economic interests really deserves to be equated with the national interest. During the 19th century these conflicts corresponded to periods when emerging sectors of the economy expanded so rapidly that it soon became apparent that they deserved the full support of the state. The performance of cotton during the late 1820s, competitive capitalist firms such as railroads in the 1850s, and export-oriented monopolies during the 1890s were so dynamic that political coalitions organized around the growth of less dynamic or declining industries eventually broke apart as new coalitions or parties representing these driving sectors became dominant. Control of the government passed to the set of elites with a new vision of conquest and freedom when those same elites were able to mobilize sufficient popular support through electoral competition and legitimize the changed concept of national interest. The "critical election" signals elites to proceed also marks the fabled realignment.

The party realignment of the 1930s was similar to those of the 19th century in that it too corresponded to a reorganization of productive forces (by virtue of markedly increased state intervention into the economy). But it was different in that it was not intended to shift the authority of the state behind an emerging driving sector. Rather, the state intervention it sanctioned was intended to protect property relations by stabilizing productive forces and market pressures. The post-1980 situation as a potential period of party reorganization appears similar to the 1930s in two respects. First, there does not appear to be an emerging dynamic sector around which reorganized coalitions can rally although "high-tech" industries (which created half of all new position created in manufacturing between 1962 and 1982)[74] may yet blossom into such a sector. Second, the growing influence of transnational planning mechanisms, such as the IMF and the Trilateral Commission, to protect the stability of multinational corporations within western capitalist nations is parallel in significance to the increased intervention of the state during the New Deal. Yet, the post-1980 situation is far more ominous. The continued expansion of multinational firms undermines the national interests of the U.S. and planners cannot be held publically accountable in the same way that New Dealers were; the globalism of multinational capital has transcended nation state accountability.

Because the party realignments are but the culmination of extensive and fundamental reorganizations of people's work lives, social and family relations, it is misleading to think of party change solely in terms of the realignment of coalitions. The scoreboard approach highlights the distinctions between the major parites. When we think in terms of realignment, we are seduced into believing that it really does matter whether or not a Republican or Democratic administration governs. Made invisible is the assumption shared by both Democrats and Republicans that social grievances cannot be explained by the dynamics of the private economy. Made invisible as well is the general problem that plagues popular governments that are tied to private economies: what does the state do with the propertyless class? How does it relate to the non-elites of the sexual-economy? Attention to this problem illuminates the long cycle of the two party system, the oscillation between Police State and Welfare State management of those who are kept from sharing political-economic power.

* * *

The re-election of Ronald Reagan in 1984, despite its landslide proportion, was not a critical election. Republicans in Senate, House and gubernatorial contests registered only modest gains. More important, however, was the legitimation of the "solution" to the post-1965 economic crisis advanced by transnational elites. The approval, although it did not result in a party realignment, is but another indication that the shift back toward the Police State is underway. *Which major party wins or looses in the shuffle of coalitions matters less than the way in which both major parties come to grips with the problem of the propertyless class*. In other words, as the new Police State gets underway, it could be administered by either Republicans or Democrats.

What most political *scientists* have missed has been the transcendence of the nation state by the largest global corporations. Their newly found power transcends the standard norms of political accountability. For example, transnational firms such as Goodyear have acquired the ability to extract, according to Harvard researchers, "some amazing concessions" at the state and local levels of government. In the town of Lawton, Oklahoma, Goodyear was able to have "interstate highways moved, access roads built, and even a school jurisdiction annexed so that the children of Goodyear managers could attend a school controlled by the Lawton City Council, over which the company would presumably have some influence."[75] At the level of the nation-state, concessions were massive increases in military spending, massive cuts in the social wage, tax relief, and deregulation. The resulting increased deficits combined with a tight monetary policy kept interest rates at a very high level. Perhaps, unanticipated, this in turn has led to a highly valued dollar which serves to augment the fiscal policies just mentioned, and, therefore, to strengthen the push to re-establish U.S. corporate hegemony with respect to the international labor market and market in raw materials.

This solution to stagflation turns on the federal government's ability to keep inflation low by keeping unemployment high and by keeping the unemployed dependent upon private employers (eroding the social wage). The effect is growth in certain sectors of the economy and recession in others or *growth recession*. This unbalanced growth and low inflation may pull the growing number of Independents (especially white students, affluent professionals, and former southern Democrats) and significant portions of key Democratic groups, such as "better-off" Catholics, union families, southerners, and city dwellers, into the Republican Party. But this "solution" also renders imports cheaper and makes it difficult for exporters to compete. The resulting huge trade deficit is but one piece of evidence which marks uneven growth. Components of heavy industry such as steel and producers of farm equipment have suffered. Should the "Reagan Revolution" drag the economy downward, the constituencies mentioned above together with Sunbelt conservatives could mount a challenge to the Republicans as "neo-liberals" re-industrialize heavy industry and recapture white males.[76] In this scenario, a realignment would benefit the Democrats. But in either case, the federal government would remain an instrument of transnational corporations and discipline for the less well off would be a key element within the political agenda.

A study of congressional donations by corporate political action committees (PACs) for the 1980 election further suggests that the oscillation in question or *party redirection*, underway since the mid-1970's, may be irreversible for the forseeable furture. This study, conducted by Dan Clawson, Allen Kaufman, and Alan Neustadtl.[77] reveals an unexpected degree of political unity among corporate executives despite their important differences. For example corporate size, market orientation (multinational or domestic), rate of growth, location (Frostbelt or Sunbelt), and organic composition (capital or labor intensive) was a "relatively insignificant" factor in predicting their 1980 political behavior. Instead there was an astonishing degree of unity: "The data unequivocally show that for everyone of these factors the corporations with the hypothesized characteristics overwhelmingly supported the conservative candidates, usually giving 75 percent or more of the donations to conservatives." In other words, the swing away from the Welfare State to the Police State (strong support of the quasi-moral legitimation of Reagonomics in 1980) seems to have been broadly encouraged by corporate elites.

It may be useful to conceptualize the historical oscillation by political parties between the Welfare State and the Police State this way:

Figure 2
Long Cycles of the Two Party System

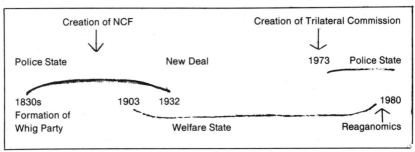

But the reorganization is stalled. The legitimation of the shift toward the Police State which the Reagan presidency has helped achieve is, at the very best, precarious. First of all, by their own standards, electoral support for the re-direction of the social order is weak. Reagan won the support of 27 percent of the potential electorate in 1980 and 32.5 percent in 1984.[78] A second factor complicating legitimation is the anti-labor bias of the New Right. In previous reorganization periods, elites bargained earnestly to win labor's support. In 1828, Jackson's anti-national bank campaign resonated with worker's distrust of monopolies. In 1860, Republicans promised workers free land. In 1896, the appeal to workers was minimal as radicals were purged, but Republicans did stress the benefits industrial workers would receive from high tariffs while their program of reciprocity and bi-metallic currency was aimed at farmers. And by 1936, FDR attempted to enlist elements of labor other than those who were in the skilled trades. The point is not that the bargaining was in the real interest of wage-earners, but that party elites believed that the support and cooperation of labor was necessary in order for the new strategy to proceed. In addition, elites during the 19th century had something to sell, namely that the future was brighter. The idea of endless expansion still held credibility. With the collapse of the economy in the 1930s, Democrats appealed to the idea of mutual responsibility. The 1980s neither holds the promise of a better future nor mutual responsibility.

Instead, Republicans are attempting to sell the past—a stronger, more powerful white-male dominated America. And it is in this respect that they are attempting to bring white male elements of labor, which is essentially Democratic, into the fold.

The implicit strategy for Republicans, if they are to turn around labor's allegiance to the Democratic party, and for Democrats, if they are to abandon labor and capture white-male support in general, is to weld together the notions of rearmament, white male authority, discipline, individual initiative, self-improvement and self-restraint and then link these notions to the promise that a brighter future can be had only by restoring "traditional morality" (or dismantling the Welfare State). In other words, the party redirection requires the political repression of feminists who challenge the validity of equal opportunity, and minorities, and dissidents who resist taking their place in a restored traditional America. Whether it is militarist aggression toward barefoot revolutionaries, discriminatory aspects of voting laws, or the neglect of the impoverishment of single mothers,[79] black and female activists have kept the issue of domination and the hope of empowerment alive. However, if there is a cutting edge to the campaign to point out the shortcomings of conservative populism and reconstituted liberalism, it may be the political activity of women.

In terms of the two party system, women are just beginning to show signs that they may vote as a "bloc." Certainly, they show evidence of voting differently than men (61 percent of men, as compared to 57 percent of women, voted for Reagan in 1984). And given their numbers (they are quite simply the majority of voters), they are rapidly becoming the most important swing constituencies. The political posture of feminists, therefore, is of primary concern to elites. This is especially true with regard to the militarization of the United States. Not only does the slashing of the social wage (which is a component of militarism) impact severely upon women (particularly single mothers)[80], but the greater need for the U.S. military presence in the Third World represents the clearest form of white-male authority. To put it another way, because militarism is the political-economic lynchpin of U.S. public policy for the 1980s, gender-based critiques of the social order must be made to appear illegitimate.

Progress toward this end is made when feminism is cast in terms of two responses. One response parallels the role of the moral guardian which many reform oriented women played in previous discipline-based coalitions. Today's "neo-moral guardian" response allows women to express themselves through the "anti-abortion movement, the anti-equal rights movement, and mass self-improvement courses like Total woman and Fascinating Womanhood." Their voice is in harmony with the evangelical song that runs throughout our history, a song which sings the praise of restoring the virtue of America. Neo-moral guardians are unable to make sense of criticism which challenges the inhumanity of the marketplace. Restoring virtue to them, instead, means defending "the material wealth of a particular class and race of people." Economically dependent upon their husbands, neo-moral guardians view the legal advance of women and the broader agenda of feminists as the erosion of the obligation which men have to them. Therefore, the subversion of male authority means not only the subversion of their own economic security but the subversion as well of their personal identity as private citizen and their self-interpretation as mother and nurturer. A public opinion poll prior to the 1984 election revealed that 16 percent of women said they were more likely to vote Democratic because Geraldine Ferraro was on the ticket, but 26 percent of the women polled said they were less likely.[81] This response, then, to the degree that it can be used to shore up male authority and the domestication of women, becomes an important element within the popular base of the Republican party.[82]

For many women, it is precisely the domesticity of the neo-moral guardian which is objectionable. From this point of view, domesticity is viewed as a constraint, as suffocation. The second response, therefore, is one based upon escape from domesticity, of individual freedom and self-improvement; in short, one of equal opportunity. It is, according to Ehrenreich and English, a response that "implicitly acknowledges the need for formal equality between the sexes. [It] offers techniques, some similar to feminist consciousness-raising, to build women's confidence and self-reliance." This is the "Equal to Men" response. It is a response which de-emphasizes social responsibility and social change and, true to the Protestant work ethic, "holds each person wholly responsible for her own condition, from the welfare mother to the million-dollar-a-year TV star." Consequently, concern is not with market or workplace relations as such but with the subordination of women within them.[83]

"Equal to Men" women are likely to feel comfortable as Democrats. The Democratic alternative, which seemingly takes into account the interests of women, does not question the priority of restoring white male authority. Rather Democrats argue that the restoration ought to include certain women. As long as some women are capable of acting as and speaking in the voice of white self-restrained males, they, and/or people of color for that matter, may also become generals, ambassadors to the United Nations or even Vice-Presidents.

These two responses illustrate the way in which policy and personal options are constrained by the structured relationship between the state and the economy. They also illustrate the lack of clarity and unreflective character of politics organized within and around the two party system. For example, the other-directedness, humility, and the unity of reflection, judgment, and emotion that is central to the experience of women as mothers is, within the first response, exploited. The female identity is contained and then employed primarily in the service of men. But because there is no legitimate political space in which women can imagine a social order free from subordination and conquest, our social norms, which reflect a distorted masculinity, are understood as human norms. Many women view the role of neo-moral guardian ("total womanhood") as "shocking, stupid, even repugnant."[84] Equal to men feminists, then, by totally negating womanhood, construct relationships which Ehrenreich and English claim are socially atomized and bereft of "human" values or what Ellis calls a tradeoff of children for "quasi-integration."[85]

Fortunately, the political involvement of women does not simply oscillate between a repressed and manipulated female identity and honorary male status. Cynthia Enloe offers contrasting examples:

Women in groups such as Britain's Women Opposed to the Nuclear Threat (WONT) and the Women's Pentagon Action in America have deliberately devised actions that have avoided topdown relationships, maximised people's spontaneous participation and drawn connections between militarism and women's ordinary lives. They have done this because they saw the qualities of equality, spontaneity and connectedness as the opposites of the quintessential characteristics of both patriarchy and of militarism.[86]

This is a remarkable development. By linking the lack of spontaneity within patriarchal and militaristic relationships, feminist activists are creating space for large numbers of people to engage in public discussions that cannot be had within the two party system. It becomes possible for people to reassess, in the light of a new perspective, old assumptions. It gives people the space to move from an object to a subject, from a thing to a person and exercise the capacity for self-reflection. The potential for deliberate and constructive social change is great. But there remains a problem.

The politicization of militarism by women is similar to the involvement of women in 19th century reform movements such as the temperance movement. Each, at an implicit level, has been an attack on the "irresponsibility of men." This is not enough, however. The problem is not just one of male irresponsibility. The problem, at the very least, has to due with a set of collective arrangements which, on the one hand, have out-distanced every other social order in terms of productivity and, on the other, have made it quite difficult for all its members to act responsibly. The critique at this level although it slips into modes that might, at times, stimulate one to become self-reflective, has yet to identify self-reflection as a principle of political work, has yet to identify politics as a *discipline*.

For example, as Enloe points out, many feminists find virtue in qualities that are opposites of partriarchy and militaries. One might infer, as does Joan Cocks in her evaluation of radical feminists, that an organizing principle of some movement activists is to present one's culture as the dominant order's perfect opposite. One harmful tendency in this is simply to appear freakish or irrational and invite repression. A second danger is to unwittingly become captured by the same way of thinking that mark the dominant order: feminists who urge women to "go back to some primordial nature untainted by male creation" share the assumption central to the dominant order that reason and emotion or the organic affinity with nature are contrary essences. Note the difference between this "reverse immage" and Ruddick's conception of maternal thinking that was rooted in the *unity* of reflection, emotion, and judgement. One position rests on the complete condemnation of the social order while the other draws forward some of its elements to create new conceptions and visions. The danger, then, is this: without a party system or a political institution which encourages us collectively as citizens to continuously discover and re-create the way we live, it is quite likely that our unfamiliarity with the process of creative politics will lead us to find comfort in untainted but more primitive modes of politics which further suppress rigorous thought.

In spite of the dangers, the two party system ought to challenged and altered so that politics does not stunt but rather enhances our capacity for self-reflection. The steps we might take to move in this direction is the subject of our final chapter.

7

CREATING SPACE FOR POLITICS

In this final chapter we shall discuss the meaning and purpose of a kind of politics that goes beyond the two party system and we shall discuss ways of getting there. First we shall look at opposition politics in the United States and the opportunities that now exist for marginalized constituencies to obtain their share of political power. In this context, we shall examine the opportunities which neo-liberals offer as an opposition force.

Then we shall move on to discuss how we might reconceptualize and restructure party politics. We shall find that critical thought is a necessary feature of the politics which we wish to see take hold but that structural obstacles such as the electoral college, single member districts, and plurality elections limit the degree to which significant social change can take place. Finally we shall find that mass protest and defiance which exposes contradictions internal to the electoral process and which makes clear to elites that a legitimation crisis does indeed exist may be the most effective and fulfilling means of creating political space for a democratic order.

Opposition Politics and the Two Party System

"A distinctive, persistent, unified structural opposition scarcely exists in the United States." So stated Robert A. Dahl in a comparative study in 1966. The array of groups organized in what is termed opposition, Dahl continues, "ordinarily affirm their support for the prevailing ideology and the basic social, economic, and political institutions; these oppositions concentrate on limited changes within the established framework of ideas and institutions." And that is precisely the point. The established framework of ideas and institutions becomes our cage without our even realizing it. Indeed, we celebrate it. The two party system *is* the hallmark of democracy. But what of third party efforts? Surely they provide an opportunity for real opposition. "Although the option of forming a new party is theoretically open," adds Dahl, "there is not a single case in American history where an opposition has formed a third party, pushed one of the major parties aside, and subsequently won a national election. The electoral record of third parties in the United States is one of nearly total failure." Concludes one of the most respected political scientists in the United States, "Parties other than the two largest have less impact on politics in the United States than in any other country examined in this volume [Great Britain, Norway, Sweden, Belgium, the Netherlands, Germany, Austria, France, and Italy]."[1]

But what would opposition politics look like? If there were unconstrained space for reflective politics, its process might look like the process whereby grassroots activism (presently separated by single issue campaigns) would be slowly transformed into a movement of broad based coalitions. Many issues would be linked and connections made. Politics as bargaining would become politics as critical thought. For example, consider the peace activism that is presently centered around the desire for a nuclear freeze. A large segment of the peace movement has been captured by those who cast the issue in terms of containing "Soviet aggression." This is frighteningly parallel to the 40 year effort of elites within the wage economy prior to the Civil War who also deflected internal critiques in order to focus public attention on what what considered then to be "Southern aggression." In part due to the constraint imposed by party politics of having to negotiate a freeze *and* "rearm America," many leaders of the movement resist exploring connections internal to the issue *which is the crux of movement politics.* Instead they prefer to work within traditional political channels (writing letters to and working with appropriate Congresspeople), proclaim the "urgency and uniqueness of the nuclear threat" which prevents the "movement" from being "sidetracked," and avoid linking other issues (which "makes it harder...for new people to become involved") to the anti-nuclear agenda.[2] The underlying assumption here is that politics consists of pressuring Congress. Protest can then be dismissed as ineffective ("so many people find it so alienating") and organizing middle and upper-class constituencies behind a particular candidate or specific policy can be made to seem the only realistic option. Moreover, in this way, the "passivity" of the propertyless class is left undisturbed. But as the strategy unfolds and more citizens are encouraged to rally around the issue, "ordinary" citizens meeting in groups at the community level begin to alter their conception of politics and their public purpose. Creatively, they begin to go beyond that prescribed approach of pressuring Congress. Much to the chagrin of establishment leaders, many small communities have taken it upon themselves to create nuclear free zones. In an unconstrained space, that is, in a space where social interaction at the community level is encouraged, the creativity that often emerges from prolonged discussion and social interaction holds the potential of transforming single issues into points of departure for deeper and broader analysis. The linkage of issues then logically follows. Let us continue with the freeze campaign as an example.

Particularly in Europe, the deployment of nuclear missiles has been aggressively resisted by women. The deployment of nuclear missiles, as one feminist pointed out, thoroughly represented the mind, body, and spirit of "erect masculinity." Like their counterparts in the West, feminists working within eastern bloc countries also have found within the peace movement the opportunity to expose the gendered nature of military aggression and the gendered nature of political and economic domination. The linkage between nuclear militarism and male domination represents one connection that exposes others.[3]

Prominent among women peace activists have been lesbians. The general alliance between lesbians and gay men within the gay liberation movement suggests that the involvement of gay men within the freeze movement may not be far off. The expression of homosexuality as an acceptable male life style mocks the male domination/female subordination relationship so central to the restoration of white male authority ("traditional America") by the New Right, which in turn is so central to militarism. This is not to suggest that gays are incapable of launching new rounds of militarism; but it does suggest that the acceptance of homosexuality for both men and women, by virtue of broadening the concepts of masculinity and femininity, may weaken the present legitimacy of male authority and female subordination.

More destabilizing would be the linkage between militarism and race. The gender-based critique by women of militarism, namely that it is rooted in an elemental desire for conquest that is characterized by violence and dispassionate and rationalized control over nature, ought to resonate with people of color if the themes outlined earlier in this study are correct. By linking militarism to sexual-racism, the common status shared by women and people of color (and to a lesser degree wage earners) as objects in a disembodied social order could be made explicit. In light of these broader explorations, freeze advocates may revise their interpretation of international politics to account for North/South hostilities. Alliances with solidarity workers could be explored. Discussion of freeze legislation might then be linked to divestment legislation or limited public control of direct foreign investment by U.S.-based multinational corporations. This recognition that social authority does have its place within a society organized around individual rights might lead to a reconsideration of the relationship between individual and social needs, rights and community, and so on.

Another related issue that makes contact with the feminist critique of militarism is that of the environment. Although the specific link might be the disposal of radioactive waste, unconstrained discussion of the matter would quite likely lead to a new understanding of our relationship to nature. This feminist-environmental bond would have profound implications for the politics of growth and conquest. Once having come full circle, citizen participants in critical thought may then have less desire for scientific styled politics. The method of separating ideas, of fragmenting complex systems so that its constituent parts appear to exist in isolation would seem silly. Instead, an *ecological* (meaning holistic, from the Greek *holos* or whole) view might take hold; reality would be understood as a web of interdependent systems, each of which is both a whole system itself and a part of other systems.[4]

Eventually the lesson learned from unconstrained social interaction might be formalized as a principle: *politics consists not of representatives telling people how to live their lives but of providing citizens with the space and encouragement to clarify the central issues in their lives.* The change would be the transformation of the state from a protector of property relations to a protector of political relations. Yet even if this sort of politics were suddenly to grow alongside the two party system *without having the alteration of the two party system as one of its major tasks,* it would, in order to impact upon national public policy, have to be processed by the two party system as it now stands. And there it would be re-transformed back into the more recognizable pluralistic model where the range of options would be structured around the politics of growth and where the bargaining process would re-fragment the matrix of progressive alliances into competitive political units, each supporting the structure of power as it struggles to survive.

* * *

Let us take a last look at this process. Suppose coalitions opposed to the restoration of "traditional America" grew to the point where they could no longer be ignored or repressed. How would the two party system come to grips with such a movement? The dynamics and the history of the two party system suggests that once progressive alliances have demonstrated broad public support either through third party efforts or through movement politics, their ability to influence public policy has often hinged on their ability to work with dissident elites within one of the major parties. Dissident elites generally representing significant but politically weak sectors of the economy often seek to bargain with disaffected constituencies in order to broaden the base of their popular support. In the 1980s, the cast of party characters that might be forced to work together in order to create an alternative to the New Right could conceivably approximate the following scenario.

Should the candidacy of Sonia Johnson, nominee for president of the Citizens Party in 1984, fail to broaden the base of the party, Citizen Party leaders and leaders of other small progressive minor parties may opt to forego national campaigns. Instead they might support (at the national level) progressive candidates such as Jesse Jackson who are involved with the building of a "party within a party strategy" similar to if not in coalition with Democratic Socialists of America.[5] Community level organizing that could be most easily translated into the legislative packaging required of party politics include campaigns for rent control, regulation of toxic chemicals in the workplace and the community, tax reform, a nuclear freeze, and the Equal Rights Amendment. Groups such as NOW, ACORN, Mobilization for Survival, Massachusetts Fair Share, 9 to 5, and left of center coalitions in New Jersey, Montana, Ohio, Illinois, and California that have coalesced women, blacks, Hispanics, environmentalists, neighborhood and tenant activists, senior citizens, and labor (such as United Automobile Workers, International Association of Machinists, the Service Employees International Union, the International Union of Electrical Workers, the Communications Workers of America, and several teachers' unions) would play key roles as *reformers*.[6] But this party-within-a-party would become a rather inconsequential left-of-center faction unless it were able and willing to bargain with major party elites who set the national policy agenda. Within the context of the two-party structure, this could be achieved only by plugging into (and attempting to influence) the national political agenda of a faction of dissident elites.

The Clawson study of 1980 congressional campaign financing referred to in Chapter 6 suggests that at that time, there were no real dissident elites. The Reagan administration strategy of protecting the interests of multinationalists through a strong dollar may exacerbate tensions within his own coalition as it becomes more difficult for midwestern auto and steelmakers, New England technocrats, north west lumber and farm equipment producers, and southern textile mill owners to compete successfully internationally. However, what we are looking for is not simply dissident elites but dissident elites located in a sector of the economy which has the potential for very rapid growth but whose growth is being stymied by policies designed to advance and protect the interests of the elites who govern. Dissident elites whose political opposition would be significant would most likely be organized around the agenda of what former Sen. Paul Tsongas (D-Mass.) has called the "new liberalism" or what has been come to be known as "neo-liberalism."

What is their agenda? Like supply-side Republicans, neoliberals have steadfastly focused on spurring economic expansion. Governmental intervention, from taxation, regulation and the bailout of failing industries to protectionist trade policies, has thus far ineffectively moved the development of property relations. But unlike Republican supply siders, neoliberals do not condemn government intervention as such. They instead have called for an "industrial policy" or prolonged governmental intervention to insure that corporations not squander their public subsidies on mergers and speculation but instead engage in "production-oriented entrepreneurialism."

From the neo-liberal point of view, the small owner-operated companies, such as Apple, that have characterized the expansion of high technology (the "information revolution") represents the model of production-oriented entrepreneurialism. Neo-liberals, such as former Senator Paul Tsongas and Gary Hart, believe that the key to economic expansion is the encouragement of high-tech industries and the installation of high technology in older industries. Three government programs often cited have been 1) basic and applied technological research, 2) an investment in so-called "human capital"—education, training and when appropriate, the retraining of the nation's workforce, and 3) rebuilding the nation's infrastructure or public communication and transportation links.[7]

The neo-liberal industrial policy would establish government councils to orchestrate market incentives to exact concessions from business (short-term trade concessions would be granted in exchange for agreements to modernize). The councils resemble FDR's National Recovery Administration in that they lean heavily upon the co-operation of government, capital, and labor. But unlike New Dealers, neo-liberals have no intention of creating a social wage. On the contrary, as columnist Joseph Kraft explained, "We're for the growth of national income, not its redistribution from rich to poor." By placing great emphasis on individual motivation and competition, the ideology of neo-liberals is closer to the New Right than it is to European style social democrats. Policies suggested by Felix Rohatyn, a leading voice in demanding fundamental changes in the relationship between government, capital, and labor, illustrate this approach. Although the federal government would be called upon to redirect capital to where it was needed (away from saving smokestack industries toward the encouragement of high-tech industries), such redirection would not be democratic. That is, because of the capacity of multinationalists to transcend the nation-state, government would not be able to coerce the private sector into redistribution schemes characteristic of the Welfare State. Within the United States, chances of Democrats becoming Social

Democrats are doomed. As the Rohatyn plan to rescue New York City in 1975 revealed, standard channels of accountability were circumvented to impose austerity and sacrifice on both public and private enterprises that were financially troubled.[8]

Not the official doctrine of the Democratic Party, neo-liberalism promises to grow in strength as a classic polar opposition force within the two party system. The fate of neo-liberalism may lie with bankers. Worried about a debt cartel in the Third World, increased military spending, and the debt crisis and the irresponsibility of corporate mergers, financiers may be seduced by the attractiveness of a "lean and mean" military and new growth opportunities in the electronics industry. In September 1982, the House Democratic Caucus published what was billed as the campaign-season program for the 1980s. It was virtually a neo-liberal manifesto: "Rebuilding the Road to Opportunity" called for a "break from the policies of the past....Decisions must be made on our spending priorities. While it may have once appeared that the federal government could have been all things to all people, that time has passed. We must be willing to say no to particular interests in order to bring overall spending under control."[9] The constraints, then, within which a progressive "party-within-a-party" must bargain are severe. Re-establishing the social wage would be out of the question. Organized labor would be offered worker retraining and computer education programs (in the context of high unemployment) in exchange for support for wage standards and automation. At best, women and blacks would be offered the opportunity to join rich white men (as junior partners) in the "real challenge" of expanding the economy, of controlling nature, and of deliberating over the rational use of force. "The litmus test of justice in a democratic society is equality,"—intones Gary Hart, a man impatient with yesterday's politics—"both equality of rights and equality of opportunity." And given the choice between the New Right and neo-liberalism, how long could progressive alliances hold out? Would white women support a "bias free" evaluation system for classifying federal employees that continued to discriminate against people of color? Would radical/cultural feminists support anti-pornography legislation which would provide the New Right legal assistance in protecting the "traditional family."? Would nuclear freeze advocates support the buildup of conventional forces which emphasize combat readiness and rapid deployment capabilities in exchange for an immediate six-month moratorium on nuclear weapons testing and deployment? Would teachers' unions be able to maintain their commitment to "jobs, peace, and justice" in the face of massive grants designed to expand high technology instruction?

It becomes apparent that the political involvement of marginal constituencies within the two party system is a one way street. You either play ball their way or you don't play at all. But this is not new. It is as old as the first direct appeals ever made to marginal constituencies. These appeals were made by Andrew Jackson, "the Father of Democracy." As a "candidate of the People," Jackson seemingly challenged the view of his opponent, John Quincy Adams that "the will of the Representative should not be palsied by the will of his constituents." Viewed as a historic turn, his efforts to enlist the support of the lowly working class has been celebrated as a sign that the two party system had grown to maturity. Robert V. Remini has nicely captured this appeal:

> To attract the vote of the several nationalities in the country, the Jacksonians utilized a wide variety of techniques.... As a start, they reminded immigrants that John Adams was the well-known "author" of the Alien and Sedition Acts, and that there was always a distinct possibility that John Quincy Adams might revive them—apparently for no other reason than that he was the son of John Adams and, as everyone said, like father like son. The Dutch in New York, New Jersey, Pennsylvania, and Delaware were solemnly assured...[that Jackson] "revered" the Dutch for their many virtues, their steady habits, and their patriotism.... Party leaders published tracts, handbills, and pamphlets in German. They sent German speaking lawyers into the heavily populated communities to organize rallies and public meetings.... In Boston, the leaders, "proclaiming Jackson as an Irishman...planted their flag on the meager of Broad Street.... In the West, poor Adams was accused of hobnobbing with Catholics, conversing in Latin with nuns and priests.... Or he was labeled a "Unitarian," not because the Jacksonians... cared, but because in many parts of the country it was just a polite way of calling a man an "atheist." Meanwhile in puritan New England, Isaac Hill published a report that the President was seen "travelling through Rhode Island and Massachusetts on the Sabbath, in a ridiculous outfit of a jockey." What was the country coming to, worried the pious Mr. Hill?[10]

This quaint characterization would be amusing if it not for the fact that it does represent, in our day as in Jackson's, the two party system grown to maturity. It cannot be otherwise.

Our politics are bounded by commitments to economic efficiency, individualism, growth, stability, expansion, conquest, competition, and force. There is no room for politics as listening and reflection, no need for the unity of reason and emotion, no space for the involvement of people of color, or women, or workers as social, self-creative beings, *as subjects*. Pandering is the only way to involve marginal constituencies and, at the same time, not tamper with our rigid and inflexible one dimensional social commitments. But there is the rub. We must acknowledge that even commitments to individualism are social-commitments. We are compelled to live a double existence. We are compelled to make shadowy reference to social needs—equality, community, democracy—even though our true spirit is the spirit of individualism. We thirst for competition. Our vision is one of achievement. Individual rights is our only serious political concern. But the genuine political involvement of people who have social identities, who see themselves not primarily as individuals but as *blacks* or as *women*, tends to erode the validity of individual rights or *privilege*, does it not? Would not this involvement contribute as well to the erosion of the legitimacy of what we know as freedom? If citizens whose identities were social in nature were permitted to run this country, would not individual rights soon be supplanted by group rights, then transformed to group or social responsibilities and then into the array of social programs where government acts as Big Brother? Our commitment to individualism and a private economy, therefore, requires the appearance of the involvement of these people without their real involvement. And this, we are told, is not pandering, it is democracy.

Our Double Existence

Where the political state has attained to its full development man leads...a double existence....He lives in the political community, where he regards himself as a communal being, and in civil society where he acts simply as a private individual, treats other men as means, degrades himself to the role of a mere means, and becomes the plaything of alien powers.
—Karl Marx, *On The Jewish Question*

In spite of the eclipse of the Welfare State, the ethos of mutual responsibility must linger. Even as 19th century notions of self-help and individual initiative are dusted off and wheeled into place, the New Right is unable to restore the Police State without "safety nets" for the "truly needy." Within our social order, the pursuit of self-interest and the quest for mutual responsibility are bound like rival siblings, forever locked in an antagonistic relationship.

But compounding the problem of the double existence appears to be the fact that we are blind to its existence. Liberals and conservatives each celebrate the concept of family without questioning the premise of organizing institutions around the individual. And social justice is consistently reduced to equal opportunity which in itself is little more than giving everyone a chance to become egoistic. And to the degree that we are unaware of that tension, we are incapable of clarifying and then creating a healthy relationship between individual and social needs.

To be sure, the concept of community within Liberal-capitalist orders has been stretched so thin and the notion of individual rights has been given so much weight that individuals have, from time to time, destroyed communities in the name of freedom. The individual's right to own slaves, now superceded by the individual's right to contaminate the environment with pesticides or to sit in research laboratories devising ways to reduce most of civilization to irradiated ruins, serve as examples. Socialist orders have been designed precisely to avoid these ills. But although socialists have recognized the degree to which individual independence, particularly in the form of property rights, undermines community, many have seemingly glossed over the way in which individual independence, particularly in the form of critical thought, contributes to community. Is some form of double existence to be desired?

Political space, that is space for independent critical thought, is needed to insure that our personal identification with social norms and standards is not due either to the absence of social processes or the presence of social pressure. Stated another way, reflective politics may require that individuals possess an important degree of economic independence. William E. Connolly has outlined a concept of freedom that contributes to the understanding of the nature of this independence. It is also one which he believes is "appropriate to socialist aspirations:"

> First, the social relations in the home, the workplace, and the community must embody, insofar as possible, that mutual respect and reciprocity that encourages people to develop as social beings, that allow each, at least often, to "obey oneself" while responding to shared norms and objectives.
>
> Secondly, the citizen must have a number of options available, options which allow each freedom and capacity to carve out a life in accordance with his own considered judgment.
>
> Thirdly, the attainment by each of self-consciousness must be encouraged and fostered. For without self-consciousness, the selection of projects (as in 2 above) is impulsive rather than reflective, and the adaptation to collective norms (as in 1 above) assumes the form of passive acquiescence rather than considered acceptance.[11]

The double existence, then, that may be essential to community is not one where lip service is paid to equality all the while inequality is rationalized. Nor is it a simple mixed economy where private ownership is preserved in order to protect individuals from reprisal by the state. Critical thought is more than the protection of individuals from the state; it is more than the Bill of Rights. A double existence may in part consist of institutional space where citizens are encouraged to explore competing or alternative interpretations of the social order. Such institutional space would serve two necessary functions.

First, access to competing perspectives would permit citizens to become aware of the limits to public policy, family, work, and social relations posed by ideas that are cherished and widely shared. Second, constraints placed upon individual action by state authorities *as well as by social norms tacitly all shared and understood* could be arrived at consciously and democratically. For example, the promotion of equal opportunity is widely accepted. Yet the constraints that it imposes upon various individuals is not consciously and publicly debated. We may say that the encouragement of many to compete for few rewards guarantees (and implicitly justifies) that most competitors will not reach their goals and that many will downright lose, in spite of their talent, intellect, and/or skill. This constraint is not made clear to those injured by the celebration of equal opportunity. A constraint is placed upon individual action that has not been democratically arrived at and is not, therefore, legitimate. The process as it is celebrated is mystified. Access to competing perspectives, however, would help to clarify the assumptions embedded in the process. Such assumptions could then be validated or revised. Inexcusable blindness of the forces shaping our lives would be lessened.

For those who are inspired by the socialist ideal, this institutional space may hold greater interest. In a socialist society, the state would *at times* have to deny the right of individuals to act in their own private interest when one's individual interest jeopardized the development of community and political relations. But when is that? The danger socialists face is that the rush from an individuated community where political voices are but a cacophony of market competitors builds momentum toward a totalistic edifice where one is no longer able to speak except in chorus with The Party. Should we, as Rousseau seems to have suggested, prohibit the accumulation of capital when it allows one to control the will of another? Should individual acts interpreted by the state as racist be prohibited? We surely are unable to clarify these matters now. Blueprints are a cure worse than the disease. But on the one hand we recognize that genuine critical thought, because it challenges the assumptions upon which the social order rests, will appear to be irrational or worse, counter-revolutionary, to many. A well intentioned socialist state may inadvertently silence its most creative thinkers. On the other hand, we realize that unchecked private rights lead to the subversion of social needs. In defense of the Bill of Rights, leaders of great social movements may be harassed, imprisoned, or even assassinated. Institutional space that guarantees public access to and the creation of interpretations which diverge from the social norms may be the best way to insure that the range of social action a community deems acceptable is *established reflectively and democratically*. Otherwise the cluster of notions which are central to any given order defines the range of socially acceptable activity without citizens ever consciously understanding that concepts in themselves are a social force. A positive double existence, therefore, is an existence in which we are at once engaged in political expression and solicitous of criticism of that political expression from a competing perspective. It is a political existence which permits and encourages citizens to *understand* the limits of the terms of their political discourse and, therefore, of the institutions in which they participate as family members, workers, and citizens.

* * *

The institution capable of providing this space is the party system, but not as it is presently structured. As Nelson Polsby has argued, the genuinely disaffected in a political system like ours are more likely to withdraw and be unavailable for political participation. They are rarely clustered in some convenient spot, geographic or social, together and able to participate easily. And, in any case, even if there were more communication within this group relevant to politics, there is little interest. And why is this? It is because the political experience within the two party system for significant numbers of women, minorities, and wage earners has been drained of meaning. *Nowhere within the two party system have they been able to clarify and express their highest aspirations as they explore competing perspectives.* A party system which provided space for politics as critical thought would be one in which the disaffected were encouraged to *express and clarify that disaffection.*

This, of course, opens the door to the "mischief of faction," social strife, and the potential legitimation of practices and beliefs which diverge from the social norm. And as we have noted, there are many students of the party system who, in the tradition of James Madison, believe that genuine political opposition is poison to the body politic. Perhaps it is worth pointing out that in Europe where factions exist in the form of ideologically distinct parties the imperatives of governing seem to blunt the edges of ideological conflict and generate a pull toward the political center. During the early part of the century in Sweden, the Socialists were against any collaboration with a non-socialist party and many were opposed to electoral politics in general only to end up collaborating with the Liberal party at the governmental level.[12] In addition, I know of no one who fears genuine opposition who is female, a person of color, or a wage earner, although, undoubtedly, there are some. Also, those justly concerned with factionalism often pay insufficient attention to the repression that is induced by institutions, such as the two party system, which effectively covers up power relations that underlie market, production, and family relations. Notes Joan Cocks, our denial of "a spontaneous place in public life" often leads us to press our grievances "within the even narrower boundaries of family quarrels, turbulent friendships, visits to the therapist, and religious urges in an era when religion itself has become merely a personal option."[13] Indeed, this kind of conflict resolution generated by the two party system regularly produces *one party regions*. The dictum that institutions which prevent fundamental peaceful change make violent change inevitable may explain a good portion of the violent history of the United States.

Providing space for politics within the party system also means that there would have to be space for parties whose primary function was not exclusively that of contesting elections. It would be unreasonable to expect progressive political activists who point to the concentration of power within the private sector on the one hand and policy option constraints within the public sector on the other to claim that the alleviation of social ills primarily depends upon who holds office. To attempt to mobilize the electorate on the basis of such a claim would be akin to fraud. Yet it would appear foolish for someone to run for office while acknowledging that his or her candidacy mattered little. Therefore, political parties that are genuinely *political* would have to become vehicles for political action that encompassed, but was not primarily organized around, electoral competition. Electoral competition, for example, might be thought of as one form of organizing, one way of doing educational work. The party, in other words, would be turned right side up. As it stands now, various constituencies are mobilized in support of individual candidates and party platforms. As more space is created for the articulation of views by those who are disaffected, individual candidates and party platforms would have to be mobilized in support of various constituencies. This brings us to the presidential campaign of Jesse Jackson and Rainbow Coalition building in general.

One reason Jesse Jackson's presidential campaign of 1984 failed in organizing a *Rainbow* coalition while it was successful in empowering blacks, enfranchising the disenfranchised, and politicizing to a considerable degree the process of party politics (no small accomplishment) may have been due, in part, to the conception of electoral politics shared by constituencies within the Rainbow. We have as yet not made the distinction between welfare politics and the politics of empowerment. The old adage—don't give a hungry person a fish, give him or her a fishing pole, helps illustrate the point. Involving Rainbow constituencies in a political process which was designed to give a voice to a few is *at best* welfare politics. The politics of empowerment, on the other hand, would rest on the involvement of Rainbow constituencies for the purpose of altering or abolishing the political process in order that the many could speak for themselves.

Because we are conceptually stuck at the level of welfare politics, political activity is divorced from the conscious process of clarifying who we are, what we are doing, and what we may be becoming. By asking women and minorities to come together in the context of an electoral campaign, the Jackson campaign, in effect, was asking women and minorities to calculate the advantage of supporting one candidate over another. Consequently, NOW endorsed the candidate closest to them ideologically *that had the best chance of winning*, the liberal Democrat, Walter Mondale.[14]

If on the other hand, the shared concept of politics were such that electoral competition was one party function in a network of organizing/educational community functions, the purpose of an electoral campaign would not be for a party staff to articulate a set of policy positions in the hope that its implied vision would resonate with a given constituency.[15] Nor would the party system, if the concept of politics were broadened to include the meaning of organizing, have the capacity to isolate and control political expression, to set apart, regulate and contain divergent points of view. Rather it would allow parties to become a central feature of the process of drawing out and making public the ideas binding alliances among constituencies within the Rainbow. What progressive party leaders thus far have failed to express is an awareness of a felt urgency among "ordinary" people to engage in political discourse. If progressive party leaders do not make space for this urgent expression, the political impulse among the disaffected dissipates, citizens withdraw from political life and activism fragments into thousands of tiny community meetings where the committed struggle to keep politics alive. Worst of all, under these conditions, the appearance of major parties as the repositories of political knowledge and political skill is maintained.

Freed from the rules governing electoral competition as we know it (*efficient* use of the candidate in terms of electoral success, for example, often dictates where and to whom the candidate speaks), progressive party leaders would be less responsible for articulating the vision for a Rainbow Coalition and more responsible for helping to create a self-feeling of a Rainbow *Community*. A central purpose of party activity, then, would be to help find ways to link ongoing community organizing activity among Rainbow constituencies and to give activists a voice and in so doing lend them legitimacy. The difference between party activity as it exists and party activity as a feature of movement building is the difference between coalitions and community, between an individualized process and a social process, between promoting a constituency's self-interest and working together to find common needs, between bargaining and listening, between telling people how to live their lives and creating the space where people are able to explore and articulate the most meaningful aspirations of their lives. And unless party activists move from the former to the latter, continued efforts to mobilize elements of a Rainbow Coalitions are apt to be counter-productive in two ways.

The first is that those who are creating space through political activism will be inadvertently pushed aside. Political activists shun electoral politics because they know it for what it often is—a cliche. Having found the self-creating experience of political activism to be enriching, they are unlikely to sustain a relationship in which political work becomes a series of hurdles to jump over. From the court house to the White House or from the slave ship to the championship is an impressive accomplishment, but it resembles individual conquest too closely. The process of becoming and of building a movement is but an afterthought.

The second is that by leaving party platforms to platform committees instead of creating a platform for those whose voice is not heard, the viewpoint of party leaders becomes stale. Disaffected constituencies that are left out have no way of getting in. The situation of the white male worker is a case in point. Neoliberals have nothing to offer. Regarded as ignorant or reactionary by left of center forces, white male workers must choose between dead end liberal agendas and the New Right. And with his dignity somewhat depleted, the New Right's offer of greater authority looks pretty good. If a progressive faction understood the need to listen to, learn from, and provide a platform to white male workers (as opposed to labor "leaders"), his voice might alter the position of the faction to the degree that he could identify with it at the same time that its self-understanding grew. For example, by accepting the division over the abortion issue as either Pro-Life or Pro-Choice, the concern of the black woman that abortion may be another form of sterilization is not woven into the progressive point of view. Nor is the view of white working class women and their husbands who are against abortion because they identify with the fetus as an innocent victim.[16]

Activists opposed to capital punishment implicitly reject the concept of punishment in general. In addition, opposition to capital punishment is often linked to arguments based on the notion of "deterrence": capital punishment ought to be opposed because it does not deter crime. The conceptions of punishment and deterrence cut a number of ways. The concept of punishment *implicitly suggests respect for responsibility* whereas the concept of deterrence implicitly suggests that criminals ought to be *used* for larger ends, namely the prevention of crime. Should we be surprised that many white working people who seek the respect accorded to responsible adults but who are themselves used as instruments in the accumulation process support capital punishment and oppose schemes of deterrence?[17]

Affirmative action is significant historically in that it represents the first time that the state has gone beyond "equality before the law" in response to demands by women, minorities, and the physically challenged to end discrimination. Yet it behooves us to understand that affirmative action suggests that women and black victims of discrimination are not responsible for their employment situation. The implication is that, unlike women and minorities, the white male earner is responsible for his employment situation. As victims of classism, white male wage earners may see affirmative action programs as themselves discriminatory. To the white male wage earner, then, the New Right's charge of reverse discrimination appears to make more sense.

Efforts to politicize underlying power relationships within the family have often led to the conflation of public and private realms. To suggest that the personal is political may be to overpoliticize the personal. One effect of this simplification may be to hasten the transformation of family relationships into contractual ones. This insensitivity to the rich, complicated, vexing but joyous emotional *and* private dimensions of family life parallels the liberal intellectual's insensitivity to the wage earner's sense of sacrifice that George Wallace had once exploited. Insensitivity of this sort today makes it appear that only the New Right is capable of addressing the dissolution of the family by market forces.

We ignore the distinction between mobilizing support and working to build institutions that allow people to speak for themselves at our peril.

Bargaining on Revolutionary Terms

We need to challenge the two party system. We need to create within the party system space for critical thought and practice, for politics. Third parties are not the answer. Within a two party structure, they must either play minor roles or become an appendage to a major party. It appears that if political space is to be created, we must take steps to create a *multi-party* system. To put it another way, we need to change the rules of the game. Lest this sound un-American, let us recall that electoral reform or rule changing has been a regular feature of party politics. The problem has been that most rule changes have been undertaken to minimize the participation of various "undesirable" constituencies. Walter Dean Burnham has categorized the "sociopolitical thrust of electoral reform" as shown below.[18]

Figure 4

Target Groups	Opponents	Rational	Sanctions
1. Urban machines	Middle-class WASPs (status anxiety) Techocratic progressives Upstate agrarians	Anticorruption Inefficiency "Sodom and Gomorrah"	Ballot reforms; special prosecutors; nonpartisanship malapportionment, discriminatory registration laws
2. Political parties	Progressives; many of the above	Unrepresentativeness; "old politics"; corruption	Detailed legislative regulation; direct primaries
3. Immigrants	Agrarians (upstate in NY); small-town and metropolitan middle class WASPs ·	Not adequately culturally developed; "Romanism"; "Anarcho-Communism"; lazy, drunk, etc.	Elimination of alien voting (Midwest and West); personal periodic registration for cities only; literacy tests
4. Populist agrarians (North and West)	Corporate elites, urban.town middle classes	Danger of "revolution by the "backward"	Electoral activity plus some corruption and "pressure" on dependent voting population
5. Populist agrarians (South)	Elites (regional and local), Democratic organization	Same as above	Same, but massive use of fraud and force, and sanctions below
6. Blacks (South)	Southern white progressives; gradually, ex-Populist white agrarians	Racism; "traditionalist Southernism"; anti-corruption	Violence and terror; later largely replaced by poll tax, literacy tests, "white primaries," grandfather clause, etc.

Rules that are responsible for transforming political expression in the United States into a two party system, as opposed to a multi-party system, are ones which are seemingly part of the background of electoral activity. They are the rules which insure that the electoral college, single member districts, and plurality elections structure our electoral experience. The common denominator of these rules is that they force coalitions where conflict exists. Much like collective bargaining where wage earners are financially dependent upon owners or the "traditional" family where the wife is financially dependent upon the husband, these political institutions are structures which create common interests at the surface level which in turn makes it more difficult to politicize the power relations that lie underneath. These rules, in effect, make it nearly impossible to create *opposition* parties or parties ideologically distinct from the ideology shared by Democrats and Republicans.[19] Let us look more closely at these rules and the institutions they help create.

When confronted with demands for reform, partisans, as Austin Ranney suggests, tend to ask, "will it hurt our party's chances to win elections?" The abolishment of the electoral college, therefore, has met stiff resistance even though it has been responsible for reversing the popular mandate in presidential contests three times (1824, 1876, and 1888). The electoral college helps both Democrats and Republicans win elections because it helps to keep the number of major parties to two. It does this in two ways. First, because presidential elections are winner-take-all situations within each state (the candidate with a plurality of popular votes gets all of the state's electoral votes), parties which lose narrowly in a state get nothing. Unless a third party expects to win in a given state, it faces great pressure to "moderate" its agenda and coalesce with a major party. The same thing happens at the national level. Because a majority of electors is needed to win the presidency, third parties which possess significant strength but are incapable of winning (as was the case with the People's Party of 1896) again face great pressure to bargain and coalesce with a major party. It is worth repeating Dahl's observation here: "...there is not a single case in American history where an opposition has formed a third party, pushed one of the major parties aside, and subsequently won a national election." The Democratic and Republican Parties are the oldest parties in the world thanks in large measure to the electoral college.

Another structural factor contributing to the maintenance of a two party system is the single member district in which voters are allowed to elect only one representative from each district. Nearly all representative assembly elections in the United states use single-member districts.[20] It is easy to grasp the effect of single member districts when we think of situations in which if we vote our conscience we will probably be "wasting our vote." For those of us to the left of the major parties, this is a recurring problem. Unenthusiastic about the Democratic or Republican candidate, we often prefer to vote for a third party more in accord with our point of view, the Citizens Party for example. But we know that by voting for the Citizens Party, we may, in effect, be wasting our vote as it tends to help the candidate of the two major parties whom we dislike most. The pragmatic response, given the structure of single member districts, is not to vote our conscience but to vote for the lesser of two evils who has a chance of winning. In 1980, 1982, and 1984, most activists disenchanted with the major parties could be found voting for the Democratic nominee (instead of minor parties we really preferred) in order not to enhance the chance of electing Ronald Reagan or one of his supporters. Under these circumstances, it makes sense for ideologically distinct factions (such as the Democratic Socialists of America or Rainbow Coalitions) to work as a party within a party rather than face the likely prospect of meeting with very little electoral success as a third party.

The third structural element which tends to force coalitions among disparate groups is the plurality election. Under plurality elections, no matter how many candidates are running and no matter how small the percentage the leading candidate gets, the candidate with the most votes wins the election. This places a very small premium on majority rule and a premium on rule by minority. Plurality elections work well in tandem with single member districts to support either one or two major parties. It is an essential component of the "waste your vote" dilemma because the winner in a three or four way contest need only obtain a plurality of votes, not a majority of votes. Party identification alone virtually insures that plurality elections will go to either one of the two major parties. Given this dynamic, it is common at the local and state level for a single party to dominate, eliminating party competition altogether. Consequently, minor parties, if they place a high priority on winning, are pressured to coalesce with a major party rather than risk coming in second or worse and losing.

The implication of this analysis is that these structural impediments to a multi-party system ought to be challenged. Surprisingly, activists have not focused their attention on the rules of the game except with regard to suffrage reform. Numerous articles suggesting that the "Green Party" experience (in West Germany) can happen in the United States have appeared without a word about these structural impediments. There have been proposals to reform the electoral college but these proposals have not come from progressive activists who desire major third and fourth parties. The 1984 campaign of Jesse Jackson has achieved a considerable breakthrough by calling attention to the "double primary." Undoubtedly this helps to politicize the rules of the game. But Jackson's analysis may be defective as we shall see and by making support for the elimination of the double primary a "litmus test" for progressives, he may be inadvertently preventing the kind of change he desires. Let us, therefore, turn to the feasibility of changing the rules in question and then move on to a discussion of the double primary.

The Electoral College

With regard to the election of the president the Constitution states:

> Article II, Section 1: Each state shall appoint, in such a manner as the legislature thereof may direct, a number of electors....The Congress may determine the time of choosing the electors, and the day on which they shall give their votes....

Altering or abolishing the electoral college does not appear to require a constitutional amendment. This view is supported by the fact that there have been various federal congressional proposals to do just that. Two of these proposals deserve our attention and probably our support. The Lodge-Gossett or proportional plan would abolish the office of elector and each state's electoral vote would be based on its popular vote. Better yet was the proposal sponsored by Senator Birch Bayh (D-Indiana) in 1977. Calling for the abolishment of the electoral college; his "direct popular vote" proposal would substitute direct election of the president without regard to state lines. The proposal also called for a national run-off between the two top candidates in the event that neither received 40 percent of the votes cast. As we shall discuss below, the run-off aspect of the proposal, in addition to the abolishment of the electoral college, further encourages the possibility of a multi-party contest at the national level.

Astonishingly, Bayh's proposal received support from the Chamber of Commerce, the AFL-CIO, and the American Bar Association, as well as Senators Hubert Humphrey, Edward Kennedy, Howard Baker, Robert Dole and President Carter. The support which this proposal enjoyed was undoubtedly due to three important factors:

1. The electoral college cuts against the grain of direct elections, a process that is widely touted as a democratic process in the United States and, as we saw is an important way of side-stepping collective processes such as nominating conventions.

2. Many federal politicians fear that the electoral college may either reverse a popular decision as it has in the past or throw the election into the House of Representatives (should no one receive a majority of electors). In either case, the result would call into question the legitimacy of popular rule. *That politicians really fear the appearance of illegitimacy should not be lost on activists.*

3. Ignorance. Judging from what our federal representatives say, it appears that most of them drip with ideology. Few understand that their own fear of popular activism was felt by the Framers as well and that our political institutions were designed to prevent the "tyranny" of the masses. But most important, many may not understand how critical the electoral college is in preserving the two party system.

It behooves us to keep in mind the power of the internal critique in this regard. It is more effective to argue that the electoral college ought to be abolished because it impairs what everyone believes to be a democracy rather than link its abolishment to the merits of a multi-party system or the need to create space for critical thought. Surely the latter would be putting the cart before the horse.

Single Member Districts, Plurality Elections

With regard to federal elections generally the Constitution states:

The Times, Places and Manner of holding Elections for Senators and Representatives, shall be prescribed in each State by the Legislature thereof: but the congress may at any time by Law make or alter such Regulations, except as to the Places of choosing Senators.

Again it appears that alteration or abolishment of single member districts or plurality elections does not require a constitutional amendment but rather simple congressional elections legislation. In fact, it is virtually certain. Prior to 1842, single member districts did not exist in Alabama, Georgia, Mississippi, Missouri, New Hampshire, New Jersey, and Rhode Island. In these states, the entire congressional delegation was elected at large by means of what was called a *general ticket*. According to Joel Francis Paschal, this method was adopted by small states in order that they might take advantage of the unified delegation that the method apparently produced. In 1842, an apportionment bill, which "touched off a violent two-year controversy," was introduced to prevent the general ticket system. In part it stated:

That in every case where a State is entitled to more than one Representative, the number to which each State shall be entitled, under this apportionment, shall be elected by districts, composed of contiguous territory, equal in number to the number of Representatives to which said State may be entitled; no one district electing more than one Representative.[21]

One opponent to the measure insisted that "as the people of the States are to elect their Representatives, they cannot be divided into districts, and those residing in a district be restricted to vote for a single representative, but *all* have the right to vote for *all* the Representatives of the state." (Original emphasis.) But as we know, there is no such "manner" of elections—which "admits of the most dangerous latitude" according to Patrick Henry. The danger of course, at least in the eyes of elites such as Henry, was the national social authority of Congress vis-a-vis the states. What egalitarian electoral schemes might Congress impose upon the states? The question ought to stir the imagination of progressive activists.

If we are able to return to at-large congressional elections within the states as easily as we left them—by congressional fiat—the possibility of creating political space within the Congress increases dramatically. The election of a state delegation at large, for example, lends itself quite nicely to *proportional representation*. In other words, the share of congressional seats awarded to any party would be equal to the share of the vote which it receives. There have been many precedents of proportional representation in the United States. One of the most well known was the proportional representation system used to elect city council members of New York City from 1936 to 1947. The process encouraged a wide range of diverse parties. In addition to Democrats and Republicans there were the American Labor Party, the Liberal Party, the Communist Party, and the Fusion forces. Having permitted the election of two Communist council members, the process was eventually terminated by a coalition of anti-communists who called it a "Stalin Frankenstein" that had "created confusion with the blessing of the Kremlin." A prominent Republican stated what we now all know, "No democratic system can exist in any form of government save under the two-party system. I want to see the two-party system restored in our city, instead of the three, four, and five party system which now exists." Blacks fought to save proportional representation arguing that if it were abolished "there will not be a single Negro in the Council." One black Republican felt that the effort to repeal proportional representation was due not to the presence of Communists but of blacks on the council. Now let us turn to the double primary.[22]

The double primary or run-off primary is an example of a *majority* election as opposed to a plurality election. Majority elections require that candidates receive *absolute* majorities, if not on the first ballot, then on the second. Because it is difficult for a candidate to obtain a majority of votes when more than two candidates are running (such as in a primary), a run-off is held between the top two vote getters to insure that the eventual winner obtains a majority.

This system of voting encourages a multi-party system and generally enhances the chances of progressive party candidates. Let us consider the 1984 presidential race. Because it is a plurality election, voters who prefer Citizen, Communist, Socialist, Socialist Worker's, Libertarian, Independent or other minor party candidates will be under pressure, as we noted above, to vote Democratic in order to stop Reagan. But what if majority rules were in effect: if no major party candidate received an absolute majority, then a run-off would have to be held between the top two contestants. Citizens would then be free to vote their conscience during the first round. The number of votes received by minor parties during this first round would increase, perhaps significantly, because under these rules more ideologically distinct campaigns would be encouraged. The DSA or Jackson forces might bolt the Democrats to form a progressive party, a party in which women would have to play a major role. Factions within the Republican party that have provided Reagan with his popular base could either split from the Republicans or enhance their bargaining position by threatening to do so. Fearing this, liberal Republicans could push for a more moderate candidate, and so on. The point is that majority elections weaken the base of the major parties as they give space to factions and minor parties that would otherwise have to coalesce. More important, the bargaining position of progressives within the Democratic Party would be more greatly enhanced than would conservative forces in either major party.

Between 1968 and 1980, Republicans, as the minority party, have won 3 out of the last 4 presidential elections. Opinion polls suggest that Republican victories are due to Democratic defections.

Figure 3
Defection Levels From Party in
President Voting, 1952-1980

	Democrats			
Year	To Rep. Candidate	To 3rd Party (if significant)	Total	By comparison, Republicans (to anybody)
1952	23%		23%	8%
1956	15		15	4
1960	16		16	5
1964	13		13	20
1968	12	14%	26	14
1972	33		33	5
1976	18		18	9
1980	26	4	30	13

1952-1968 mean defection: 18.6 Democrat: 10% Republican
Post 1968 mean defection: 27% Democrat; 9% Republican

Although Republican presidents have been elected by Democratic defectors, Democrats may have more to fear from an electoral process that encourages diversity and discourages artificial coalitions, especially if women, blacks, and/or workers are among those seeking more ideologically distinct parties.

Majority elections, therefore, seem to help left-of-center candidates get into a run-off situation and thereby publicize and legitimize left-of-center positions. The educational significance if not the general competitive advantage for minority factions within the context of majority elections is considerable. Although studies are lacking in this area, recent elections in Denver and Boston support this contention. In Denver, Federico Pena, an Hispanic initially given little chance of winning, won a plurality of votes during the first round and bested his opponent, "the city's no-nonsense district attorney," in the run-off. In Boston, two left-of-center candidates, Mel King and Ray Flynn, finished first and second respectively in the preliminary round, while

Ray Flynn won the run-off. In a city besieged with racial tension, Mel King, a black man, was constantly referred to as the candidate who "can't win." Would he have gotten as far as he did had there not been the run-off? I do not think so. As Connolly has pointed out, "Voters *seeking* to maximize the impact of their vote, cast it with a general *understanding* of the electoral consequences flowing from the election system within which they vote."[24] During the preliminary round, the "don't waste your vote" rationale was inoperative. Voters knew that they were not under pressure to choose between the establishment candidate(s) and the closest rival. If this analysis is correct, it was in large part because of a majority election that a progressive black man in a racially divided city was given a great deal of attention, further legitimacy statewide and, to a degree, national recognition.[25] Let us turn, then, to the special conditions of the South.

Majority elections are held in the South. However, they are not held in the general elections *but in the Democratic primaries only.* Between 1902 and 1939, nine southern states instituted majority election within the context of *primary* elections.[26] There is reason to believe that this practice was not motivated by racial prejudice. As Key suggests, the logic of public accountability requires direct primaries rather than the convention system of nominating candidates when a single party determines the results of elections in advance. Following the demise of the Republican party in the aftermath of Reconstruction, southern Democrats, if they were to be popularly elected *had to be elected* by a primary within the Democratic party. If the logic of public accountability, in addition, requires that winners of elections receive a majority of votes (as they would if there were two parties), then a run-off or second primary would also logically follow. In other words, there is reason to believe that majority elections in southern primaries may be due to the fact that it has been uniquely a one party region.

Whether or not these majority elections impair black representation is somewhat controversial although the Jackson campaign leads one to believe that they do. Recent studies, which differ with respect to the size of the sample and region, draw conflicting conclusions.[27] Evidence also suggests that racial bloc voting may persist even if blacks get the Democratic nomination as white Democrats would flee to the Republican party.[28] It appears that our attention has been drawn to majority (double primary) elections because our attention has been diverted from a critical inspection of the Democratic party and the two party system. Is the problem that majorities are required or that the Democratic party encourages white supremacy within the South as the two party system discourages multi-racial coalitions nationally?

Perhaps the issue ought to be broadened. Through a variety of measures such as the poll tax and the literacy test and through violent intimidation, such as lynching, blacks had been effectively disenfranchised at least until the Voting Rights Act of 1965. *Yet one partyism and white supremacy remain dominant features of the two party system.* Rule changes are of critical importance; but there is reason to believe that majority elections may be one way to subvert and destroy one partyism and white supremacy. Rather than pushing for the elimination of run-off elections, however, the reverse strategy may be effective. Together with pointing out the limitations of the two party system, namely that it encourages racial/gender systems and often leads to one partyism, supporters of the Rainbow Coalition who seek to see more women, blacks and progressives in Congress might argue for the abolishment of the electoral college, single member districts and in support of proportional representation at the municipal and state levels. With regard to plurality elections and double primaries, it may be more fruitful to suggest that as long as majority elections are required in primary elections *they ought to be required in general elections.* If majority elections were required at the level of general elections, the prospects of developing Rainbow Communities and political muscle in the guise of progressive parties or in southern Democratic state parties abandoned by whites would be enhanced.

* * *

Too often we implicitly suggest that our social ills are like the separate parts of a machine, that each can be located, identified, and removed without appreciating their interconnection with other parts. As though there were no political structure blocking movements necessary to support radical ideas, public ownership has been demanded, militarism has been attacked as gender based, and calls for black nationalism have been issued for more than a hundred years. Yet, however critically we may move within our political institution we are held back by the limitations of those institutions and we are captured by them unless the institutions themselves become the object of our criticism. The politicization of the rules which govern electoral competition may be valuable primarily in that it broadens our understanding of the centerpiece of the party system and our democratic order. Broader understandings alter our expectations, clarify how institutional designs impact upon political work, allow us to envision alternative institutions, and help us as citizens to revise our political commitments. But as most activists know, revised political commitment is more apt to invite repression than it is to lead to progressive change.

Our political work may have the greatest impact if two objectives are fulfilled. The first objective is to expose antagonisms that may be embedded in our most cherished political concepts or ideals. By doing this we are engaging in internal critiques or critiques which rest on the norms and standards of the system itself. The second objective is to insure that elites understand the reality and possibility of a general legitimation crisis, that movement politics provides an alternative source of dignity for marginal constituencies, and that we, as individuals no longer need to accept their system as our own once space is created for us as citizen subjects. By virtue of fulfilling the first objective, activists will have taken a step toward fulfilling the second. But questioning the system's legitimacy is best accomplished when the mode of questioning itself is "illegitimate," that is, when it violates the law. In other words, political ends and political processes essential to them are one and the same, a relation. The protection of our understanding of freedom (property rights, conquest, and control, etc.) requires the kinds of electoral processes we know as the two party system. *We can only hope to achieve real political ends through processes essential to them.* We can only hope to reach a place where competing experiences and critical thought are valued by publicly practicing the politics we seek. Such practice, while possible in isolated private groups, is not publicly possible; no institutions exist to support it. Our choice is to withdraw, which elites count on, or to challenge the current public political practices by means of civil disobedience. Piven and Cloward in *Poor People's Movements*, by pointing out that the gains of the 1930s and 1960s were due not to formal organizations but to *mass defiance*, suggest that the latter option is more effective.

The electoral process is tailor-made for activists who wish to engage in revolutionary bargaining. It is among the most cherished of all public processes and it is filled with antagonisms. Moreover, it is the lynchpin of our system's legitimacy. One must constantly recall Madison's claim (in *Federalist No. 10*) that the great problem to be solved was to "secure...private rights against the danger of...faction, and at the same time...the spirit and form of popular government." The stability and durability of private rights turns on mass acceptance of the rules of the game. But we have seen that it has become increasingly difficult to preserve our form of popular government and private property rights. So difficult, in fact, that Trilateralists have admitted to the necessity of inducing or coercing "some measure of apathy and non-involvement on the part of some individuals and groups." *To participate all the more boldly and in a fashion that encourages the critical thinking on the part of some individuals and groups is our most effective bargaining chip.* An example is in order.

Consider voter registration. Introduced in larger cities during the late 19th century, voter registration was used to "control the possibly dangerous or subversive potential of mass urban electorates...."[29] Along with the poll tax, literacy tests, municipal reform, civil service requirements, and property tests it reflected the vision of reformers that highly individuated de-personalized parties could provide efficient (for business) public services and infrastructure in urban areas. The protests of blacks, immigrants, and workers which had been bubbling to the surface in party politics throughout the 19th century had to cease. Consequently, effective barriers to the political participation of these constituencies were erected. It may behoove us to consider voter registration in this light and not simply as a nuisance with which we must comply year after year.

Although the most obvious barriers have been removed, the less obvious ones remain. In this sense registration is rather insidious. Studies reveal that registration, as it fails to curb fraudulent voting, obstructs voter participation, in some instances explaining as much as one third of the decline in voter turnout when it fell precipitously during the first two decades of this century.[30] In the 1980 presidential election, 47 percent of eligible voters or 76.5 million people refused to participate. Recognizing that registration is an effective barrier and that mass protest movements can play a catalytic role in the context of progressive social change, Piven and Cloward have begun mobilizing the tens of thousands of social service professionals (Human Service Employees Registration and Voter Education or Human SERVE) in a campaign to register the "millions of unregistered clients of the welfare state." Piven and Cloward hope to "increase the electoral participation of people at the bottom, and to politicize the terms of their participation....Mass registration through the welfare state will provoke furious opposition by the parties, by their key constituencies, and by the business community."[31]

The objectives of Piven and Cloward seem to be right on target. Their emphasis on provoking a certain "level of conflict" as a necessary condition of change and of disrupting the Democratic party in order to transform it is a penetrating and candid assessment that seems to grasp the reality of our political history. But cooperation with registration reform permits the creation of another set of obstacles. For example, registrars often use their "discretion" to refuse to deputize volunteer assistant registrars despite their legal authorization to do so. Registration by postcard is often impeded when such specialized cards are not distributed. In Michigan, where labor is well organized, voter registration is the domain of the city clerks, who, as Blair Clark points out, "often close down the process arbitrarily just when political interest is at its peak."[32] These reforms run into these kinds of problems because registration itself is not the problem. The analysis and activism of Piven and Cloward fail to make the most central fact clear: our form of democracy only works when certain constituencies do not vote. Or to put it another way *our democracy works only when there is no democracy.* That's the contradiction. Voter registration is a method of disenfranchising the politically alienated. As responsible citizens, should we be organizing registration drives or exposing the contradiction of which registration is an essential part?

How might we make this contradiction clear or as Martin Luther King, Jr. might say, how might we make the invisible visible? The answer, I believe, may lie in the recognition that we are experiencing a legitimation crisis. Because we tend to identify with our institutions and because we tend to believe that our institutions are part of the solution to our problems, this crisis has provided space for the New Right to restore "traditional America." But simmering below this conscious re-affirmation of traditional America lies disaffection, a disaffection which Burnham describes as political alienation:

> Convinced that both party organizations are hopelessly corrupt and out of reach of popular control, a minority which is large enough to hold the balance of power between Republicans and Democrats tends rather consistently to vote for the lesser, or lesser known, of the two evils....A Great many American voters...are quite intelligent enough to perceive the deep contradiction which exists between the ideals of rhetorical democracy as preached in school and on the stump, and the actual day-to-day reality as that reality intrudes on his own milieu. Alienation arises from perception of that contradiction, and from the consequent feelings of individual political futility arising when the voter confronts an organization of politics which seems unable to produce minimally gratifying results. The concentration of socially deprived characteristics among the more than forty million adult Americans who today are altogether outside the voting universe suggests active alienation...on a scale quite unknown anywhere else in the Western world.

The question, therefore, becomes how can we make that alienation conscious and focused? How can we draw to the surface and make clear what the two party system inhibits and represses? Following Piven and Cloward's lead, we ought to synthesize movement and electoral politics through defiant mass protest. The process I shall describe shall be called *Freedom Voting.*

Much like the Freedom Rides of the 1960s which challenged the legitimacy of specific laws, Freedom Voting is a direct challenge of the legitimacy of personal registration requirements. Whereas registration campaigns are concerned with enfranchising the disenfranchised, Freedom Voting is concerned first with reasons for their disaffection and alienation. Whereas registration campaigns respect laws safeguarding voter registration, Freedom Voting would defiantly call them into question and demand their alteration or abolishment. The process would consist of the mobilization of "the people at the bottom" (the same citizens Piven and Cloward would hope to register) for the purpose of voting *without first having registered to vote*. The process would also be initiated in the context of presidential primaries so that 1) the action could be linked to a progressive party coalition (such as the Rainbow Coalition) and candidate (such as Jesse Jackson); 2) the issue could be politicized in several states over a prolonged period; 3) others would be encouraged to participate as the process was repeated and momentum built; and 4) the presidential candidates, and citizens generally, would be compelled to come to grips with the bias internal to our electoral process.

It would be important for the participants, and especially candidates that headed the movement, to clarify the reasons behind the action. Points similar to the following could be made:

1. The United States is alone in placing the onus of registering on the individual citizen. All other developed countries produce voting lists and do not leave it to the individual to register as elector.

2. Our system of voter registration does not prevent voter fraud. If fraud is the reason for voter registration we would do well to follow the example of other countries. Accurate registers are considered so important in Canada, for example, that the length of Canadian election campaigns is determined by the time deemed necessary to enroll the electorate.

3. While foreign systems differ from one another greatly, they all share a vital willingness to accept responsibility to initiate voter registration, usually register 90 to 99 percent of the voting-age population and have fairly high voter participation rates.

4. Several nations, such as Austrailia, have compulsory registration. It is similar to our own compulsory *military* registration for males 18 years of age. The point here is to illustrate how as a nation we are capable of accepting compulsory registration and that our government is capable of administering such a program.[33]

The repeated (within the context of a presidential primary) arrest of thousands of the poorest citizens attempting to vote would make crystal clear for the world to see what normally goes unseen and that is that the government of the United States *does not permit the enfranchisement of all its citizens* or, as Walter Dean Burnham argues, "the American political system is...significantly less democratic today then is any other Western political system which conducts free elections."[34] Hopefully the national self-awareness that actions of this sort might help to generate would channel the political alienation of so many citizens into the creation of richer democratic institutions. The international impact of such actions might create a political climate in this country parallel to the situation of the early 1950s. Then, the obvious repression of blacks in the context of scornful indictments of the Soviet system exposed the double standard that contributed to

Brown vs. the Board of Education. Perhaps registration laws would be revised, at a minimum, to compare with those of Europe.

*   *   *

What we need is more sense of the wonder of life and less of
this business of making a picture.

—Robert Henri

Robert Henri's understanding of the art spirit is applicable to politics. Freedom Voting or other direct actions intended to challenge the legitimacy of the rules governing the party system are needed. And to be sure, they may provide the disenfranchised with a degree of bargaining power which they would not have had by playing by the rules. But this is a bonus really. We engage in political struggle because it enriches our lives, because it is fulfilling.

The great artist Titian as he lay dying at the age of 99 is suppose to have said, "I am just beginning to get the idea." While in his 80s, the American artist Robert Brackman, after having been told that someone saw more color in his work, stated simply that he was beginning to see more color. Beethoven rewrote certain passages of his 9th symphony some 200 times. The struggle internal to art differs from the creative struggle in politics primarily because each is structured differently. But structures are social conventions; the structure differs because we permit it to differ. We need to recognize that politics, like art, can be a self-creative experience in which self-discipline and passion embrace.

We seem to oscillate between two empty conceptions of politics. In each conception, there is primarily a means to some perceived worthy goal. One is the Liberal conception, where politics is an instrument to preserve and protect property relations, and opportunities for rationalized conquest. The other is a radical conception of politics often associated with the socialist ideal. It too is a means, a means to reach the good society where the opacity, division, indirectness and cross-purposes of social life are overcome.[35] Each conception leads to political alienation. Rationalized conquest destroys people and other living things. And on the other hand, the opacity, division, indirectness and cross-purposes of social life may be dealt with more sanely and humanely, but they cannot be overcome. Given these two conceptions, politics seemingly leads to either self-destruction or burnout.

The struggle to challenge the party system has very specific goals. But if we look for results, let that looking not be our only motivation. If we hope to win elections, let us remember that we are engaged in politics because to express an idea, or to reflect upon oneself, or to think honestly and publicly is in itself worthwhile and satisfying.

A poet friend of mind once said to me, "I believe it was Neitzsche who said 'Life without music would be a....'" And he stopped short, imploring me to complete the sentence.

I said, "Let's see. Life without music would be....something terrible...a void, a prison, a nightmare....I don't know."

Smiling whimsically, the poet knew he had gotten the best of me. I was conceptually off track. The categories I had thought of simply meant "bad." Neitzsche's understanding of music, and one must presume other forms of self-creative expression, was unavailable to me. Having seen that I was lost my friend permitted me to share Neitzsche's insight: "Life without music would be a *mistake*."

Politics as a life giving experience is also a form of self-creative expression. We ought to be furious over its betrayal. To call the two party system the maker of democratic government is as odd as if the prohibition of music were to be called art.

FOOTNOTES

Footnotes Chapter 1

1. Cited by William Chambers and Walter Dean Burnham, *The American Party System* (New York: Oxford University Press), p. 50fn.

2. Thomas Ferguson, "Strategies for A New Economy," *The Nation*, August 6-13, p. 109.

3. Whether one is considered an adult at 18 years of age or older, until 1920 only a minority of adult citizens were permitted to vote, given the disfranchisement of women and minorities. Since 1920, barriers to voting such as registration combined with high levels of political alienation have generated low participation rates, thus insuring that presidents are elected by a minority of the nation's adult citizens.

4. V.O. Key, Jr., *Politics, Parties, & Pressure Groups*, Fifth Edition (New York: Thomas Y. Crowell Company, 1964), p. 203.

5. Waltern Dean Burnham, *The Current Crisis in American Politics* (New York: Oxford University Press, 1982), p. 17.

6. Barbara Epstein, *The Politics of Domesticity* (Middletown, Connecticut: Wesleyan University Press, 1981), pp. 22, 37.

7. See Alice Cook and Gwyn Kirk, *Greenham Women Everywhere* (Boston: South End Press, 1983).

8. Hannah Josephson, *The Golden Threads* (New York: Duell, Sloan and Pearce, 1949), p. 231.

9. Howard Zinn, *A People's History of the United States* (New York: Harper Colophon Books, 1980), p. 116.

10. Philip S. Foner, *We, the Other People* (Chicago: University of Illinois Press, 1976), p. 77, 105.

11. *New Left Notes*, 27 June 1967, cited by Sara Evans, *Personal Politics* (New York: Vintage Books, 1980), pp. 190, 191.

12. Aileen S. Kraditor, *The Ideas of the Woman Suffrage Movement 1890-1920* (New York: Doubleday & Company, Inc.,1971), p. 187

13. This is not to say that party issues are not cast in moral terms. The most effective elimination of serious political economic opposition has been drenched in the morality of "anti-communism."

14. "Single women head more than half of the country's poor families, and two out of every three adults below the poverty line are women. Those women lucky enough to have full-time jobs make, on the average, 59 cents for every $1 earned by a man; the unemployment rate for women in December 1982 was 10.3 percent, the highest since the end of World War II. For black women, the rate was 18.6 percent." See "What Women Want," *The Nation*, May 28, 1983, p. 658. For an

217

analysis of the role of suffragists during the Red Scare, see Alan P. Grimes, *The Puritan Ethic and Woman Suffrage* (New York: Oxford University Press, 1967).

15. Andrew Kopkind and Alexander Cockburn, "The Left, The Democrats & the Future," *The Nation*, July 21-28, p. 42; for an analysis

17. See Robert L. Allen, *Reluctant Reformers* (New York: Anchor Books, 1975), pp. 148, 149.

18. Aileen S. Kraditor, "The Liberty and Free Soil Parties" in Arthur M. Schlesinger, Jr., ed., *History of the United States Political Parties* (4 vols.; New York: Chelsea House Publisher, 1973), Vol. I, pp. 741, 746.

19. Wilfred E. Binkley, *American Political Parties* (New York: Alfred A. Knopf, 1943), p. 183.

20. Cited by Kraditor in Schlesinger, Jr., p. 751.

21. Federick J. Blue, *The Free Soilers* (Urbana, Illinois: University of Illinois Press, 1973), p. 4.

22. From Madison's point of view the weakening of property rights was "incompatible with personal security" and adverse to the "aggregate interests of the community."

23. It should be pointed out that several historians, including W.E.B. DuBois, have argued that the first Emancipation Proclamation of 1863 was not the result of the party system rewarding the work of abolitionists but rather part of the Union's military strategy to enlist the massive number of slaves that were aiding the federal army as soldiers (150,000) and laborers (several hundred thousand). Allen, *Reformers*, pp. 31, 182.

24. Throughout this study the Rainbow Coalition is viewed favorably. The anti-semitism expressed by some of its leaders, however, was disquieting. Jesse Jackson's apology, in this regard was a refreshing and positive act.

25. Cited by Rachel Gorlin, "Backing Mondale inspired some, divided others," *In These Times*, June 13-26, p. 11.

26. Samuel Eliot Morison, *The Oxford History of the American People* (Vol. III; New York: Mentor, 1972), p. 38.

27. See the 1983 census report, "America's Black Population: 1970 to 1982" and the National Urban League report of 1978.

28. Harvard Sitkof, *A New Deal For Blacks* (Oxford University Press, 1978), p. 20.

29. Manning Marable, *How Capitalism Underdeveloped Black America* (Boston: South End Press, 1983), pp. 180-193.

30. In addition to the eruption of extremely volatile political economic issues, the proliferation of so many minor parties prior to the Civil War may have been due to the fact that the structure of the party system was still in the process of being established. Single-member districts, which political scientists claim help limit the number of

major parties to two, were not established until the mid-1840s. Other regulations which limit multi-party activity, such as the state regulation of printing and distributing ballots, also were not yet in evidence.

31. The broad coalition of minor parties including the Barnburners and Libertymen formed the Free Soil Party in 1848 which became the Free Democratic party when the Whigs assumed national office. During the early 1850s, as the Whig party broke apart, a number of factions together with the Know Nothing's, a nativist party, formed the Republicans.

32. Philip Foner, *Labor Movement in the United States, Vol. 1*, (New York: International Publishers, 1975), p. 233.

33. Cited by Norman Ware *The Industrial Worker: 1840-1860* (Chicago: Quadrangle Books, 1964), p. 215.

34. Zinn, p. 233.

35. Lawrence Goodwyn, *The Populist Moment* (New York: Oxford University Press, 1978), p. 4.

36. Philip S. Foner, *History of the Labor Movement in the United States* (4 vols.; New York: International Publishers, 1975), II, p. 331.

37. Key, p. 259; Lawrence Goodwyn, "Organizing Democray: the limits of Theory and Practice," *Democracy*, January 1981, pp. 56-57.

38. Mike Davis, "Why the US Working Class is Different," *New Left Review*, Sept-Oct 1980, No. 123, p. 5.

39. Edward S. Greenberg, *Serving the Few* (New York: John Wiley & Sons, Inc., 1974), p. 125.

40. Gabriel Kolko, *Main Currents in Modern American History* (New York: Harper & Row, 1976), p. 131-137.

41. For a discussion of the failure of minimum wage legislation, see Kolko, p. 326.

42. David Milton, *The Politics of U.S. Labor* (New York: Monthly Review Press, 1982), pp. 12, 15.

43. Goodwyn, "The Current Crisis," p. 56.

44. The percentage of the total U.S. workforce that is organized has dropped from roughly 30 percent after WW II to about 20 percent today.

45. Thomas Ferguson and Joel Rogers, "The Reagan Victory," in *The Hidden Election* (New York: Random House, 1981), ed. by Ferguson and Rogers, pp. 21-24; see Andrew Kopkind and Alexander Cockburn, "The Left, the Democrats & the Future," *The Nation*, July 21-28, 1984 for the data cited.

46. Vincent Harding, *There Is a River* (New York: Vintage Books, 1981), p. xix.

47. Jean Caini, Public Speech, Northampton MA.

48. Charles Taylor, "Interpretation and The Sciences of Man," *Review of Metaphysics*, Spring 1971, pp. 4-51.

49. Sara Evans, *Personal Politics* (New York: Vintage Books, 1980), pp. 134, 206.

50. Frances Fox Piven and Richard A. Cloward, *Poor People's Movements* (New York:Vintage Books, 1977), p. 36.

51. Davis, "The Barren Marriage," p. 82.

52. Evans, pp. 171, 172, 224.

53. Jeremy Brecher, *Strike* (Boston:South End Press, 1972), p. 15.

54. See Joan Cocks, "Wordless Emotions: Some Critical Reflections on Radical Feminism," *Politics and Society*, Vol. 13, No. 1, 1984, p. 33.

Footnotes Chapter 2

1. "'Industrial Policy'—Now The Bad News," *The Nation*, June 4, 1983, p. 687.

2. Cited by Sara Evans *Personal Politics* (New York: Vintage Books, 1980), p. 5.

3. Michael Polanyi has called this tacit dimension the "...propositions and opinions shared by a group and so obvious to it that they are never fully or systematically articulated." Cited in *The Passions and the Interests* by Albert O. Hirschman, (Princeton, NJ: Princeton University Press, 1977) p. 69.

4. Robert Henri, *The Art Spirit* (New York: J.B. Lippincott Co., 1923), p. 15; references to gender have been amended.

5. R.H.Tawney, *Religion and the Rise of Capitalism*, (New York: Harcourt, Brace and World, Inc., 1954), pp. 27-28.

6. Cited in Tawney, p.29.

7. Tawney, pp.30-35.

8. Cited in Tawney, p.68.

9. This characterization of the shift of ideas is drawn from a similar characterization by Tawney, p. 19.

10. See Charles Taylor's interpretation of the development of the "modern subject" in Chapter 1 of *Hegel* (London: Cambridge University Press, 1975).

11. In fact, as Robert Higgins has pointed out, the early modern state, whether "absolutist" as in France or "republican" as in England, was a target of Liberal/market proponents just because it embraced mercantile policies (i.e., it heavily regulated the emerging bourgeoisie). These regulations were, in part, created to raise revenues for the (mostly military) costs of uniting and defending the "nation." It should also be pointed out that as the state became the source of social authority and trade the center of public life, production was separated from the home and made part of public life as well. Therefore, as the importance of religion was push into private life so was the role of women. Public authority, both political and economic, became essentially white male authority.

12. Cited by Jurgen Habermas, *Theory and Practice* (Boston: Beacon Press, 1974), Translated by John Viertel, p. 61.

13. Joan Cocks, "Wordless Emotions: Some Critical Reflections on Radical Feminism," *Politics and Society*, Vol. 13 No. 1, pp. 40, 41.

14. The Age of Faith seems to be a part of the Age of Reason still.

15. We shall come back to the question of discrimination in Chapter 4; see Christine DiStefano, "Legitimation Crisis Reconsidered: Women, Personal Identity, and the State." Graduate seminar paper, University of Massachusetts, Amherst, 1979. p. 52; Carol Gilligan, "In a Different Voice: women's conceptions of the Self and Morality," *Harvard Education Review* 47 (1977), p. 484.

16. Albert O. Hirschman, *The Passions and the Interests* (New Jersey: Princeton University Press, 1977) This theme is located by Hirschman in the writings of numerous modern thinkers. Many of our contemporary problems may be due less to the intentions of the "ruling class" than to the unintended consequences of the kind of reasoning that we all share to some degree.

17. Hirschman, p. 41, 48-56.

18. Helvetius and the Duke of Rohan cited in Hirschman, p. 43 and p. 34 respectively. Ruckelshaus cited in *The Morning Union* Springfield, MA., June 23, 1983, p. 5.

19. Simone de Beauvoir, *The Second Sex*. Translated by H.M. Parshley. (New York: Bantam Books, 1968).

20. Dorothy Dinnerstein, *The Mermaid and the Minotaur* (New York: Harper Colophon, 1976), p. 179.

21. See DiStefano, 1979.

22. Cited in DiStefano, DiStephano's characterization, p. 35.

23. Ulrike Prokop, cited in DiStefano.

24. Cocks, p. 44.

25. Robert Higgins, *Legitimacy in American Politics* (Amherst: unpublished dissertation, University of Massachusetts, 1982), p. 189, 194.

26. Winthrop Jordan, *White Over Black* (Durham, N.C.: University of North Carolina Press, 1968), p. 38. Cited in Higgins, p. 200.

27. Higgins, p. 201.

28. George Rawick, *The American Slave* (Westport, Con.: Greenwood Press, 1972), p. 133. Cited in Higgins, p. 202.

29. Higgins, pp. 213, 214. Max Weber, *The Protestant Ethic* (New York: Charles Scribner's Sons, 1958), pp. 158-159.

30. George Frederickson, *The Black Image in the White Mind* (New York: Harper and Row, 1971), p. 49. Cited in Higgins, p. 229. The other information was drawn from Eugene Berwanger, *The Frontier Against Slavery* (Chicago: University of Illinois Press, 1967), Chapters Two, Six. Cited in Higgins, pp. 230, 231.

31. Cited by Howard Zinn, *A People's History of the United States* (New York: Harper Colophon Books, 1980), p. 195.

32. Jacquelyn Dowd Hall, *Revolt Against Chivalry* (New York: Columbia University Press, 1979), pp. 146, 147; Higgins, pp. 231-238; also see Forrest Wood, *Black Scare* (Los Angeles: University of California Press, 1968.

33. John Locke in 1697.

34. Charles Schultze, *The Public Use of Private Interest* (Washington, D.C.: The Brookings Institution, 1977), pp. 16-18.

35. See Cocks, p. 42.

36. Kenneth M. Dolbeare, *American Public Policy* (New York: McGraw Hill, 1982), p. 75.

37. James O'Connor, *The Corporations and the State* (New York: St Martins' Press, 1974), p. 6.

38. Bryan Magee, *Men of Ideas* (New York: Oxford University Press, 1982), p. 3.

Footnotes Chapter 3

1. See George Novack, *America's Revolutionary Heritage* (New York: Pathfinder Press, 1976), p. 117.

2. Margit Mayer and Margaret A. "The Formation of the American Nation-State," *Kapitalistate*, No. 6, Fall 1977, pp. 57, 58.

3. The Constitution, therefore, was intended to block such political thrusts as Shays' Rebellion. Often, it seems, we are told the reverse, that the Constitution was intended to help indebted farmers like Daniel Shays.

4. Notice how freedom, individualism, and equality merge here. The assumption is that one is free and equal as long as one can enter into contracts voluntarily and receive equal protection under the law; the substantive inequality or the impoverished sense of community that may result from such arrangements merits no consideration.

5. Mayer and Fay, pp. 61, 12.

6. Mayer and Fay, p. 62.

7. Cited by Philip S. Foner, *History of the Labor Movement in the United States* (New York: International Publishers, 1975), Vol. 1, pp. 88-89.

8. Howard Zinn, *A People's History of the United States* (New York: Harper & Row, 1980), p. 99.

9. These Virginian planters, led by Madison and Jefferson, had first organized opposition to the policies of Federalist in the House of Representatives. The presidencies of Jefferson, Madison, and Monroe (from 1801 to 1825) are known as the Virginia dynasty.

10. Philip Foner, Vol. 1, pp. 84, 85; V. O. Key, Jr. , *Politics, Parties, & Pressure Groups* (New York: Thomas Y. Crowell Company, 1964), p.

202; Wilfred E. Binkley, *American Political Parties* (New York: Alfred A. Knopf, 1943), p. 51.

11. Claude G. Bowers, *Jefferson and Hamilton* (Boston: Houghton Mifflin Company, 1953), p. 67.

12. The federal excise tax was eventually repealed while Jefferson was president in 1802; Leland D. Baldwin, *Whiskey Rebels* (Pittsburgh: University of Pittsburgh Press, 1939), pp. 61, 64, 86, 221, 264.

13. Samuel Eliot Morrison, *The Oxford History of the American People* (New York: Mentor, 1964), Vol. II, p. 79.

14. Thomas Ferguson and Joel Rogers, "The Reagan Victory," in *The Hidden Election* (New York: Pantheon, 1981) which they edited, p. 7.

15. The acts did, however, give American manufacturers a monopoly of American markets; Joseph Charles, *The Origin of The Party System* (New York: Harper & Row, 1956), p. 24.

16. Samuel Bowles and Herbert Gintis, *Schooling in Capitalist America* (New York: Basic Books, 1976), p. 157; Charles, p. 24.

17. Binkley, p. 104.

18. It is unfortunate that party elites today are not as candid. That government encouragement of property relations or what we call freedom is not a neutral process is an important point that needs to be thoroughly discussed publicly.

19. Mayer and Fay, pp. 45, 46

20. Novack, p. 164.

21. Louis M. Hacker, *The Triumph of American Capitalism* (New York: Van Nostrand and Reinhold Co. , 1946), p. 305.

22. Hacker, pp. 301-306.

23. Hannah Josephson, *The Golden Threads* (New York: Russell and Russell, 1949), p. 104.

24. Michael Holt, "The Democratic Party: 1828-1860" in Arthur M. Schlesinger, Jr. , *History of United States Political Parties* (4 vols. ; New York: Chelsea House Publisher, 1973), Vol. I, p. 515.

25. It was in this context that freedom vis-a-vis slavery acquired its meaning. Again we see the meaning of freedom: individual freedom from the state to engage in trade and production for profit.

26. Holt, p. 531; Binkley, pp. 197, 213.

27. Holt, p. 527.

28. Kinley J. Brauer, *Cotton Versus Conscience* (Lexington, KY: University of Kentucky Press, 1967), p. 50.

29. Binkley, p. 223.

30. Foner, p. 283; thus we can see that even during the earliest days of *laissez faire*), the role of the state at all levels was quite active.

31. See Foner, Vol. 1, Ch.10.

32. It is important to understand that most key party leaders opposed to the expansion of the slave system were not opposed to slavery as such.

33. Norman Ware, The Industrial Worker: 1840-1860 (Chicago: Quadrangle Books, 1964), p. 201; Foner, Vol. 1, pp. 192, 245.

34. I am referring to the Missouri Compromise which divided the Louisiana Purchase territory at the latitudinal line of 36 degrees 30 minutes. North of this compromise line was closed to slavery with the exception of Missouri, which was admitted to the Union as a slave state (while Maine was admitted as a free state). Thomas Jefferson felt that the controversy was "more ominous than any that had confronted the American people from the battle of Bunker Hill to the Treaty of Paris. " Glover Moore, *The Missouri Controversy: 1819-1821* (Gloucester, MA: Peter Smith Publishers, 1953), pp. 253-254.

35. Indeed, as political positions hardened, parties, for the first time began to adopt "lists of resolutions" or platforms.

36. Douglass C. North, *The Economic Growth of the United states: 1790-1860* (New York: Prentice Hall, 1961), pp. 192-197.

37. North, p. 196.

38. Also increasing the marketing of food from the Northwest to the East and to the Old World was the repeal of the British Corn Laws, the Crimean war and the Irish famine in the latter part of the 1840's; North, p. 141.

39. Michael F. Holt, "The Antimasonic and Know Nothings," in Schlesinger, Jr. , I, p. 598.

40. The ratio of cotton to slave prices (expressed in cents per pound of cotton to hundreds of dollars for the average slave) was 4 to 1 in 1805, 1 to 1 in 1837, and on its way to becoming . 6 to 1 by 1860; Louis M. Hacker, *American Capitalism* (New Jersey: D. Van Nostrand Co. , Inc. , 1957), p. 48.

41. Binkley, p. 213.

42. Wright was an abolitionist and a champion of woman's rights who also believed in the elimination of clerical influence in education. She founded experimental communes and is credited with being the ideological parent of the Workingmen's party.

43. Robert Allen, *Reluctant Reformers* (New York: Anchor Press, 1975), p. 44.

44. See Ware, p. 189; the ten hour movement was contributed to by the militancy of "factory girls," some of whom earned $2. 50 for a 72 hour week. Foner, Vol. 1, p. 207.

45. Eric Foner, *Politics and Ideology in the Age of the Civil War* (New York: Oxford University Press, 1980), p. 70; P. Foner, Vol. I, p. 207.

46. Many elites and workers understood that most urban workers neither possessed the skills nor the money to move west.

47. Cited by Zinn, p. 276.

48. Richard Hofstader, *The Age of Reform* (New York: Vintage Books, 1955), p. 55.

49. Philip Foner, Vol. I, p. 286.

50. Foner, Vol. 1, p. 247.

51. Binkley, p. 213.

52. David Gordon, Richard Edwards and Michael Reich *Segmented Work, Divided Worker* (New York: Cambridge University Press, forthcoming), mss. p. 68; Gabriel Kolko, *Main currents in Modern American History* (New York: Harper & Row, 1976), p. 2.

53. Gordon, et al, p. 75.

54. Kolko, p. 8; it is worth noting that regulation and government intervention into the economy came at the behest of capitalists alarmed by the unfettered conditions of free enterprise.

55. Brownlee, p. 294.

56. Brownlee, pp. 294-295.

57. In part, this was contributed to by a severe drought; James Sundquist, *Dynamics of the Party System) (Washington, D. C. : The Brookings Institution, 1973) p. 114; Lawrence Goodwyn, The Populist Moment* (New York: Oxford University Press, 1978), pp. 22, 23.

58. For an analysis of the economic constraints imposed by 19th century monopolies, see Karl Marx, *Capital III), p. 1003; cited by Paul M. Sweezy, The Theory of Capitalist Development* (New York: Monthly Review Press, 1970), p. 272.

59. Roughly a third of black women worked outside the home.

60. Commons cited in Jeremy Brecher, *Strike* (Boston: South end Press, 1972), pp. 25, 26; the work of Herbert Aptheker cited by Zinn, p. 204; for a detailed explanation of how blacks and whites were locked into a cycle of poverty via the sharecropping system, see William H. Harris, *The Harder We Run* (New York: Oxford University Press, 1982), pp. 10-13.

61. Carl N. Degler, "The Nineteenth Century," in William H. Nelson, ed. , *Theory and Practice in American Politics* (Chicago: University of Chicago Press, 1964), p. 35.

62. Goodwyn, p. 236.

63. Allen, pp. 51-85.

64. Several states and territories had adopted school and wider forms of suffrage before then. See Aileen S. Kraditor, *The Ideas of the Woman Suffrage Movement 1890-1920* (New York: Anchor Books, 1965), p. 3.

65. Brownlee, pp. 350-352.

66. Degler, p. 37.

67. Sundquist, p. 117.

68. Leon Friedman, "The Democratic Party," in Schlesinger, Vol. II, pp. 903, 904.

69. William A. Williams, *The Roots of the Modern American Empire* (New York: Random House, 1969), pp. 166-169.

70. Goodwyn, p. 4.

71. New Orleans, 1892; the Homestead Strike, 1892; the Coal Creek Rebellion, Coure d'Alene, 1892, the Great Northern Strike, the Pullman Strike; see Jeremy Brecher, *Strike* (Boston: South End Press, 1972)

72. Binkley, p. 317; P. Foner, Vol. II, p. 339-341.

73. Commission to Central and South America, 1884, cited by Williams, p. 284.

74. Brownlee, p. 352; Kolko, pp. 37, 38.

75. Goodwyn, p. 217.

76. Goodwyn, p. 218.

77. See Richard Hofstadter, *The Age of Reform) (New York: Vintage Books, 1955), pp. 49-50.*

78. Allen, p. 81.

79. If there were a proportional representation or majority elections ideologically distinct parties would fare better. We shall come back to this discussion in Chapter 7.

80. Senator William M. Stewart of Nevada ($40,000,000); Senator John P. Jones of Nevada (Comstock Lode, $25,000,000); the Hearst interests in California ($75,000,000); and Charles E. Lane of California ($20,000,000).

81. Leaders of the fusionist wing were Senators William Allen and Mario Butler, James Weaver and Jerry Simpson. Those responsible for purging labor included Herman E. Taubeneck, A. J. Warner, and Senator William A. Peffer of Kansas; Goodwin, p. 230; P. Foner, Vol. II, pp. 327-329.

82. Again, note the effect of winner take all single member districts.

83. Foner, Vol. II, pp. 327-329; see Kraditor, p. 187 and Allen, p. 73.

84. Kolko, p. 103.

85. Sundquist, p. 191.

86. Mike Davis, "The Barren Marriage of American Labour and the Democratic Party," *New Left Review*, No. 123, September 1980, fn. p. 48; Otis L. Graham, Jr., "The Democratic Party," in Schlesinger, Vol. II, p. 1943.

87. See Davis, p. 43.

88. Sundquist, p. 223.

89. See Edward S. Greenberg, *Serving the Few* (New York: John Wiley & Sons, Inc., 1974), p. 115.

90. See Greg Mitchell, "Upton Sinclair's EPIC Campaign," *The Nation*, August 4-11, 1984, pp. 75-78.

91. Sundquist, p. 200.

92. See George H. Mayer, "The Republican Party, 1932-1952" in Schlesinger, Vol. III, p. 2262.

93. Between 1918 and 1929, industrial production increased 50% while the factory workforce actually declined by 6%; Davis, p. 44.

94. Martin Sklar, "On the Proletarian Revolution and the End of Political-Economic Society," in *Radical America*, May-June 1969;

Trent Schroyer, *The Critique of Domination* (Boston: Beacon Press, 1973), p. 229.

95. Merele Fainsod and Lincoln Gordon, *Government and the American Economy* (New York: W. W. Norton & Co., 1941), p. 715; Sundquist, p. 188.

96. In 1930 Bernard Baruch had suggested that antitrust laws be modified so that "uneconomic competition" could be controlled by business itself, under government supervision. In 1931 the Committee on Continuity of Business and Employment of the Chamber of Commerce had put forward similar plans as had Gerard Swope, president of General Electric. Frances Fox Piven and Richard A. Cloward, *Poor People's Movements* (New York: Vintage Books, 1977), p. 111.

97. Kolko, pp. 119-119.

98. Fainsod and Gordon, p. 573.

99. Kolko, p. 129.

100. Greenberg, p. 111.

101. Greenberg, pp. 103-111.

102. Hoover had called the initial framework of the NIRA the "most gigantic proposal of monopoly ever made in history," and said that it would "drive the country toward the Fascism of which it was a pattern." See William Myers and Walter Newton, *The Hoover Administration* (New York, 1936), pp. 4, 119-120; cited in Kolko, p. 119.

103. Brownlee, p. 421; Kolko, p. 129; Fainsod and Gordon, pp. 586, 587.

104. Greenberg, p. 120.

105. Frances Fox Piven and Richard A. Cloward, *Poor People's Movements* (New York: Vintage Books, 1979), p. 87.

106. Sundquist's is a good example of this type of analysis; pp. 200-204.

107. Sundquist, pp. 200, 245, 246.

108. See Davis, p. 55 fn; Sundquist, p. 227.

109. See James Weinstein, *The Corporate Ideal in the Liberal State* (Boston: Beacon Press, 1968), pp. 180, 181, 208.

110. P. Foner, Vol. III, p. 61.

111. Note labor's very weak inclusion in the "Rainbow Coalition."

112. P. Foner, Vol. III, pp. 70-71.

113. Fainsod and Gordon, p. 575.

114. See Fainsod and Gordon, p. 574; Kolko, pp. 125-127.

115. Piven and Cloward, p. 117; Davis, p. 49; Kolko, p. 134.

116. An organization composed of the nation's twelve largest corporations was making their support contingent upon FDR avoiding such measures as the 30 hour week. See Richard O. Boyer and Herbert M. Morais, *Labor's Untold Story* (New York: UE, 1955), p. 281.

117. Piven and Cloward, p. 131.

118. Piven and Cloward, p. 133; for a discussion of labor's support of FDR against the Court as well as the influence of the left within labor, see Milton, pp. 73, 90, Ch. 6.

119. Lorin Lee Cary, "Institutionalized Conservatism in the Early CIO," *Labor History*, 12 (Fall, 1972), p. 494; cited by Davis, p. 51.

120. For a more positive interpretation of Lewis and his role in the New Deal, see Milton, pp. 73, 74, Ch. 4.

121. See Milton, p. 107 and the *Congressional Record* for documentation by the LaFollette Committee on Civil Liberties, 1936.

122. Davis, p. 54.

123. Walter Dean Burnham, *The Current Crisis in American Politics* (New York: Oxford University Press, 1982), p. 256.

124. Thomas Ferguson and Joel Rogers, *The Hidden Election* (New York: Pantheon, 1981), p. 8.

125. See James Sundquist, *Dynamics of the Party System* (Washington, D. C. : The Brookings Institution, 1983), p. 5.

126. Sundquist, p. 298.

127. Everett Carl Ladd, Jr. and Charles D. Hadley use the term "transformation," in part because they too see "critical realignments...as effects of other major changes occurring in the society." Their analysis, however, gets bogged down in an over emphasis on the impact of technology. Obscured are changing power relationships between different social classes; see *Transformations of the American Party System* (New York: W. W. Norton & Co. Inc., 1975).

128. "There shall be no discrimination on account of race, creed or color."

129. Davis, pp. 58, 60 ff, 63, 64.

Footnotes Chapter 4

1. "Critical Notes on the Article 'The King of Prussia and Social Reform,'" in Lucio Colletti (ed.), *Early Writings: Marx* (London: Penguin Books, 1975), pp. 411, 412.

2. Marx in Colletti, p. 412.

3. Marx in Colletti, p. 408.

4. This linkage is made implicitly by characterizing the Soviet Union as an "evil empire" and explicitly by such New Right gurus as George Gilder; see Gilder's *Wealth and Poverty* (New York: Basic Books, 1981).

5. Notice how an examination of property relations is deflected and an explanation of inequality is grounded in character defects.

6. Barbara Leslie Epstein, *The Politics of Domesticity* (Middletown, Connecticut: Wesleyan University Press, 1981), pp. 68-69.

7. John Kasson, *Civilizing The Machine* (New York: Penguin Books, 1980), pp. 18, 8.

8. As the Cherokees, Creeks, Choctaws, and Chickawas were being removed from the eastern half of the continent and as the northern half of Mexico was being taken, Ralph Waldo Emerson could conclude that "our whole history appears to be a last effort of Divine Providence on behalf of the human race." Walt Whitman argued that political and economic expansion generated "unparalleled human happiness and national freedom." Andrew Jackson, as slaveowner, called the acquisition of more territory for plantations "extending the sphere of freedom." And Thomas Hart Benton of Missouri, a Jacksonian Democrat, called the conquest of Asian markets the "highest pinnacle of wealth and power," a "symbol of freedom and of national greatness...." As William Williams illustrates, sentiments of this sort mark every phase of our history; see William Appleman Williams, *Empire As A Way Of Life* (New York: Oxford University Press, 1980), pp. 84-88. Frederick Jackson Turner's conception of the conquest of the western frontier is similar; it "promoted individualism, economic equality, freedom to rise, democracy." Cited by Alan P. Grimes, *The Puritan Ethic and Suffrage* (New York: Oxford University Press, 1967), p. 15.

9. This is Robert Higgins' term; see Chapter 2.

10. William Leiss, *The Domination of Nature* (New York: George Braziller, 1972), p. 57.

11. "Public schools, parks and gardens, art galleries and museums, Sunday schools and tract societies all represented attempts to extend the

sphere of...instruction; to counteract the turbulence and corruption of American life by...establishing monitors over it...the almshouse, orphanage, penitentiary, reformatory, and insane asylum all were erected and meticulously systematized to deal with the deviant and the dependent.... The order, supervision, industry, and temperance of institutional life, authorities believed, would counteract the chaotic and corrupting forces of the larger society and transform social victims into respectable citizens." (Kasson, pp. 63, 64.) It is ironic that this seems to be precisely the kind of trouble socialist societies get into when they are imbued with ideologies suggesting that the just society can be engineered.

12. Charles Foster, *An Errand of Mercy* (Chapel Hill, N.C.: University of North Carolina Press, 1960), p. 222.

13. George Frederikson, *The Black Image in the White Mind* (New York: Harper and Row, 1971), p. 4; typical was the attitude of John Pintard who found that the "scabby sheep" Irish who lived in "that sink of pollution" would have nothing to do with Protestant crusades; see Wyatt-Brown, *Lewis Tappan and the Evangelical War Against Slavery* (Cleveland: The Press of Case Western Reserve University, 1969), p. 63; Robert Higgins points out that the Irish, up until 1650, were not peasants of the European type: "they lived a way of life of which the English had no recent experience or understanding, and which appeared to the English as barbarian and savage.... Irish sexual and family practices encouraged the English sense of the Irish as an entirely different order, appearing, by evolving English standards as licentious. The Irish intermarried with relatives forbidden by English kinship rules, engaged in trial marriages, and allowed for easy divorce by man *or* woman. See Robert Higgins, *Legitimacy in American Politics* (Amherst: doctoral dissertation, University of Massachusetts, 1982), pp. 195, 224.

14. Kasson points out that work was a form of control and moral instruction. The movement for shorter hours meant only mischief, idleness at best, "at worst vicious amusements, drink, gambling, and riot." The Lawrence Company regulations stipulated that all employees "on all occasions, both in their words and in their actions show they are penetrated by a laudable love of temperance and virtue, and animated by a sense of their moral and social obligations." Kasson, p. 75.

15. Wilfred E. Binkley, *American Political Parties* (New York: Alfred A. Knopf, 1958). pp. 123, 124.

16. Note the contradiction: the industrial order which required the divorce of emotion from reason (in the context of work) also required the linkage of reason and emotion (in the context of politics).

17. For a discussion of the relationship between craft production and fraternalism, see Mary Ann Clawson, "Early Modern Fraternalism

and the Patriarchal Family," *Feminist Studies* (6, no. 2, Summer 1980), p. 371; "Fraternalism and Class Formation in Europe and the U.S., 1600-1900," Ph.D. dissertation, SUNY at Stony Brook, 1980, pp. 168-170, 153; an additional unpublished work of Clawson's that is useful in the exploration of the various forms of patriarchalism is "Fraternal Orders and Class Formation in the Nineteenth Century," August 1983.

18. Philip Foner, *Labor Movement in the United States, Vol. 1* (New York: International Press, 1975) p. 225.

19. What most worried evangelist-entrepreneur Lewis Tappan "was the alarming spread of 'wasteful and vicious habits,' as hundreds of rural men and women poured into the city to mingle with Irish immigrants, all looking for work and mostly finding crime, slums, whiskey, and poverty." Bertram Wyatt-Brown, p. 21.

20. Paul Kleppner, "The Greenback and Prohibition Parties," in Arthur M. Schlesinger, Jr., *The History of United States Political Parties* (4 vols., New York: Chelsea House Publisher, 1973), vol. 2, pp. 1567, 1568; Foner, vol. 1, p. 225.

21. Michael Holt, "The Antimasonic and Know Nothing Parties," Schlesinger, Jr., 1 p. 593; Mark L. Berger, *The Revolution in the New York Party Systems: 1840-1860* (London: Kennikat Press, 1973), pp. 15, 16, 53, 54. The term "Know Nothings" was due to the fact that the party had its origin in a secret fraternal order. The response of participants when asked about their activity was typically, "I know nothing."

22. Holt, p. 594.

23. Holt, p. 601.

24. For a discussion of reactive attitudes and critical thought see William E. Connolly, *The Appearance and Reality in Politics* (New York: Cambridge University Press, 1981), pp. 52, 53.

25. In several states Republicans formed alliances with Know Nothings. In Ohio, for example, Salmon P. Chase, once a Liberty organizer, was the Republican nominee for governor while the rest of the ticket was composed of Know Nothings. In New York, some Republicans worked to foster nativism as well as anti-Nebraska (Kansas-Nebraska Act) sentiment in order to create a loose coalition between the two forces. In some areas, the Republican name was dropped when it was offensive to Know Nothings. Many Republican state platforms contained Know Nothing planks. Republican National Chair Edwin D. Morgan recruited nativist speakers to campaign in Pennsylvania and New Jersey. James W. Barker, an organizer of the Order of the Star Spangled Banner, was pressured into joining the Republicans while the national platform contained terms which were well known Know Nothing rhetoric. See Holt, pp. 607, 616, 617; Berger, p. 131.

26. While between 1820 and 1860 the number of immigrants reached approximately 5,000,000, between 1860 and 1890 nearly 13,500,000 immigrants arrived.

27. Vincent Harding, *There Is a River* (New York: Vintage Books, 1983), p. 126.

28. In areas in which the Free Soil movement had widespread support, "Negro exclusionist" sentiments were strong. During the 1840's and 1850's efforts were made to prevent black immigration and to remove blacks who were already residing in midwestern states. In 1851, Indiana prevented all blacks from entering the state as did Illinois in 1853. Iowa passed an exclusionary law in 1851 and four states—Illinois, Indiana, Oregon, and Kansas—passed referenda (averaging 79.5 percent of the vote) excluding free blacks. The belief underlying these actions, it appears, was that the enfranchisement of blacks would encourage blacks to "marry our sisters and daughters, and smutty wenches to [marry] our brothers and sons." During this time period, Democrats and the fledgling Republicans "time and again used the issue of interracial marriage and sex to attack one another." Eugene Berwanger, *The Frontier Against Slavery* (Chicago: University of Chicago Press, 1967), pp. 36, 139, 140, cited by Higgins, p. 230; the last quote is Higgins'.

29. Harding, p. 155; Dudley O. McGoverney, *The American Suffrage Medley* (The University of Chicago Press, 1949) p. 17.

30. The Free Soil Party was a coalition of those factions in the late 1840's anxious to forge an expansionary program free of ties to the declining slave mode of production. Included in this coalition were the Liberty Party, Barnburners, and Conscience Whigs. See Chapter 3.

31. See Frederick J. Blue, *The Free Soilers* (Urbana, Ill.: University of Illinois Press, 1973), p. 87.

32. Harding, p. 265.

33. Higgins, pp. 233-234.

34. The Black Codes of 1865 were laws which restored white supremacy as southern states rejoined the union. Although they varied from state to state, several states imposed restrictions on land and property ownership or rental and/or restricted travel and employment opportunities, bound blacks to jobs and land controlled by whites, penalized blacks for loitering, and made unpaid child labor among blacks relatively easy. Black codes, states Harding, were the slave codes revived. And under no circumstances whatsoever "did any of these newly loyal states make provisions for black men to govern themselves, vote, or hold office, or for black children to receive publicly funded education;" Harding, pp. 313, 314.

35. Williams, p. 119.

36. See Gabriel Kolko, *Main Currents in American History* (New York: Harper & Row, 1976), p. 287 for data on killing of Filipinos.

37. See Carl Boggs, "The Blues Tradition," *Socialist Review* 38, 1978, p. 119; Paul Garon, *Blues and the Poetic Spirit* (London: Edison Press, 1975).

38. See Peter N. Carroll and David W. Noble, *The Free and the Unfree* (New York: Penguin Books, 1982), pp. 320, 321.

39. V.O. Key, Jr., *Southern Politics* (New York: Alfred A. Knopf, 1950), p. 541.

40. Epstein, p. 73.

41. This was the Masonic view of women in the 18th century. Its significance is that as a fraternal order based upon the collaboration between scientists and artisans, the image revealed is the concept of woman shared by men at the moment they begin to break away from orthodox Puritanism. See Clawson, dissertation, pp. 328-331.

42. In addition, spinning and a large part of the weaving had been the work of women in the home. See Hannah Josephson, *The Golden Threads* (New York: Duell, Sloan and Pearce, 1949), p. 49; another reason consistent with the dynamics of the sexual-economy is one noted by Ehrenreich and English. Everything that seems uniquely female "becomes a challenge to the rational scientific intellect. Woman's body, with its autonomous rhythms and generative possibilities, appears to the masculinist vision as a 'frontier,' another part of the natural world to be explored and mined." Ehrenreich and English, pp. 18, 19.

43. The new role as moral guardian, therefore, did not violate the concept of women as domestic; rather it was an extension of it. Physicians and educators still argued that the female brain and nervous system were incapable of sustaining intellectual effort. Consequently, the emergence of the cult of True Womanhood (in the 1820-1860 period) encouraged women to embody four qualities: piety, purity, submissiveness, and domesticity. Guidebooks to marriage declared that "The female breast is the natural soil of Christianity." See Rossi, p. 252; Epstein, pp. 76-81.

44. The auxiliaries were reminiscent of the relationship between female operatives and owners of the Lowell textile mills. The female operatives who worked in Lowell and the other mill towns from 1814 to 1850 and who were positioned as a bulwark against a debased proletariat, far from belonging to "a downtrodden class...came from precisely the same stock, with the same traditions, as the overseers, agents, and even the Boston investors themselves." Josephson, p. 62. With regard to fraternal orders, lodges had excluded women and blacks and with the rise of nativism at the turn of the 20th century, immigrants were excluded as well. Germans, however, were viewed as less a threat to the American cultural homogeneity and moral standards than were the Irish, Italians, Poles, and Eastern European Jews; see Clawson, dissertation, pp. 342-346.

45. Rossi, pp. 252, 256.

46. Epstein is referring specifically to the campaign against intemperance; pp. 23, 73, 90.

47. Ellen DuBois, *Feminism and Suffrage* (Ithaca, New York: Cornell University Press, 1978), p. 104; Epstein, pp. 89, 90.

48. Biologists of the period "proved" that there was a hierarchy of evolution: "WASPs would be in the lead, followed by Northern Europeans, Slavs, Jews, Italians, etc., with negroes trailing in the far rear." See Ehrenreich, p. 117.

49. See Epstein, p. 142; Angela Y. Davis, *Women, Race And Class* (New York: Vintage Books, p. 187).

50. Kraditor, pp. 20, 21.

51. Grimes, pp. 83, 89, 99, 102.

52. James Weinstein, *The Corporate Ideal in the Liberal State* (Boston: Beacon Press, 1968), p. 155.

53. Robert K. Murray, *Red Scare* (Minneapolis: University of Minnesota Press, 1955), pp. 13, 14, 194, 212, 213.

54. The territorial legislature of Wyoming adopted woman suffrage in 1869 in order to "civilize" the state. Populated with "Chinese coolies," Irishmen, Negroes, Union troops and Confederate soldiers, women were needed to "make the streets safe from injury and disrespect, to build churches and erect schools, and to restore as far as possible the niceties and amenities of...civilized communities...." Similarly in Utah, whose territorial legislature adopted woman's suffrage in 1870, the Mormon Church urged passage to maintain its power in Utah by attracting Puritan women who were "sober, moral, just, and industrious." See Grimes, pp. 34, 44, 57-60; no small consideration among Mormons, however, was the need for women to support the practice of polygamy. In 1896, with four western states having adopted woman's suffrage (Wyoming, Colorado, Utah, Idaho), Republicans supported "admission of women to wider spheres of usefulness, and welcome their cooperation in rescuing the country from democratic mismanagement and Populist misrule." Women "were increasingly coming to be looked upon as the custodians of public as well as private morality." In 1881, temperance leaders in addition to the Prohibition Party formed the Home Protection Party. This name was taken from the title of petitions that had been presented to national and state legislatures by the WCTU, which had enjoyed success in organizing the Woman's Crusade in closing saloons several years earlier. Several states passed prohibition laws during the early to mid-1890's. But then the tide turned as the "liquor interests," among whom were many immigrants, fought back. Between 1887 and 1890, ten prohibition campaigns were lost, and in Rhode Island a prohibition amendment was rescinded. See Kleppner, pp. 1574, 1575.

55. Hofstadter, pp. 136, 137.

56. Ehrenreich, pp. 186, 187.

57. Richard Edwards, *Contested Terrain* (New York: Harper Colophon Books, 1979), pp. 32, 33; W. Elliot Brownlee, *Dynamics of*

Ascent: A History of the American Economy (2nd ed.; New York: Alfred A. Knopf, 1974), p. 303.

58. Brownlee, p. 392.

59. Ehrenreich, pp. 201-202.

60. In Boston some of the older Mugwumps were Charles Francis Adams, Thomas Wentworth Higginson, and Edward Atkinson. Younger and perhaps the more leading Mugwumps in Boston were Moorfield Storey, William Everett, John F. Andrew, Richard Henry Dana, Josiah Quincy, George Fred Williams, and Winslow Warren. Most of these Mugwumps were Harvard graduates; nearly all were lawyers. They had the support of leading Boston businessmen such as John Murray Forbes, Robert Treat Paine, and Henry L. Pierce. They also enjoyed the support of investment houses and the presidents of a variety of colleges such as Harvard, Amherst, and Williams. See Geoffrey T. Blodgett, "The Mind of the Boston Mugwump," in Felice A. Donadio, ed., *Political Parties in American History: 1828-1890* (New York: G.P. Putnam's Sons, 1974), 881-883. Similarly, in New York City, Mugwumps consisted of professionals, bankers, merchants, journalists and the "better" politicians had been displaced from position's of political influence by lower and immigrant classes, especially the Irish. Among those advocating scientific reform were William F. Havemeyer, Judge James Emott, Robert Roosevelt, Charles Richard O'Connor, Joseph H. Choate, R.A. Hunter, George W. Benster, James Whitten and E.L. Godkin. See Alexander B. Callow, Jr., "The Crusade Against the Tweed Ring," in Callow, *American Urban History* (2nd ed.; New York: Oxford University Press, 1973), p. 5.

61. Hofstadter, p. 178; civil service reform was achieved through the Pendelton Act of 1883, which had bipartisan support and which made entrance to the "classified service" contingent upon competitive or merit examinations; Blodgett, p. 895.

62. Callow, p. 238.

63. Progressives were in some ways descendants of the Mugwumps. Also a faction within the Republican Party, they were almost entirely Anglo-Saxon and professional. Their support of Sunday laws and prohibition reveals the degree to which they were influenced by Protestant clergy. Progressives also strongly supported voter registration, the poll tax, literacy tests, the primary system, the direct election of senators, the referendum, and the "imperialist policies of the era." Hofstadter, pp. 144, 274; for a discussion of who the Progressives were and what they stood for, see David M. Kennedy, *Progressivism* (Boston: Little, Brown and Company, 1971).

64. This reform made it easier for self-disciplined experts and professionals to displace the grocers, saloon keepers, livery stable proprietors, owners of small hotels, druggists, clerks, bookkeepers, skilled, and unskilled workers from city government. It was more

difficult for members of the lower classes to wage a campaign city-wide than it was within their own wards where a network of personal relationships made electoral competition feasible. It also contributed to the erosion of ethnic customs and traditions or the "Americanization " of the immigrant. See Samuel P. Hays, "The Politics of Reform in Municipal Government in the Progressive Era," *Pacific Northwest Quarterly*, LV, 4 (Oct. 1964), pp. 161, 162.

65. See Weinstein, pp. 93-95.

66. The list of great strikes, not coincidentally, that occurred at the turn of the century, reads "like a roster of the consolidations: the railroads, McCormick, Carnegie (Homestead), Pullman, General Electric, U.S. Steel, International Harvester;" Edwards, p. 50.

67. With a membership of over 100,000, the Socialist Party, at one time, had 1,200 officeholders in some 340 municipalities and controlled about one third of the organizations in the American Federation of Labor; Weinstein, pp. 135-137; Weinstein is referring to those areas where "their organization had not been suppressed."

68. Weinstein, pp. 135-138.

69. Joseph Schaffner in 1914 and Meyer Jacobstein in 1920 each reported "astonishing changes" in the attitudes of immigrants toward employers once industrial unions were recognized. Other pioneers in this reform effort were Robert A. La Follette, Jr., Felix Frankfurter, the Filene brothers, Frances Perkins, Rexford Tugwell, and Sidney Hillman; see Steve Fraser, "Dress Rehearsal for the New Deal: Shop-Floor Insurgents, Political Elites, and Industrial Democracy in the Amalgamated Clothing Workers," in Frisch and Walkowitz, pp. 214-216, 221, 239, 241.

70. The crushing defeat in 1904 of Judge Alton B. Parker, the Democratic presidential nominee, along with an old-fashioned laissez faire platform, suggested that public support for governmental nonintervention had waned. Moreover, with the National Association of Manufacturers becoming a dominant force in the Republican Party, Republicans in 1908 took a decidedly anti-labor stand with the nomination of William Howard Taft and alienated native industrial workers. Organized labor, therefore, was ready to switch its allegiance from the Republican to the Democratic or Socialist parties. See Wilfred E. Binkley, *American Political Parties* (New York: Alfred A. Knopf, 1958), pp. 358-363.

71. Indeed, Steve Fraser suggests that Hillman along with the ACW "prefigured the essential ideological assumptions, programmatic reforms, and political realignments characteristic of the New Deal." Fraser, pp. 212, 241.

72. Fraser, p. 225.

73. Fraser, pp. 225, 234.

74. Fraser, p. 232.

75. Fraser, pp. 219, 241.

76. There is wide agreement that the AAA added to the poverty of blacks, who in 1931 registered unemployment rates of 58.5 percent for women and 43.5 percent for men; see Richard Sterner, *The Negro's Share* (New York, 1943), p. 362. Making its objective the raising of cotton prices, the AAA created an artificial shortage by paying southern farmers to plow up cotton. Large landowners benefited as cotton prices rose. Tens of thousands of black sharecroppers, however, were displaced. Many black farmer owners became tenants. Others lost their jobs, were forced to work for lower wages, or forced to migrate to the cities. Moreover, not a single black served on an AAA county committee throughout the South; William H. Harris, *The Harder We Run* (New York: Oxford University Press, 1982), p. 100; Harvard Sitkoff, *A New Deal for Blacks* (New York: Oxford University Press, 1978), p. 53. The FERA, which was the first agency to work directly to alleviate the plight of the poor, was seemingly unconcerned with the complexities of racial discrimination. In Jacksonville, Florida, for example, black families on relief outnumbered white families three to one. But FERA money was divided proportionately on the basis of the entire (non-relief) population data. Therefore, 15, 000 black families received 45 percent of the funds while 5, 000 white families received 55 percent.

77. The FHA refused loans to blacks moving into white areas and warned in its *Underwriting Manual* that property value declined when blacks moved into predominantly white areas. The WPA and the PWA may have lowered the occupational level of black workers because the relief work provided rarely was equal in skill with the work blacks performed in the private sector; see Leslie H. Fishel, Jr., "The Negro in the New Deal Era," *Wisconsin Magazine of History*, vol. 48, no. 2/Winter, 1964-1965, p. 113; Harris, pp. 101, 106. The National Industrial Recovery Act (NIRA) permitted southerners to pay whites more than blacks. The practice was purposely hidden through job classification schemes suggesting the discrimination was conscious. In addition, the NIRA and social security, which was intended to provided old age insurance, denied blacks benefits by exempting job classifications in which blacks were heavily employed, such as agriculture and domestic service; Harris, pp. 102, 105; Fishel, pp. 113-114.

78. Democrats excused their failure to respect blacks by pointing to the necessity of placating the Democratic white supremacists of the South. For example, Roosevelt explained that he could not back an anti-lynching bill "now" because Southerners would "block every bill I ask Congress to pass to keep America from collapsing." Cited by Sitkoff, p. 46; obviously in FDR's mind the lynching of blacks was separate from a collapsing America.

79. In Philadelphia, St. Louis, Detroit, Baltimore, Chicago, New York City, Washington, D.C., Pittsburgh, Cincinnati, Newark, and Cleveland, the percentage of blacks increased severalfold between 1910

and 1940; Sitkoff, pp. 90-91. Northern states with large black urban populations controlled 157 electoral votes, 31 more than the South; see Gordon, p. 599. By 1936, it was believed that blacks held the balance of power in a close election in 17 states with a total of almost 300 electoral votes. Sitkoff, p. 91.

80. Sitkoff, pp. 39, 40, 88-92.

81. Frederick Turner, *Beyond Geography* (New York: The Viking Press, 1980), pp. 278, 281, 282.

Footnotes Chapter 5

1. I do not believe I am blaming the victim. Rather I believe I am pointing to a feature of repression that is often overlooked, namely that repression often flows more from a set of ideas shared by people at all levels of society than from the conscious intentions of those who wield vast amounts of power.

2. Chile, El Salvador, South Africa and the Philippines come to mind.

3. For a full discussion of the dynamics of identity and the discrepancy between the public and private self see William E. Connolly, *Appearance and Reality in Politics* (New York: Cambridge University Press, 1981), Chapters 3 and 6.

4. Or as Morris Janowitz suggests, "ideology requires thorough-going affirmation and produces comprehensive observance." *The Reconstruction of Patriotism* (Chicago: The University of Chicago Press, 1983), p. 8.

5. Less educated and lower income people expressed greater opposition until the pulling out of Vietnam became official policy in 1969. See Kenneth M. Dolbeare and Murray J. Edelman, *American Politics* (Lexington, Ma: D.C. Heath, 1974), p. 405.

6. Sennett and Cobb focus primarily upon white male workers of European ancestry. Richard Sennett & Jonathan Cobb, *Hidden Injuries of Class* (New York: Vintage Books, 1973), p. 124.

7. Connolly, pp. 161-167.

8. Michael H. Best and William E. Connolly, *The Politicized Economy* (Lexington, MA: D.C. Heath and Company, 1982), p. 215.

9. Ely Chinoy's study of auto-workers supports this theme. He found that workers did not aspire to move up in the auto industry. Rather they envisioned themselves owning their own businesses; cited by Mary Ann Clawson, "Fraternalism and Class Formation in Europe and the U.S., 1600-1900", Ph.D. dissertation, SUNY at Stony Brook, 1980, p. 3; within the black community there has been a continuous stream of thought, at least since Booker T. Washington, suggesting

that dignity lay in black capitalism. However, within the black community, this approach has only been one among many. For a discussion of the orientation of black leadership see James A. Harrell "Negro Leadership in the Election Year 1936," *The Journal of Southern History* Vol. XXXIV, Feb-Nov 1968, pp. 546-564 and Robert Allen, *Reluctant Reformers* (Washington D.C.: Howard University Press, 1983), Ch. 7; Although women have had less reason to aspire to ownership, there is reason to believe that many women have identified with the process of accumulation. For example, see the "rationalist solution" as described by Barbara Ehrenreich and Deirdre English. *For Her Own Good* (New York: Anchor Books, 1979), p. 169.

10. Original emphasis; Vincent Harding, *There Is A River* (New York, Vintage Books, 1983), p. xix.

11. Madison's *Federalist No. 10* and George Washington's "Farewell Address" are the most well known examples of this fear. See Noble E. Cunningham, Jr., ed., *The Making of the American Party System* (New Jersey: Prentice-Hall, Inc., 1965).

12. Madison, *Federalist No. 10*, my emphasis; Cree and Brown cited by Austin Ranney, *Curing the Mischiefs of Faction* (Los Angeles: University of California Press, 1976), pp. 36, 37.

13. See John H. Bracey, Jr., August Meier, and Elliott Rudwick, eds., *Black Nationalism in America* (New York: The Bobbs-Merrill Co., 1970).

14. The percentage of the population in cities over 8,000 in 1840 was 8.52. By 1900 this percentage had grown to 33.10. Cities had become a ready market for manufactured goods at the same time that they provided a vast, inexpensive market in labor. Access to transportation was located in the cities as were a wide range of activities which contributed to economic development such as state-financed social services (public schools, hospitals, churches, asylums, almshouses, taverns, clubs, theaters, parks), and information about social-political-economic conditions which financiers and manufacturing elites required in order to plan investment strategies. And given the elaborate system of infrastructure located in urban areas, decisions by urban representatives regarding specialized land-use patterns, the building of complex water and sewage systems, bridges, lighting systems, tax rates and assessments, and high rise structures were impacting upon the development of the economy far beyond the boundaries of the municipality.

15. Samuel P. Hays, "The Politics of Reform in Municipal Government in the Progressive Era," *Pacific Northwest Quarterly*, LV, 4 (Oct. 1964) p. 166.

16. Richard Hofstadter, *The Age of Reform* (Vintage Books, 1955), p. 177.

17. Herbert Gutman, "An Iron Workers' Strike in the Ohio Valley, 1873-74," cited by Hays, p. 166.

18. Cited by Ranney, p. 119.

19. Cited by Ranney, pp. 119-120.

20. In addition to Jim Crow legislation during the Progressive Era, poll taxes, literacy tests and voter registration in the urban areas were intended to filter out "impure" elements. See Walter Dean Burnham, *Critical Elections and the Mainsprings of American Politics* (New York: W.W. Norton & Company, 1970), Ch. 4.

21. Ranney, p. 47.

22. Burnham suggests further that the legal regulation of election rules (reforms consisting of ballot reforms such as the Austrailian ballot which made voting a straight ticket much more complicated, non-partisanship malaportionment, discriminatory registration laws, e-limination of immigrant voting, detailed legislative regulation, poll tax, literacy tests, "white primaries") in addition to violence and terror were intended to derail the influence of immigrants, Populist agrarians, blacks, urban machines, and political parties themselves;Walter Dean Burnham, *The Current Crisis in American Politics* (New York: Oxford University Press, 1983), pp. 138-139.

23. Ranney, pp. 65-67.

24. La Follette and Norris cited by Ranney, pp. 124-125.

25. V.O. Key, Jr., *American State Politics* (New York: Alfred A. Knopf, 1956), p. 133.

26. Nelson W. Polsby, *Consequences of Party Reform* (New York: Oxford University Press, 1983), p. 159.

27. See Edward Merriam, *Primary Elections* (Chicago: The University of Chicago Press, 1908).

28. The demise of this attractive feature of politics in part accounts for the decline in electoral participation that follows anti-party reforms. In other words, such reforms have contributed to political alienation.

29. Larry L. Wade, *The Elements of Public Policy* (Columbus, Ohio: Charles E. Merrill Publishing Co., 1972), p. 127; Kevin Phillips and Paul H. Blackman, *Electoral Reform and Voter Participation* (Washington, D.C.: American Enterprise Institute for Public Policy Research, 1975), p. 1.

30. See Martin P. Wattenberg, *The Decline of American Political Parties 1952-1980* (Cambridge, MA: Harvard University Press, 1984).

31. See Wattenberg, pp. 71, 90.

32. Jean Bethke Elshtain, "Democracy and the QUBE Tube, " *The Nation*, August 7-14, 1982.

Footnotes Chapter 6

1. James O'Connor, *Fiscal Crisis of the State* (New York: St. Martin's Press, 1973), pp. 23, 24.

2. Barry Bluestone and Bennett Harrison, *The Deindustrialization of America* (New York: Basic Books, Inc. 1982), pp. 138, 139.

3. Thomas Ferguson and Joel Rogers, eds., *The Hidden Election* (New York: Pantheon Books, 1981), p. 9.

4. For a discussion of the economic theory during this time frame, see Michael H. Best and William E. Connolly, *The Politicized Economy* (Lexington, MA: D. C. Heath and Co., 1982), Ch. 1.

5. See Frances Fox Piven & Richard A. Cloward, *The New Class War* (New York: Pantheon Books, 1982).

6. Wolfe, p. 21.

7. "In 1952, among members of the IMF, the United states share of exports had been 20. 8 percent, while Japan's share was 1. 7 percent. Twenty years later, the United states share had dropped to 13. 2 percent, while Japan's had more than quadrupled to 7. 6 percent. In 1971, when the U. S. trade balance finally turned sharply negative, Japan and West Germany commanded an aggregate trade surplus of $12 billion. " Ferguson and Rogers also point to "rapid economic integration, sharp increases in the mobility of capital, heightened competition among the major industrial powers, and the disintegration of traditional labor markets." Ferguson, p. 13; Harrison and Bluestone cite the drop in the U. S. corporate share of the total direct foreign investment flows of the thirteen countries in the Organization for Economic cooperation and Development from 61 percent during 1961-67 to 30 percent during 1974-78, p. 142; Kevin Phillips, by surveying the withdrawal of U. S. Air Force bases in various parts of the world, draws the parallel to "Rome's fatal withdrawal of its legions in the fifth century." While not as convincing, perhaps, to economists, Phillips' analysis strikes an important cord of "offended national pride." See *Post Conservative America* (New York: Vintage House, 1982), pp. 26, 27.

8. The Trilateral Commission, founded in 1973, was an attempt by political and economic elites of Japan, the United States, and Western Europe to overcome the mounting tensions between these capitalist blocs as the U. S. international position declined. Its purpose has been to co-ordinate political-economic policy in order to optimize global capitalist production under unfavorable circumstances. See Holly Sklar, ed., *The Trilateral Commission and Elite Planning for World Management* (Boston: South End Press, 1980).

9. See Ferguson, pp. 10-12.

10. O'Connor, p. 14.

11. Harrison and Bluestone seek to point out that the growth in the Sunbelt, which is taking place at the expense of the Frostbelt is extraordinarily uneven; p. 33.

12. Harrison, pp. 141-146.

13. Harrison and Bluestone, p. 147.

14. Murray Weidenbaum, chair of the Council of Economic Advisors in 1981-82 has argued that regulations imposed $100 billion of annual costs on business prior to the ascendancy of the Reagan administration. Weidenbaum's claim appears to be specious. He claimed that 80% of the federal regulatory budget was devoted to "the newer areas of social regualtion, such as job safety, energy and the environment, and consumer safety and health." Economists William Tabb, however, points out that Weidenbaum counted as "newer" areas of social regulation the Food and Drug Administration (created in 1931), the Coast Guard, Customs Service, the Bureau of Alcohol, Tobacco and Firearms. Are Weidenbaum's exaggerations due to the desire on the Right to silence environmental, consumer, and labor activists? See Frank Ackerman, *Hazardous To Our Wealth* (Boston: South End Press, 1984), p. 52.

15. See Harrison for a comprehensive discussion of this development; p. 17.

16. Wolfe, p. 166; Harrison, p. 209.

17. For a full discussion of the "Nixon shocks" and the alarm it created among multinationalists, see Jeff Frieden, "The Trilateral Commission: Economics and Politics in the 1970s," pp. 68-70, in Sklar.

18. See Laurence H. Shoup and William Minter, "Shaping a New World Order," in Sklar, pp. 139, 148.

19. Frieden, pp. 68, 69.

20. Cited in Frieden, p. 69.

21. Many have claimed that Deep Throat and the revelations of White House tapes represented the handiwork of transnationalists working through the CIA.

22. Cited by Laurence Shoup, "Jimmy Carter and the Trilateralists: Presidential Roots," in Sklar, footnote pp. 200, 201; for an account of the influence of transnationalists in the campaigns of 1980 see Ferguson and Rodgers.

23. Twenty-six trilateralists were in the Carter administration; see Holly Sklar and Ros Everdell, "Who's Who on the Trilateral Commission," in Sklar, pp. 91, 92.

24. Some investment bankers (such as Felix Rohatyn and George Ball), fearful of Reagan's projected defense spending and its impact on inflation supported Carter. Important multinationalists who played a key role in Reagan's campaign were George Schultz, Charles W. Robinson, Caspar Weinberger, William Casey, William P. Rodgers, John McKetta, and Henry Kissinger among others.

25. Population shifts correspond to the shift in employment opportunities. Thus 11.7 million people migrated to the South and to the West during the 1970's. Note Harrison and Bluestone, had all these

people come from the six New England states, "this entire region would have been left without a single man, woman or child." Harrison, pp. 99, 100, 165, 166.

26. *Business Week*, July 2, 1979, p. 79.

27. See Ferguson and Rodgers, pp. 16-18; the organizations they cite as playing an important role in this campaign were the American Security Council, the National Strategy Information Center, the Georgetown Center for Strategic and International Studies, the (U.S.) Atlantic Council, the Paris-based Atlantic Insitute, the London-based International Insitute for Strategic Studies, and the Committee on the Present Danger, see Jerry Sanders' *Peddlers of Crisis* (Boston: South End Press, 1983).

28. Frances Fox Piven & Richard A. Cloward, *The New Class War* (New York: Pantheon, 1982), pp. 26, 31.

29. For the names of such bankers, see Ferguson, p. 18; note that by mid-1978 Carter had cut CETA funding and federal aid to states and government spending was reduced below the amount budgeted to most departments—quoted from "Election and the Business Cycle," *Dollars and Sense*, Oct.—1984, pp. 4, 5.

30. Cited by James Phillips, "Renovation of the International Economic Order," in Sklar, pp. 485, 490.

31. Piven and Cloward's analysis from the Left in *The New Class War* and Kevin Phillips' analysis from the Right in *Post Conservative America* both seem to reach this end.

32. Michael J. Cozier, Samuel P. Huntington, Joji Watanuki, *The Crisis of Democracy: Report on the Governability of Democracies to the Trilateral Commission* (New York: New York University Press, 1975), pp. 75, 113, 114.

33. Cited by Wolfe, p. 211.

34. Paul Wyrich, a key leader of the New Right, argues that "The very essence of the New Right is a morally based conservatism. As a matter of fact, our view is not based in economics but in a religious view." Phillips, p. 48.

35. Also of concern to Phillips in this regard is the effort on scholars to wrap the cloak of Christianity around corporate imperatives. Michael Novak, for example, writes that the "corporation mirrors God's presence also in its liberty, by which I mean independence from the state." Phillips, pp. 13, 159.

36. Harrison and Bluestone, p. 196.

37. "...small businessmen, farmers, artisans, white-collar workers and some professional elements." Phillips, p. 197.

38. Richard Senntt and Jonathan Cobb, *The Hidden Injuries of Class* (New York: Vintage Books, 1973), pp. 22, 135, 136.

39. This is one sign that many Pro-lifers may be more concerned with the sexual freedom of women than they are with "saving lives."

40. W.E. Connolly, *Appearance and Reality in Politics* (New York: Oxford University Press, 1981), pp. 67, 68.

41. Labor union households voting Republican increased from 40 to 48 percent from 1976 to 1980 (which was greater than among non-union households); see Walter Dean Burnham, "The 1980 Earthquake," in Ferguson and Rodgers, p. 131.

42. Lewis Chester, Godfrey Hodgosn, Bruce Page, *The Presidential Campaign of 1968* (New York: The Viking Press, 1969), pp. 17, 45, 200, 363.

43. Phillips, p. 47; James Sundquist, *Dynamics of the Party System* (Washington, D.C., The Brookings Institution, 1983), pp. 359, 418; for a discussion of Dixiecrat strategy, see Austin Ranney, *Curing the Mischiefs of Faction* (University of California Press, 1975), p. 182.

44. Burnham cited by Piven and Cloward, p. 3; See Philips for data concerning social-issue voters, p. 49.

45. Cited by Michael Omi and Howard Winant, "By the Rivers of Babylon: Race in the United States," Part One, *Socialist Review* No. 71, Vol. 13, No.5 Sept.-Oct., 1983, p. 34; their discussion of programmatic strategies can be found in Part II, No. 72, Vol. 13, No. 6, Nov.-Dec., 1983, pp. 46, 47.

46. The labor movement, as has been suggested, has been impaired by the apparent fraternal desire among many white male workers to secure degnity through the maintenance of white male authority. In addition, the decline of "smoke stack" industries and the decline in relative strength of white male wage earners (who no longer constitute a majority of industrial workers) has weakened the solidarity and, therefore, the political significance of union members.

47. Barbara Ehrenreich and Deirdre English, *For Her Own Good* (Garden City, New York: Anchor Books, 1978), p. 317.

48. A proponents of this viewpoint might be Robert Allen, *Reluctant Reformers* (Washington, D.C.; Howard University Press, 1983), see postscript.

49. Stephen B. Oates, *Let the Trumpet Sound* (new York: Harper & Row, 1982), p. 179.

50. This idea is a paraphrase of J.N. Findlay, "The Contemporary Relevance of Hegel," in *Hegel* (New York: Anchor Books, 1972), edited by Charles Taylor, p. 4.

51. Those who stress the non-violence of King's strategy fail to grasp the function that confrontation and violence played. Granted, the non-violent protest by Blacks themselves was essential in preventing black activists from being cast in racist images; however, the making of the invisible visible required forcing the "oppressor to commit his brutality openly." The effectiveness of non-violence depended upon confrontational provocation and the eliciting of violence.

52. Omi and Winant, Part Two, p. 35.

53. Sara Evans, *Personal Politics* (New York: Vintage Books, 1980), p. 25.

54. Angela Davis, *Women, Race & Class* (New York: Vintage Book, 1983), Chp. 1; Evans, pp. 51, 53.

55. Christine Di Stefano, *Legitimation Crisis Reconsidered: Women, Personal Identity, and the State*, unpublished paper, 11, 12, 51, 52.

56. I agree with DiStefano who argues that many feminists and egalitarian thinkers fear that recognition of significant biological differences makes women vulnerable to a justification of unequal treatment. "While this fear is well based, it is important to remember that 'different' does not necessarily translate into 'unequal.' In fact, failure to acknowledge differences may result in nothing more than pseudo-equality." DiStefano, pp. 16, 17.

57. D.W. Winnicott cited by Ulrike Prokop, "Production and the Context of Women's Daily Life," *New German Critique*, No. 13, Winter 1978, pp. 21-23.

58. Prokop, p. 24.

59. Sara Ruddick, "Maternal Thinking," *Feminist Studies*, no. 2, Summer 1980, pp. 348-351.

60. Cited by Ruddick, p. 353.

61. Evans, pp. 40, 65.

62. Ortner and Carlson cited by DiStefano, pp. 23, 24.

63. There is a danger in focusing on process, however. It encourages us to wallow in the complexities of our inner life and neglect the complexities of social life. See Joan Cocks, "Wordless Emotions: Some Critical Reflections on Radical Feminism," *Politics and Society*, Vol. 13, No. 1, 1984, p. 49.

64. See Distefano for a discussion of these landmarks and the female identity, p. 43.

65. I am refering to radical, socialist, and psychoanalytic feminists. I exclude liberal feminists such as the National Organization for Women which seems to be captured by the traditional instrumental version of politics. See Elshtain, Chp. 5, for a discussion of the various distinctions among feminists.

66. This is Harrison and Bluestone's citation, p. 19.

67. Sklar, pp. 37, 38.

68. Zillah Eisenstein, *The Radical Future of Liberal Feminism* (New York: Longman, 1981), pp. 244-248; DiStefano, p. 61; Carter quoted by Kim Kelber, "Carter and Women: The Record," *The Nation*, no. 20 (24 May 1980), p. 267.

69. George Gilder, *Wealth and Poverty* (New York: Basic Books, 1981), pp. 70, 71, 114, 115, 135; there are a number of studies linking

military spending increases and cuts in social programs impacting most heavily upon women. NOW estimates that every time the Pentagon's budget goes up $1 billion, 9,500 jobs for women disappear in the transfer from civilian to military production; see *In These Times*, Feb. 15-21, 1984, p. 4.

70. Much like Reagan's appointment of Sandra Day O'Connor, the selection of Geraldine Ferraro as a female running-mate represents the recognition of feminism by party elites as a significant political force. But it also reveals the tremendous co-optive capacity of party politics; women in prominent positions must speak in a male voice.

71. Ellen Willis, "The Politics of Abortion," *In These Times*, June 15-28, 1983, p. 12.

72. Walter Dean Burnham, *Critical Elections* (New York: W.W. Norton & Co., 1970), p. 15.

73. Cited by Alexander Cockburn and James Ridgeway, "The World of Appearance: The Public Campaign," in Ferguson and Rodgers, p. 91.

74. *Dollars & Sense*, No. 78, July-August 1982, p. 6.

75. Barry Bluestone and Bennett Harrison, *The Deindustrialization of America* (New York: Basic Books, 1982), 183.

76. See "Cracks in the Empire," *Dollars & Sense*, December 1984, No. 102, pp. 3-5.

77. Entitled "Corporate PACs for a New Pax Americana," this as yet unpublished study is part of a larger research project that is in progress; contact Dan Clawson, Department of Sociology, University of Massachusetts, Amherst.

78. Nevertheless, Reagan's popularity is roughly equivalent to those candidates who won critical elections: FDR won 32. 6 percent of the potential electorate in 1932, McKinley 40.6 percent in 1896, and Lincoln 32.6 percent in 1860. In 1828, often considered a critical election, Andrew Johnson won only 25 percent. However, the party system in 1825 is considered to have been rather rudimentary. Notice, though, how much easier it was for elite to legitimate white male authority and the Police State of the 19th century when the franchise was severely restricted. Assuming that women are at least half of the real potential electorate, Jackson won 12.5 percent, Lincoln 16.4 percent, and McKinley 20.3 of the real potential electorate. Compensating for the exclusion of minorities drops these figures even lower.

79. "In 1981, 68 percent of all single mothers with at least one child under 6 and one or more older children were poor." See Nancy Folbre, "Motherhood—the Forgotten Issue," *The Nation*, October 20, 1984, p. 378.

80. For a discussion of the impact of militarism upon women's lives, see Cynthia Enloe, *Does Khaki Become You?* (Boston: South End Press, 1985).

81. *Time*, November 19, 1984, p. 45.

82. Ehrenreich and English, pp. 320, 321.

83. Ehrenreich and English, p. 321.

84. See Jean Bethke Elshtain, *Public Man, Private Woman* (New Jersey: Princeton University Press, 1981), p. 315.

85. Ellis, pp. 12, 13.

86. Enloe, p. 7.

87. Cocks, pp. 33, 37; note that Cocks also reminds us that the "truths radical feminism has to tell, not only to women but to all of post-Enlightenment theory and society, are so various that they cannot be taken up in a single essay."

Footnotes Chapter 7

1. Robert A. Dahl, *Political Oppositions in Western Democracies* (New Haven: Yale University Press, 1966), pp. 34, 60, 62; as Dahl notes, the Republican Party during the 1850s did not destroy the Whigs, rather it was built upon the ruins of the Whig party which was destroyed by conflict of competing modes of production.

2. This position has been expressed by Theo Brown, executive director of Ground Zero in *Nuclear Times*, February 1984, p. 13.

3. For those who view international politics through an East/West conceptual lens, a feminist critique of Soviet militarism might be found compelling. It would offer anti-communists a fresh approach. The likelihood of this particular unfolding of issues, is small, however. Male bonding, in any case, would be severely tested.

4. For a theoretical formulation which incorporates a holistic approach to all sides of social life, see Michael Albert and Robin Hahnel, *Marxism and Socialist Theory*, (Boston: South End Press, 1982).

5. We shall discuss the feasibility of organizing a "rainbow coalition" below. Given the structure of the party system at this point, however, such a coalition is unlikely. Examination of the roots of racism and sexism would require the kind of self-examination that is filtered out by party politics.

6. John Atlas, Peter Drier and John Stephens, "Progressive Politics in 1984," *The Nation*, July 23-30, 1983, pp. 82, 83.

7. Sam Zuckerman, "Can 'neoliberalism' Save Capitalism?", *The Guardian*, Oct. 20, 1982; John B. Judis, "Neoliberal Hart: stagnation is result of public spending, " *In These Times*, March 21-27, 1984.

8. See Harrison and Bluestone, pp. 210-214.

9. Zuckerman.

10. Robert V. Remini, *The Election of Andrew Jackson* (New York: J.B. Lippincott Company, 1963), pp. 104, 105. Robert V. Remini, *The Election of Andrew Jackson* (New york: J.B. Lippincott Company, 1963), pp. 104, 105.

11. William E. Connolly, *Appearance and Reality in Politics* (New York: Oxford University Press, 1981), pp. 184, 185.

12. Dahl, p. 135.

13. Joan Cocks, "Worldless Emotions: Some Critical Reflections on Radical Feminism," *Politics and Society*, Vol. 13, No. 1, 1984, p. 43.

14. On December 10, 1983, the NOW board voted 32 to 5 in support of Mondale; in all fairness to NOW, however, Jesse Jackson had not been in the race very long and he had been the leading minority *anti-abortion* spokesperson.

15. For example, Jesse Jackson switched his position from Pro-Life to Pro-Choice as he entered the presidential race. If this switch had been an effort to help express the demands of active women it would have been good; however, it appears to have been an effort to win the support of women. The distinction is a very important one.

16. Christine DiStefano points out that many have adopted the term "productive freedom" in order to get beyond this.

17. I am not suggesting that these considerations undermine the position of activists opposing the death penalty nor am I suggesting that such a view pays insufficient attention to the racism embedded in organized support for capital punishment. I am suggesting, though, that a party which helps to draw out and clarify the views of the disaffected is likely to undermine the support of the New Right.

18. Walter Dean Burnham, *The Current Crisis in American Politics* (New York: Oxford University Press, 1982), p. 138.

19. Single member districts, plurality elections and the electoral college are the major obstacles preventing a multi-party system. There are, however, many other obstacles from public financing rules, equal time and fairness doctrine requirements, and financial contribution disclosure requirements; see Polsby, pp. 81-85.

20. Alternatives to single member districts which encourage several parties rather than two are proportional representation, multiple-member district systems, and list voting; see Douglas Rae, *The Political Consequences of Electoral Laws* (Yale University Press, 1967). Note also that single member districts lends themselves to "gerrymandering" or the drawing of district lines in order to exclude the participation of certain voters within a given district.

21. Joel Francis Paschal, "The House of Representatives: 'Grand Depository of the Democratic Principle'?", *Law and Contemporary Problems*, Vol. 17, Spring 1952, p. 277.

22. Belle Zeller and Hugh A. Bone, "The Repeal of P.R. in New York City-Ten Years in Retrospect," *The American Political Science Review*, Vol. 42, No. 6, Dec. 1948, pp. 1127-1149.

23. Polsby, p. 87.

24. Connolly, p. 13.

25. One should also add that the process undoubtedly contributed to the eventual victory of Ray Flynn, a progressive as well.

26. Alabama, 1931; Arkansas, 1939; Florida, 1929; Georgia, 1917; Louisiana, 1922; Mississippi, 1902; North Carolina and South Carolina, 1915; Texas, 1918; Tennessee and Virginia continue to nominate by a plurality; V.O. Key, Jr., *Southern Politics* (New York: Alfred A. Knopf, 1950), p. 417, fn.

27. A study conducted by Profs. Charles Bullock and Lock Johnson of the University of Georgia suggests that when blacks ran first, they won the runoff against whites about two-thirds of the time. A study under preparation for a lawsuit to eliminate runoff primaries in Mississippi reportedly shows at least 100 instances at county or lower levels where blacks have been defeated in runoffs by white-bloc voting; see David Moberg, "Unease Rises with the Runoff as an Issue, " *In These Times*, May 9-15, 1984.

28. See David Moberg, "Unease Rises with the Runoff as an Issue, *In These Times*, May 9-15, 1984.

29. Walter Dean Burnham, *Critical Elections* (New York: W.W. Norton & Co., 1970), p. 81.

30. Walter Dean Burnham, *The Current Crisis in American Politics* (New York: Oxford University Press, 1982), pp. 61-87.

31. Richard A. Cloward and Frances Fox Piven, "A movement Strategy to Transform the Democratic Party," in John S. Friedman, ed., *First Harvest* (New York: Grove Press, 1983), pp. 278, 287.

32. Blair Clark, "Enfranchise the Poor—A Goal for '84," *The Nation*, April 25, 1984, p. 481.

33. With the exception of No. 4, these points were quoted directly from Keven Phillips and Paul Blackman, *Electoral Reform and Voter Participation* (Washington, D.C.: American Enterprise Institute, 1975), pp. 23, 26, 33.

34. Walter Dean Burnham, *The Current Crisis in American Politics* (New York: Oxford University Press, 1982), p. 121.

35. This is Charles Taylor's criticism of the "terribly unreal notion of freedom" in Marx; see *Hegel*, pp. 557-558.

INDEX